Presented To:

_____

From:

_____

Date:

_____

THE
Seer

EXPANDED EDITION

THE
Seer

EXPANDED EDITION

THE PROPHETIC POWER OF VISIONS, DREAMS, AND OPEN HEAVENS

EXPANDED EDITION
with Devotional

JAMES W. GOLL

DESTINY IMAGE® PUBLISHERS, INC.

P.O. Box 310, Shippensburg, PA 17257-0310

"Promoting Inspired Lives."

This book and all other Destiny Image, Revival Press, MercyPlace, Fresh Bread, Destiny Image Fiction, and Treasure House books are available at Christian bookstores and distributors worldwide.

For a U.S. bookstore nearest you, call **1-800-722-6774.**

For more information on foreign distributors, call **717-532-3040.**

Reach us on the Internet: **www.destinyimage.com.**

ISBN 13 TP: 978-0-7684-4110-9

ISBN 13 Ebook: 978-0-7684-8856-2

For Worldwide Distribution, Printed in the U.S.A.

12 13 14 / 20 19 18

DEDICATION

With a grateful heart I wish to acknowledge the team efforts of the excellent staff at Destiny Image, our wonderful staff at Encounters Network, the intercessory force of our prayer shield, and the support of my dear family. Blessings upon blessings to all of you.

Having moved in and out of various circles of the prophetic movement for the past 35 plus years, I have had the opportunity of tasting and participating in a wide variety of prophetic expression. I am grateful to the Lord for this diverse exposure and trust that the reader will benefit from those years of preparation and cross-pollination to compose this book.

With a heart of honor to whom honor is due, I wish to dedicate this book to three fathers who have immensely impacted my journey. They are each unique seers, each with 80 plus years of life experience—John Sandford, Bob Jones, and Paul Cain. Thank you, Lord, for these fatherly seers who have pioneered a way for the next generation of eagles to arise and fly!

James W. Goll
Encounters Network
Franklin, Tennessee

ENDORSEMENTS

James Goll is one of the most respected prophetic patriarchs of our time. He has incredible prophetic insight and amazing foresight that merge in a way that I have never experienced in anybody else. This gives James the extraordinary ability to understand the spirit world and articulate it in a manner that launches believers into their divine destiny.

Before my friend James Goll wrote *The Seer*, I taught people that there was no difference between a prophet and a seer. Then I bought James' book and read it in one night! I was stunned by his revelation on the seer and the way he described the distinctions between different prophetic people. I have recommended this book to literally thousands of Christians all over the world. We also have a bi annual school of the prophets at Bethel Church, and we use *The Seer* as part of our curriculum.

Every person who wants to grow in the prophetic ministry needs to read this book. This book unearths mysteries hidden since the days of King David's seer named Gad. A decade from now, *The Seer* will be referenced as one of the fundamental, reformational resources of our time. James lays a foundation with this book that will be built upon for generations. Thank you, James, for being a prophet to this generation, but even more, for being a father to multiple thousands of Christians.

Kris Vallotton
Co-founder of Bethel School of Supernatural Ministry
Author of seven books, including *The Supernatural Ways of Royalty*
Senior associate leader of Bethel Church, Redding, California

In his book, *The Seer,* James Goll takes you on a journey through time back to the beginnings and endings of the seer and demonstrates how in modern times we are still seeing and needing the seer ministry to be relevant. James gives accounts of his own life as a seer and shows the reader the ups and downs through teaching how the seer in him has matured. I highly recommend this book to all those who are prophetically seeing, so they can develop their anointing.

Dr. Jeremy Lopez
Founder of IdentityNetwork.net

Few can broach the biblically real, yet spiritually ethereal role of the seer like James Goll. The seer's life is itself a metaphor, and James captures this distinction with both the seasoned skill of a prophetic veteran and the insight of one with heightened spiritual acuity honed by years spent walking with God. For those who have a revelatory gift, this book may make your entire life make sense.

John Paul Jackson
Streams Ministries

When I first entered the world of spirit-filled believers, I had been a pastor for 14 years. The first prophet I met was very eccentric; I didn't understand his symbolic language, and I was confused. In the years to come, I met many prophetic people. I can still remember the night I sat across the table from James Goll and began asking him questions about the prophetic realm and the various ways God reveals things through both hearing and seeing.

James was very helpful in helping me understand the ways we can hear and see the activity of God in our lives. I have had James over the years speak at my church and at my conferences on the prophetic. He has the unique gift of being able to explain the realm of mystery in ways that are comprehensible to those who have not yet experienced those realms. He gives to the uninitiated in the prophetic realm clarity of understanding and the hope that even the uninitiated can be apprehended by the grace of God and the Spirit of God and enter into the prophetic seer realm themselves. I highly recommend James' book, *The Seer*.

Randy Clark
Founder, Global Awakening

James Goll is a personal friend and a co-minister in the Kingdom. I love it when our paths coincide at events and happenings. Whatever time I spend with James is always interesting, funny, and insightful.

This book is a fascinating mix of biblically based research and inspiring revelation. It is full of principles, guidelines, and values regarding how the prophetic person should operate. A true prophetic voice has both foresight and insight regarding future events and the ways of the Lord. This is a book that will enable and empower people to see more in the Spirit and develop the capacity to interpret what they see more effectively.

James is a great storyteller and understands life as a journey. *The Seer* follows that perspective faithfully, as James helps us to navigate the pathways that are common in the development of prophetic people. This book is rich with experience and revelatory insights. It provides us with places to stand, ponder, and be transformed. Do not use this book in a superficial manner. This material has been hard fought for and gained through much struggle, pain, and sacrifice. Great things never come easy. This book will save you from the pitfalls, dead ends, and wrong turns that you would have made by yourself. James is a traveler, a pioneer and a trailblazer. Follow his footsteps; drink from the imprints that he makes as he walks you through into a place of passionate pursuit of God's intimacy and presence.

This book is more than a manual, though it blends the mystical with the practical in a powerful way. This book is not a study guide; it's a map that takes you into uncharted territory and tells you where all the necessities for living this life are located. There are clues in the manuscript that tell you how to travel. You will need to keep this book close. On your own journey you will refer to it often. In my meditation suite at home, I have a small bookcase near my writing desk. These are all the books that I would save if there were a fire. They are all the reference tools that I both love and need for my own journey. *The Seer* is on that bookcase; it's that important.

Graham Cooke
Brilliantbookhouse.com

CONTENTS

FOREWORD

We live in a day when all too many "scholars" and even believers have reduced the Word of God to a purely rational and logical explanation. Granted, the Word of God appeals as reasonable and logical in its unfolding to the human mind, provided that mind is surrendered, yielded, and in the process of being transformed by the Spirit! The natural mind is not capable of receiving anything whatsoever from the Spirit of God. The Scriptures are God-breathed, and the breath of God is the Spirit of God. In fact, the breath of God was experienced by all those who penned the sacred writings. In order for that to occur, the individuals who wrote had to have experienced the experience of being moved by the breath, the wind, and the Spirit of God.

In the beginning, the wind and breath of God, the Spirit of God, brooded, hovered, and vibrated over chaos and brought about order. The Spirit of God manifests the presence of God. You cannot know the presence of God purely by logic and reason. The presence of God can only be known by experience, and that experience is tantamount to revelation. Your eyes have to be opened, your heart has to become vibrant and alive, and your ear has to be attuned to a level beyond the normal octaves that the human ear can hear. Jesus Himself quotes the prophet Isaiah in Mark's Gospel while explaining the parable of the soils, and says that the problem with the human condition in its fallen state is that it has affected the eyes, the ears, and the heart.

The actual words of Isaiah are as follows:

> *Render the hearts of this people insensitive, their ears dull, and their eyes dim. Otherwise they might **see** with their eyes, **hear** with their ears, **understand** [actually the word implies "to discern"] with their hearts, and return and be healed (Isaiah 6:10).*

When the Spirit is released both upon and within people, their eyes, ears, and hearts are opened to a world beyond their limited seeing, hearing, feeling, and discerning. That world is the more real yet invisible world. It is the world from which the visible world derives its existence. When people are brought out of the realm of darkness and ignorance, the realm of the fallen nature and the realm of the powers of darkness, and translated into the Kingdom of God's beloved Son, the Spirit reveals Him to their hungry hearts, minds, and souls.

The testimony of Jesus is the spirit of prophecy (see Rev. 19:10). There is a Man in the glory, and He is ordering our lives anew by His Spirit brooding deep within us and opening up to us worlds beyond our natural ways of knowing. What makes us uniquely the people of God is that we are called to be people of the Spirit. Immersed in that Spirit, our speech changes, because our eyes, ears, and hearts have been opened to see beyond the world in front of our eyes to the world that lies behind what our eyes can see.

In the Old Covenant, Jeremiah tells us that the earmark of true prophets was that they stood in the divine council and conclave (see Jer. 23:18). In the New Covenant, the Day of Pentecost caught the entire Church up into the divine council. Potentially, every believer has access to that which exists before the very throne of God. The reason I say "potentially" is because many of God's children fail to yield themselves to the experience of the Spirit of God and reduce everything to a logical explanation. They are even "taught" by so-called enlightened theologians that certain experiences are no longer valid for today since they supposedly ceased when the last of the original apostles of the first-century died.

Liberal theology isn't the only dangerous thing the Church needs to watch out for. Fundamental theology that takes away the experience of the Spirit in its fullness is just as damaging to the saints of God. Over 49 percent of the book we call the Scriptures is visionary experience, ecstatic experience, and prophetic experience—even in the New Testament! How can we expect to experience the truths of almost half of the Scriptures by logic and reason alone? It is impossible.

The coming of the Spirit at Pentecost was the beginning of an ongoing event for the Church throughout the ages. We need to be continually immersed in the world of the Spirit if we are to see, hear, feel, and discern the things that the Spirit of God intends for us to know and understand. Without that immersion and direct experience, we will fail to fulfill our destiny, fail to honor God's eternal purpose, and fail to know the Father as Christ intends for us to know Him.

James Goll, a seasoned, powerful, inspiring prophetic voice to the nations, has had a long history of seeing, hearing, discerning, and speaking of the things that *"eye has not seen, and ear has not heard, and which have not entered the heart of* [natural] *man"* (1 Cor. 2:9). The Spirit has found in James Goll a yielded vessel who loves the Father and has the heart of the Father. His reach extends far and wide, and his depth can only be appreciated by getting to know the man in his person and his ministry.

James has done us a great service by taking the time to clarify the nature of what it means to see, hear, and discern by and in the Holy Spirit. In these last great days of visitation, God is growing up a people who can be effective in bringing the things of the invisible world to bear on the visible world. There is a great ingathering taking place, and it is on the increase, but not because of pure human logic and reason. The harvest is being gathered, because the Spirit is moving again over the chaos of people's lives and giving them direct experiences with God through His Son the Lord Jesus.

It is imperative that we know what it means to see, to hear, and to discern the things of the world to which we truly belong. The world of the Spirit is a world where Christ is seen in all His glory, seated on the throne at the very center of the universe, and ordering all things after the counsel of His will.

Step by step, James will carefully explain to you the nature of the prophetic experience at every level: to hear from God, speak for God, to experience seeing something that relates to the nature of God and His purpose, and to discern the genuine experience of God in the Spirit from the false experiences that are counterfeited by the powers of darkness. His research is biblical and thorough, and his experience testifies to the truths of the Word he teaches and upholds. Take your time as you embark on this study, for it is more than a book; it is indeed a study. It will prepare the way in your heart and life for an eye-opening, ear-opening, heart-opening, and Heaven-opening experience of real life in the Spirit.

Thanks, James, for caring enough to share the Father's heart by sharing your heart. We are a generation in need of hearing what the Spirit is saying, and we want to thank you for helping us to do just that!

Mark J. Chironna, PhD
The Master's Touch International Church
Orlando, Florida

UNDERSTANDING
THE SEER REALM

In order to understand the seer realm, one must first understand the differ-ence between the seer and the prophet. Most people in the Body of Christ see no difference. I believe it is critical that we understand these distinc-tions. What is the difference between a *prophet* and a *seer*? The distinction will become clearer, I hope, in the pages that follow, but for now let us say that *all true seers are prophets, but not all prophets are seers.*

Another way to look at this is to turn it around and think of a great pro-phetic river flowing from the throne of God that breaks into two streams—the *prophet* and the *seer*—which then give different degrees or dimensions or facets of prophetic impartation. Either way, it should be clear that both streams are important for the full expression of the Lord's prophetic word to His people in our day.

There is a new anointing for a new generation, an enablement and a grac-ing to unveil God's purposes and desire, both verbally and visually. This pro-phetic anointing is manifested in a variety of dimensions that express the diversity of God's approach to working in our world.

Prophetic ministry is established on prophetic vision, and it is this vision that sustains that ministry. The prophetic light of vision introduces us to the process of change, a change which is the key to growth and understanding.

The Holy Spirit is the source of vision. Though there is only one Holy Spirit, He works in a variety of ways. As Paul said to the church at Corinth, there are varieties of gifts and varieties of effects. This diversity applies to visionary states and experiences. Once we understand different visionary states, we will have a better idea of how the prophetic seer anointing works.

Chapter One

SEER AND PROPHET:
TWO PROPHETIC STREAMS

The Nile is truly one of the great rivers of the world. Including its tribu-
taries, the Nile is also the longest river in the world, running over 4,100
miles from its beginning in the heart of the African continent to its mouth in
Egypt, where it flows into the Mediterranean Sea. For thousands of years, the
waters of the Nile have sustained the lives of those who dwell along its banks
and on its flood plain. Few other rivers have been as vital to the rise or fall of
human culture and civilization along their banks as has the Nile.

As mighty as the Nile is, however, it begins its life as two rivers, rather
than one. The White Nile flows from Lake Victoria in Tanzania, and the Blue
Nile from Lake Tana in Ethiopia. These two watercourses come together in
Khartoum, in the Sudan, to form the Egyptian Nile, which then runs over
1,600 miles northward on its way to the sea. Two separate streams, each
strong and significant in its own right, join together, with each adding its
strength to the other to form one mighty river that nurtures and sustains life
along its entire course.

In the spiritual realm, the flow of the prophetic from Heaven to earth
resembles the Nile River. Just as the White Nile and the Blue Nile join to

create the greater river called the Egyptian Nile, two streams of prophetic anointing come together to feed the greater concourse of the mighty prophetic river of God on earth. We can call these two streams the stream of the *prophet* and the stream of the *seer*.

Another way to look at this, as I mentioned in the introduction to this section, is to turn it around and think of a great prophetic river flowing from the throne of God that breaks into two streams—the *prophet* and the *seer*—which then give different degrees or dimensions or facets of prophetic impartation. Either way, it should be clear that both streams are important for the full expression of the Lord's prophetic word to His people in our day.

PROPHECY AND PROPHET DEFINED

In order to understand the difference between the prophet and the seer better, we need to define some foundational terms. Many Christians today are confused about the prophetic—what it is and how it operates. First of all, then, what do we mean by the word *prophecy*?

Kenneth Hagin, the late father of the modern faith movement, stated:

> Prophecy is supernatural utterance in a known tongue. The Hebrew word "to prophesy" means "to flow forth." It also carries with it the thought "to bubble forth like a fountain, to let drop, to lift up, to tumble forth, and to spring forth." The Greek word that is translated "prophesy" means "to speak for another." It means to speak for God or to be His spokesman.[1]

According to Dick Iverson, former senior pastor of Bible Temple in Portland, Oregon:

> The gift of prophecy is speaking under the direct supernatural influence of the Holy Spirit. It is becoming God's mouthpiece, to verbalize His words as the Spirit directs. The Greek word *propheteia* means "speaking forth the mind and counsel of God." It is inseparable in its New Testament usage with the concept of direct

inspiration of the Spirit. Prophecy is the very voice of Christ speaking in the church.[2]

Iverson's last statement is one of the best definitions of prophecy I have ever heard: prophecy is the *very voice of Christ* speaking in the Church!

The late international Bible teacher Derek Prince, the spiritual father who impacted my life more than any other leader, defined prophecy in the following way:

> The gift of prophecy is the supernaturally imparted ability to hear the voice of the Holy Spirit and speak God's mind or counsel. Prophecy ministers not only to the assembled group of believers, but also to individuals. Its three main purposes are:
>
> To edify = to build up, strengthen, to make more effective.
>
> To exhort = to stimulate, to encourage, to admonish.
>
> To comfort = to cheer up.
>
> Thus prophecy overcomes two of satan's most common attacks: condemnation and discouragement.[3]

David Pytches, a respected author and former Spirit-filled Anglican bishop, says:

> The gift of prophecy is the special ability that God gives to members of the body of Christ to receive and to communicate an immediate message of God to His gathered people, a group among them, or any one of His people individually, through a divinely anointed utterance.[4]

I assimilate all these understandings by stating that prophecy means the expressed thoughts of God spoken in a language that no people, in their natural gifts of speech, could articulate on their own. The substance and nature of prophecy exceed the limits that the human mind is capable of thinking or imagining. Its purpose is to edify, exhort, and comfort either individuals or the corporate Body of Christ. Although prophecy comes *through* the mouth or pen of people, it comes *from* the mind of God.

A prophet or prophetess then, is a spokesperson for God, one who hears the voice of the Holy Spirit and speaks or pens God's mind or counsel through a "divinely anointed manner."

The word *prophet* appears more than 300 times in the Old Testament and more than 100 times in the New Testament. In the Old Testament, the Hebrew word used most often for "prophet" is the word *nabiy'* (nahbi). Here are a few examples.

According to Genesis, Abraham was a prophet:

> *Now therefore, restore the man's* [Abraham's] *wife, for he is a prophet* [nabiy'], *and he will pray for you and you will live. But if you do not restore her, know that you shall surely die, you and all who are yours* (Genesis 20:7).

The same was said about Moses:

> *Since that time no prophet* [nabiy'] *has risen in Israel like Moses, whom the Lord knew face to face* (Deuteronomy 34:10).

As spokesman for his brother, Aaron was also a prophet:

> *Then the Lord said to Moses, "See, I make you as God to Pharaoh, and your brother Aaron shall be your prophet"* [nabiy'] (Exodus 7:1).

God called Jeremiah as a prophet even before he was born:

> *Before I formed you in the womb I knew you, and before you were born I consecrated you; I have appointed you a prophet* [nabiy'] *to the nations* (Jeremiah 1:5).

Malachi spoke of a prophet who would appear in the last days:

> *Behold, I am going to send you Elijah the prophet* [nabiy'] *before the coming of the great and terrible day of the Lord* (Malachi 4:5).

From Jesus' own words in Matthew 11:14, we know that this Scripture in Malachi refers to John the Baptist.

In a verse that many people believe refers to Jesus, the Messiah, God promised to raise up another prophet as a spiritual successor to Moses:

> *I will raise up a prophet* [nabiy'] *from among their countrymen like you, and I will put My words in his mouth, and he shall speak to them all that I command him* (Deuteronomy 18:18).

The word *nabiy'* has to do with hearing and speaking, with being a "mouthpiece" for God, declaring that which one has heard. A *nabiy'* prophet is a person who speaks on behalf of a superior. In Aaron's case, this was Moses and, ultimately, God. In the case of every biblical prophet, in fact, God was the superior for whom they spoke. Their words originated with Him. He planted His word in their hearts and mouths, and they in turn declared it to the people. In short, *nabiy'* prophets are speakers who declare the word that God has given to them.

IMPARTING THE PROPHETIC

God imparts this prophetic word in a number of ways. All prophecy comes from God through the Holy Spirit, but it operates differently in different people. The Old Testament uses several different Hebrew terms to describe the various modes of impartation.

First, according to Strong's Concordance, there is *nataf*, which means "to let drop like rain." This describes a slow, gentle process where the prophetic word comes upon us little by little and accumulates in our spirits over a period of time. It is like being in a certain place and having the mist of God descend around us and slowly permeate our spirits. Some have described it as being like a sponge that gradually soaks up and absorbs the "raindrops" of the prophetic presence of the Lord until they fill up and overflow.

The second Hebrew word listed in Strong's Concordance for prophetic impartation is *massa*, which refers to the "hand of the Lord" that releases the "burden of the Lord." When God's hand comes upon us, He imparts something to us—a prophetic "burden"—and when His hand lifts, that burden remains. The Lord deposits something in our spirits that was not there before; and even after He lifts His hand, we carry that burden as a word or commission from Him. He lays on us a "burden" for a particular situation, and we may carry that impartation for days, weeks, months, or even years.

For example, it might be a burden over the abortion situation in the United States. God's hand comes upon us and then departs, leaving behind a supernatural enablement of grace, a Holy Spirit endowment to prophesy and intercede in a way we never could before. I have addressed this theme thoroughly in my book *Kneeling on the Promises: Birthing God's Purposes Through Prophetic Intercession*.

Another word found in Strong's Concordance for prophetic impartation is *nabiy'*, which as we have already seen, is the action of "flowing forth," or "bubbling forth like a fountain." This perfectly describes the inspirational gift of prophecy we see so often in meetings, particularly in a setting of a plurality of elders and seasoned, gifted individuals working together as a coordinated team—the "prophetic presbytery" (see 1 Tim. 4:14).

THE SEER REALM

Within the overall realm of the prophet lies the particular and distinctive realm of *the seer*. Remember that I said all true seers are prophets, but not all prophets are seers. The word *seer* describes a particular type of prophet who receives a particular type of prophetic revelation or impartation.

According to Strong's Concordance, the Old Testament uses two words primarily to refer to a seer: *ra'ah* and *chozeh*. *Ra'ah* literally means "to see," particularly in the sense of seeing visions. Other meanings include "to gaze," "to look upon," and "to perceive." *Chozeh* literally means "a beholder in vision" and can also be translated as "gazer" or "stargazer."

With these definitions now in place, the distinction between a prophet (*nabiy'*) and a seer (*ra'ah* or *chozeh*) becomes a little clearer. When it comes to prophetic revelation, a prophet is primarily an inspired hearer and then speaker, while a seer is primarily visual. In other words, the prophet is the *communicative* dimension, and the seer is the *receptive* dimension. Whereas *nabiy'* emphasizes the active work of the prophet in speaking forth a message from God, *ra'ah* and *chozeh* focus on the experience or means by which the prophet "sees or perceives" that message. The first places emphasis on a prophet's relationship with the people; the second places emphasis on a prophet's revelatory relationship with God.

Apparently, seers were commonly employed in the royal court to offer counsel to the king. Asaph and Gad were both seers in King David's court:

> *Moreover, King Hezekiah and the officials ordered the Levites to sing praises to the Lord with the words of David and Asaph the seer. So they sang praises with joy, and bowed down and worshiped* (2 Chronicles 29:30).

> *When David arose in the morning, the word of the Lord came to the prophet Gad, David's seer, saying, "Go and speak to David, 'Thus the Lord says, "I am offering you three things; choose for yourself one of them, which I will do to you"'"* (2 Samuel 24:11-12).

In contrast, Nathan also served King David, but the Bible calls him a prophet:

> *The king said to Nathan the prophet, "See now, I dwell in a house of cedar, but the ark of God dwells within the tent curtains." And Nathan said to the king, "Go, do all that is in your mind, for the Lord is with you." But in the same night the word of the Lord came to Nathan, saying, "Go and say to My servant David, 'Thus says the Lord, "Are you the one who should build Me a house to dwell in?"'"* (2 Samuel 7:2-5)

Asaph was a seer and Gad was a seer, but Nathan was a prophet. Notice also that Second Samuel 24:11 refers to Gad as both a prophet and a seer.

One interesting verse that contains all three Hebrew words is First Chronicles 29:29:

> *Now the acts of King David, from first to last, are written in the chronicles of Samuel the seer* [ra'ah], *in the chronicles of Nathan the prophet* [nabiy'] *and in the chronicles of Gad the seer* [chozeh].

Another Scripture clearly reveals the influence of prophets and seers in ancient Israel and their position as spokespeople for God:

> *He* [Hezekiah] *then stationed the Levites in the house of the Lord with cymbals, with harps and with lyres, according to the command of David and of Gad the king's seer* [chozeh], *and of Nathan the prophet* [nabiy']; *for the command was from the Lord through His prophets* (2 Chronicles 29:25).

Nabiy' prophets and *ra'ah* and *chozeh* seers are all legitimate expressions of God's prophetic stream. As far as prophetic gifting is concerned, prophets and seers are equally valid. First Samuel 9:9 says,

> *Formerly in Israel, when a man went to inquire of God, he used to say, "Come, and let us go to the seer"* [ra'ah]; *for he who is called a prophet* [nabiy'] *now was formerly called a seer* [ra'ah].

All true seers are prophets, but not all prophets are seers. A prophet may have the particular grace to hear and proclaim the word of the Lord and yet not necessarily function as profusely in the revelatory visionary capacity as a seer does. The seer, on the other hand, may move quite remarkably in this visionary dream capacity, yet not be as deep in the inspirational audible graces of hearing and speaking. Nevertheless, both move and operate in the prophetic realm, but in different capacities or dimensions.

The seer realm describes a whole other aspect of the way the prophetic operation occurs. Generally speaking, seers are people who see visions in a consistent and regular manner. For the most part, their prophetic anointing is more *visionary* than auditory. Rather than receiving words that they attempt to repeat or flow with, they often see pictures that they then describe. These pictures may be in the form of waking visions, or as dreams while sleeping.

I know many prophetic *nabiy'* people who are not seers at all and who do not move in dream realms, but are nonetheless strong prophetic vessels. At the same time, I know other people who are profoundly gifted in "seeing"— they see angels, demons, lights and colors, dreams and visions—but who do not manifest as much in the inspirational capacity to encourage people spontaneously and verbally.

One of the differences is that, whereas the prophetic word of a *nabiy'* is often spontaneous and activated by faith, that of a *ra'ah* or *chozeh* seer is more dependent upon the manifested presence of God. Many seers will see something beforehand. For example, before going to a meeting or strategic appointment, a seer may receive a picture of a certain person at that meeting sitting in a certain place dressed in a certain color. The seer may even be given the person's name. Later, in the meeting, the seer will begin scanning the crowd looking for that particular person. If that person is actually there, this becomes a "green light" for the seer to move forward. For seers, seeing in the natural what they had already seen in the spirit activates their faith and calls forth courage within them.

This kind of prophetic anointing has a lot to do with quietly waiting on God. There are times, as observed from my own experience and that of others, when one waits on God for what seems to be an extended period of time, only to have Him come at the last minute. Quite often, impartation in the seer realm comes only after a time of patient waiting and contemplative meditation upon the Lord. I have often heard it stated: God is slow but He is always on time! But thank the Lord, if we wait, He will come!

LATTER-DAY PROPHETIC STREAMS

In recent years, we have witnessed the re-emergence of two distinct prophetic streams that first appeared over 50 years ago: the seer visionary stream and the *nabiy'* verbal stream. As spiritual fathers, Bob Jones perhaps represents the first, while Bishop Bill Hamon exemplifies the second. Founder and director of Christian International Ministries in Florida, Dr. Hamon described the mid-twentieth-century emergence of these two prophetic streams that have reappeared in recent years:

> Two streams of restoration came forth in 1947-48. One was the Latter Rain Movement, which restored the practice of... the laying on of hands...as well as extensive congregational prophesying....They emphasized moving into the prophetic realm by faith, grace and gifting. The other restoration stream was what was termed "The Healing and Deliverance Movement." Their restorational emphasis was laying on of hands for healing, deliverance and world evangelism by preaching with signs and wonders. Both groups were of God and were valid ministries.[5]

One of the father figures in the Latter Rain Movement was a man named David Shoch, while William Branham was a strongly anointed leader in the Healing and Deliverance Movement. One was a *nabiy'* prophet, while the other was a *chozeh* seer. Each movement had different manifestations and operations.

These parallel streams appeared in the mid-1940s and began to wane in the early 1950s, but both have re-emerged over the past 20 years or so. As a matter of fact, the current expression of the modern prophetic movement in America appeared in the late 1980s, centered in multiple locations: yet was distinctly at that time in Kansas City Fellowship (later Metro Vineyard Fellowship, then Metro Christian Fellowship, and today IHOP-KC) in Kansas City, Missouri. Its then lead pastor was, Mike Bickle, along with prophets such as Bob Jones, John Paul Jackson, Paul Cain, and others. At that time, I also, was recognized as one of the "Kansas City Prophets."

Central to this new emphasis on prophecy were three core convictions: "that the prophetic gift should be restored in the Church, that prophecy is a natural, biblical means for God to speak to his people, and that...this increased prophetic activity is a sign of the emergence of the last-days victorious Church."[6]

Modern-day prophecy in the Church consists of three parts—revelation, interpretation, and application. Great care must always be exercised because of the danger of fallible human instruments misconstruing either the interpretation or the application or both, which happened fairly often in the early days. The movement has grown to encompass multiple streams and locations and has matured greatly since that time, as have its practitioners.

Clearly, the central prophetic figures in the early portion of the Kansas City prophetic movement were Bob Jones and Paul Cain. Both have amazing stories of their own.

Paul was born to a mother who was miraculously healed of terminal tuberculosis, heart disease, and cancer shortly before his birth. He received his first visit from the Lord when he was eight. Even as a teenager, he was on the healing circuit, prophesying to people by telling them their names, their ailments, and that God was healing them. By the 1950s he had a full-time traveling ministry and a television program. Then, like so many revivalists of that period, he seemed to go into an eclipse. He ceased his traveling ministry, gave up his television show, and retreated out of the public eye to rekindle his love for God and devotion to holiness. Paul was released by the Lord in later years with a surge of impact. Since then, he has been to the mountaintop of global ministry, to the pits of failure, and then again in a mode of restoration.

Bob Jones, on the other hand, had an angelic visitation in his youth by an angel of the Lord when residing in rural Arkansas. It was years later, after being in the military, that Bob truly surrendered his heart to Jesus and responded to the calling on his life as a seer prophet. Bob was brought back from a near-death experience to be commissioned by the Lord to anoint leaders who would participate in the end-time harvest of one billion souls coming into the Kingdom.[7]

In addition to these two streams, I believe there are many other smaller streams of prophetic anointing that are variations of the others. The Christian Church today is experiencing her greatest period of prophetic impartation since the first-century. The river is widening, deepening and growing. Let the river flow!

Two Prophetic Streams: Contrasts and Comparisons

By contrasting and comparing the prophet and seer streams, we can gain a better understanding of how the two work together and complement each other in bringing out the fullest expression of God's prophetic revelation.

In general, as we saw before, the *nabiy'* prophetic anointing tends toward the audible and verbal and is more a communicative dimension. Prophets in this stream often work in a plurality of leadership. Seasoned and gifted individuals, both men and women, minister through the laying on of hands, relating prophecy to individuals or to the corporate Body as it is revealed to them. This ministry often utilizes the spiritual gifts of tongues and the interpretation of tongues, prophecy, and words of knowledge. *Nabiy'* prophets "hear" a word in their spirits and begin by releasing this unction. This kind of prophecy tends to be more spontaneous and with a faster flow than "seer" prophecy, with inspiration as the general tone.

Ra'ah or *chozeh* seers, on the other hand, tend more toward single-person ministry versus the plurality of a team. The seer anointing emphasizes visions and the revelatory gifts mingled with the gift of discerning of spirits rather than the audible, speaking gifts. Within the visionary dimension there are two basic levels of "seeing": *visual and actual*.

Visual "seeing" involves insights, revelations, warnings, and prophecies from the Spirit of God that may come in supernatural visual dreams. In such instances, people see God's revelation while their spirits simply observe and receive the message. Even though asleep, these people may see the heavens opened as Ezekiel did in Ezekiel 1:1 or as John did in Revelation 4:1. The special characteristic of an open-Heaven type of vision is that the higher celestial realms are disclosed, and views, patterns, and heavenly sights of God become seeable.

In contrast, *actual* "seeing" involves supernatural dreams in which God's tangible presence is evident or manifested. To see the Lord in a dream is *visual*, but for Him to manifest Himself to the person dreaming is *actual*.

Because seers prophesy primarily by sharing what they have seen, they often operate at a slower pace than *nabiy'* prophets due to the fact that they are trying to describe supernatural pictures in their own words. Unlike the generally spontaneous nature of *nabiy'* prophecy, seers often receive information ahead of time to share at a later date.

Seers often are dependent upon angelic visitations and the manifested presence of God. Consequently, these prophetic vessels may appear to have certain limitations until they sense the anointing. This was supposedly the case with William Branham, one of the leaders of the Healing and Deliverance Movement in the '40s and '50s. One day in the late 1940s, he had an angelic encounter that brought with it gifts of healing and a word of knowledge. From that day on, William Branham moved in a very high level of specifics, but with some limitations. Sometimes he would not be able to do anything until his angels showed up. When the angels came, he received release because revelation began to flow.

Prophets and seers represent diversities in the prophetic anointing. As stable and consistent Dr. Bill Hamon said, both are valid ministries, and both are needed in the Church today. God never does anything by accident or without purpose. It is important for all of us to nurture appreciation and respect for all who carry genuine prophetic giftings, no matter how those giftings manifest.

After all, both prophet and seer are servants of the same Lord and have the same goal: to speak that which God has given to them in order to exhort, edify, and comfort the Body of Christ. In a dream I had once, Paul Cain came to me and said, "The seer hears as much as he sees; it's just a different deep touch from the same dear Jesus."

Whether *nabiy'* or *ra'ah*, audible or visual, all prophecy comes from the same source: God the Father through Jesus Christ by the present-day ministry of the Holy Spirit. The purpose of both the prophet and the seer is to reveal the glorious wonders of Jesus Christ and God's purpose in each generation, as well as to bring an awareness of eternity, Heaven and hell, and the Father's great presence among His people—whether by audible or visual means, and whether by spontaneous inspiration or by reflective contemplation.

PRAY FOR VISION

There are two scriptural prayers that I have prayed regularly, even daily, for over 25 years. I have prayed them over myself, over my family and, through the years, over countless other people. Both prayers have to do with the seer anointing—the capacity to "see" in the spiritual sense.

The first of these is Paul's great prayer in the first chapter of Ephesians:

> [I pray] *that the God of our Lord Jesus Christ, the Father of glory, may give to you a spirit of wisdom and of revelation in the knowledge of Him. I pray that the eyes of your heart may be enlightened, so that you will know what is the hope of His calling, what are the riches of the glory of His inheritance in the saints, and what is the surpassing greatness of His power toward us who believe. These are in accordance with the working of the strength of His might which He brought about in Christ, when He raised Him from the dead and seated Him at His right hand in the heavenly places, far above all rule and authority and power and dominion, and every name that is named, not only in this age but also in the one to come* (Ephesians 1:17-21).

Every born-again believer has two sets of eyes. We have our physical eyes, with which we view the physical, created world around us. Paul also talks about a second set of eyes—the eyes of our hearts, or our inner self—which can be enlightened to perceive spiritual truth.

Paul said, *"I pray that the eyes of your heart may be enlightened...."* I pray the prayer something like this: "Lord, give me that spirit of wisdom; grant me that spirit of revelation so that I will be captured by Jesus Christ." Then I pray over the eyes of my heart: "Release shafts of revelation light into them, that I might know the hope of Your calling, that I might know the glorious inheritance that lives inside of me, and that I might know the surpassing greatness of Your power that works in me."

I pray this way and encourage you to do the same because I am convinced that any believer can develop the seer capacity. All prophecy, including the seer dimension, is a sovereign gift of God, but I do not believe it is an exclusive gift. Paul's prayer makes it clear that if you pray over the eyes of your heart, God will give you the spirit of wisdom and revelation in the knowledge of Him. This means you will come to know the Lord in a way you never could on your own or in your own wisdom.

The other Scripture I have prayed constantly for years is found in Second Kings chapter 6. Here is the situation: The king of Aram wants to capture the prophet Elisha and has sent his army to surround the city of Dothan, where Elisha is living. Elisha's servant sees the great army and is terrified:

> *Now when the attendant of the man of God had risen early and gone out, behold, an army with horses and chariots was circling the city. And his servant said to him, "Alas, my master! What shall we do?" So he answered, "Do not fear, for those who are with us are more than those who are with them." Then Elisha prayed and said, "O Lord, I pray, open his eyes that he may see." And the Lord opened the servant's eyes and he saw; and behold, the mountain was full of horses and chariots of fire all around Elisha (2 Kings 6:15-17).*

This Scripture shows that we can pray for someone else to be enlightened. Elisha was a seer; he saw something his servant could not see, and he prayed, *"O Lord...open his eyes that he may see."* It was such a simple prayer, and yet the Lord answered it. He enabled the servant to see into the spiritual realm. Through the prayer of a seer came an impartation to another of the capacity to see.

Nabiy' and *ra'ah,* prophet and seer—both carry the prophetic anointing, and both have a significant ministry from the Lord. Much has been written and taught about the *nabiy'* prophetic stream, but less has been composed about the *ra'ah* and *chozeh* stream of more visionary prophecy. To understand better, we first need to take a closer look at the different varieties of the prophetic anointing. So come on the journey with me, and let's learn to bless and receive from both streams of the prophetic movement in our day that together comprise one great river of God.

Chapter Two

DIMENSIONS OF THE PROPHETIC ANOINTING

They called it "the storm of the century."

In March 1993, a friend and I were traveling in New England, where I was scheduled to speak at a total of six meetings in three different cities. Our itinerary included New Haven, Connecticut; Providence, Rhode Island; and Kingston, Massachusetts. I believe the very names of these cities were significant, particularly in light of what happened. New Haven is a place of peace, a place of respite and rest. Providence has to do with the will of God, and Kingston (or Kings*town*) refers to the place where the king lives and from where he rules.

We were in New Haven, Connecticut, when the entire upper third of the eastern seaboard of the United States was slammed with a snow and ice storm propelled by 80 mile-per-hour winds. Holed up in our little cottage in the hills, we watched as snow and sleet in equal measure blew down.

In the end, only three of the six scheduled meetings took place, and attendance at those three was only about one-fourth of what it would have been otherwise. Nevertheless, that trip turned out to be a true divine appointment for us. Because of the storm, there were no meetings at all that Saturday, but it turned out to be a real joy for me that they did not happen. Rather than feeling remorse or worrying that we had somehow missed God and ended up in the wrong place at the wrong time, we knew we were exactly where we were supposed to be. While we were snowed in, watching the awesome power of nature and of nature's God, we had some wonderful time of just waiting on the Lord.

As we waited and prayed together, simply meditating before God's presence, He brought me into a realm where I began speaking prophetically, even though no one else except my friend was there to hear me. I felt at that time that the Lord was sharing part of His heart with me.

While watching a news broadcast, we heard the local story of a pregnant woman who went into labor during the storm and had to be dug out of her house in order to go to the hospital. She reached the hospital just in time to give birth to a healthy baby boy, whom she and her husband named Joshua. As a result, the local news media began referring to the blizzard as "the Joshua Storm."

As I pondered on that name, I felt the voice of the Lord inside me saying quietly, "Yes, there is a new anointing for a new generation: My Joshua generation." Like Joshua of old, who succeeded Moses as leader of the Israelites, a "Joshua generation" receives the baton from the generation that has pioneered and gone before it. It is a generation that takes the promises spoken to an earlier generation and crosses over into the "Promised Land" to possess it and to conquer the enemies that are there.

Today there is a new anointing for a new generation, a Joshua generation of people who will be born into the things of the Spirit in the midst of a great spiritual storm that is sweeping across our land. Let's take a closer look at this anointing.

UNDERSTANDING THE PROPHETIC ANOINTING

Many Scriptures throughout the Bible speak of the anointing. Psalm 92:10 says, *"You have exalted my horn like that of the wild ox; I have been anointed with fresh oil.*"Fresh anointing oil is what we need if we are going to be able to fulfill that which the Lord has already spoken of so clearly.

Isaiah 10:27 speaks of the power of the anointing to break the yoke of bondage, evil, and oppression:

> *It shall come to pass in that day that his* [the king of Assyria's] *burden will be taken away from your shoulder, and his yoke from your neck, and the yoke will be destroyed because of the anointing oil* (NKJV).

The anointing also carries the power to do good and bring healing:

> *You know of Jesus of Nazareth, how God anointed Him with the Holy Spirit and with power, and how He went about doing good and healing all who were oppressed by the devil, for God was with Him* (Acts 10:38).

Essentially, the anointing is the supernatural enablement or grace—the manifested presence of the Holy Spirit—operating upon or through an individual or a corporate group to produce the works of Jesus. It means God with you and God in you; you are talking His talk and walking in His shadow.

As an anointed people, we as the Body of Christ have been called to carry a prophetic-type burden that will cause us to live on the cutting edge of God's eternal purpose. The prophetic ministry is but one aspect of the fivefold calling of apostles, prophets, evangelists, pastors, and teachers. As such, it is resident to a degree in every ministry and more evident and active in certain ones. God's ultimate weapon is a man or a woman who has encountered the prophetic anointing. God does not anoint *projects;* He anoints *people!*

People anointed with a prophetic ministry speak the word of the Lord in the name of the Lord. They carry weight in the Church by virtue of the ethical, moral, and spiritual urgency of their message. Their credentials, credibility, and status as prophetic vessels stem not from birth or by official designation, but by the power of their inner call and by the response of those who hear them.

The single most characteristic mark of true prophetic people is the evidence that they have stood in the counsel of God and have therefore faithfully declared what they heard from His mouth. According to William Robertson Smith, it is this divine word that distinguishes a prophet:

> The possession of a single true thought, not derived from current religious teaching, but springing up in the soul as a Word from Jehovah, Himself, is enough to constitute a prophet.[1]

Usually, prophets make no special claim to be heard, but are content to speak and act and leave the matter there, confident not in themselves, but in the fact that they have heard from God and that every word from Him will find fulfillment. Their primary concern is not with the distant future, but to tell forth the will of God in the crisis of their own days. Prophets, then, are essentially interpreters of God.

The prophecies of the Old Testament prophets foreshadowed Christ. The major task of New Testament prophets and beyond has always been to declare that in Christ all the prophecies of the Bible have been fulfilled:

> And likewise, all the prophets who have spoken, from Samuel and his successors onward, also announced these days [i.e., the life, death, and resurrection of Jesus Christ] (Acts 3:24).

> As to this salvation, the prophets who prophesied of the grace that would come to you made careful searches and inquiries, seeking to know what person or time the Spirit of Christ within them was indicating as He predicted the sufferings of Christ and the glories to follow (1 Peter 1:10-11).

> For the testimony of Jesus is the spirit of prophecy (Revelation 19:10b).

Remember that prophecy itself is the expressed thoughts of God spoken in a language that no people in their natural gift of speech could articulate on their own. The substance and nature of prophecy exceed the limits of what the natural mind could conceive. Prophecy comes *through* the mouth of people, but *from* the mind of God—spiritual thoughts in spiritual words.

The prophetic anointing of the Spirit makes itself known in a wide variety of ways. People are different, with different personalities, cultures, ethnic backgrounds, and gifts. As Rick Joyner often states, no two snowflakes are alike! It should not be surprising, then, that there is a greatly divergent expression of the ministry and office of the prophet. Although there surely are more, I want to look a little more closely at 12 variations of this prophetic grace. These various models represent what the Spirit is doing and desires to do in the Church. Together they present a more complete picture of the fullness of the Lord's prophetic anointing.

Dreamers and Visionaries

Obviously, these are prophetic individuals who move primarily in the realm of dreams and visions—seers, in other words. Depending upon the particular sphere of ministry and authority God has given them, they may be released into a large public platform, or their prophetic sphere may be reserved for smaller settings such as their local church, business, family, or home group. In some cases their calling may be primarily private in nature, limited to their personal prayer closet and shared only with family members, or, as occasion permits, a few other people. The Lord does not give a prophetic anointing in a void. Large or small, every dreamer and visionary has a "market" or a sphere that he or she can influence.

The main purpose of this dream-and-vision anointing is to awaken the people of God to the spirit realm. It is a miraculous manifestation of the Spirit that creatively illuminates truth and can confirm the direction of God that has been given to others. A good biblical example is the prophet Zechariah (see Zech. 4.) In our own day, Bob Jones, John Paul Jackson, Paul Cain and others exemplify this seer prophet realm in an unusual manner.

Prophets Who Proclaim God's Corporate Purpose

People who display this expression of the anointing, while true prophetic vessels, may rarely or never prophesy over individuals in personal ministry. Their sphere of operation and authority is different. Especially gifted to discern the times and the seasons, they give clarity to the overall direction and purpose of the Body of Christ, enabling and encouraging the Church to rise up into full maturity.

Paul is the perfect New Testament example. Although an apostle and a teacher, Paul also walked under a strong prophetic anointing that revealed itself as a profound revelatory gift for uncovering and explaining the large corporate purpose of the Church.

One contemporary example could be Rick Joyner. Although Rick is an authentic seer, his emphasis is not on individual, personal prophecies. Rick is almost always found in the sphere of prophetically declaring and interpreting the corporate purposes of God for our day. Dr. Bill Hamon's teaching and many books also reveal God's overall prophetic purpose for His corporate Church, while Francis Frangipane, Tommy Tenney, and others point to the corporate direction the wind is blowing, too.

Prophets Who Proclaim God's Heart Standards for His People

People under this anointing challenge the Church by calling for holy thoughts, intentions, motives, convictions, and methodologies in every arena of life. That is what it means to proclaim God's heart standards for His people. Their purpose is to usher in the fruit of the Spirit, nurture the character of Christ, and promote purity and holiness. Biblical examples of this prophetic anointing would be Jeremiah in the Old Testament and John the Baptist in the New Testament.

A good contemporary example of this anointing was the late David Wilkerson, who released the plumb line of God into the Church even as he declared the standards of holiness in a prophetic manner. Just because he did not see visions, or individually lay hands on people, or call people out by name does not mean he was not prophetic. On the contrary, perhaps he was a prophet evangelist, releasing the Word of God in an evangelistic manner that changed lives. Thank God for others like Steve Hill and Michael Brown, who call us into radical obedience to the Word of God.

Prophets Who Proclaim
the Church's Social Responsibilities and Actions

This expression of the prophetic anointing calls to the Church to care for the widow, the orphan, the poor, the oppressed, and the prisoner—in short, all the needy who have no power and no champion for their cause. The purpose is to establish righteousness and justice. Amos in the Old Testament was just such a prophet. In the fifth chapter of the book that bears his name, he says, *"But let justice roll down like waters and righteousness like an ever-flowing stream"*(Amos 5:24).

In recent years, Norm Stone, with Walk America for Life, has been this kind of prophet. His lifestyle goes somewhat against the grain of the Church and the nation. God has given him a unique and unusual prophetic call to prayer walk across the United States from border to border—seven times— declaring the atrocities of abortion and pricking the hard hearts of the Church and of the nation to convict us of our social and moral responsibility. Though often a thankless job, it is a vitally needed ministry.

Another dear friend of mine in Nashville, Tennessee, is Scott MacLeod with Provision International. Though he is first a prophetic psalmist, he has given his life to the ministry of the poor in the inner-city projects of the city I live in. Mark Roye, who heads up our own Compassion Acts, is such a champion, as is Patricia King, with her global thrust of justice and mercy. They are some of the growing number of champions who call us to put feet to our faith by taking the prophetic to the streets.

Prophets Who Speak Forth the Administrative Strategy
of God With a Political Slant

Wait a minute! Prophets with an *administrative* gift? Isn't that a right brain/left brain conflict? Not at all! Moses was a prophet, and so were Joseph and Daniel. All three of these Old Testament men of God carried a strong prophetic anointing, yet all were extraordinarily gifted with administrative and leadership ability.

Moses needed quite a bit of political savvy to lead 3 million people out of 400 years of slavery and get them organized into a coherent nation. Joseph moved in the seer realm as an interpreter of dreams. His prophetic gifting to see what was coming put him in a unique position to speak the counsel of God to those who were in political authority. As second-in-command to Pharaoh, Joseph was a powerful and able administrator. Daniel also moved in the seer realm of revelatory dreams and visions, yet he was the most capable of all the leaders and administrators under the king of Babylon.

During my teenage years, the Lord laid on my heart a couple of prayers that I began to pray regularly. The first was, "Lord, raise up your Josephs. Raise up your counselors to the Pharaohs." Sometimes God puts something within you, and you don't even fully understand why it's there, let alone how it got there. All you know is that God has dropped into your spirit a deposit of grace that inspires you to begin praying for something or someone specific that you would never have dreamed of yourself. As a young man, I felt a burden to pray for the Lord to release counselors to those who were in authority.

The other prayer I began to pray was, "Lord, I ask that you give me a heart of purity." Jesus said, *"Blessed are the pure in heart, for they shall see God"* (Matt. 5:8). Oh, how I wanted to see the Lord! I cried out for a heart of purity, and I still do.

As God imparts this "political savvy," those who receive it reveal deep administrative skills and devise strategies that release and help foster the wise and smooth implementation of God's purposes. This is just what Joseph did in Egypt as he prepared the country to survive during seven years of famine.

Today, Dr. Kingsley Fletcher exemplifies this grace in an amazing manner. He is both a senior pastor of a church in North Carolina and a king of the nation of Ghana, calling forth change in society. There are many such statesmen and stateswomen whom God is raising up for such a time as this.

What a concept to strategically know by revelation what to do and how to implement it! Lord, expand our horizons and raise up these history-makers!

Prophetic Worship Leaders Who Usher in the Manifested Presence of God Through Prophetic Worship

Prophetic worship leaders help release people into the liberty of both expressing their love for God and receiving God's love. Under their prophetic leadership, the gifts of the Spirit flow and operate more freely. Because they are carriers of the Spirit, they can help lift others into His marvelous presence where change occurs. Jesus is truly exalted and enthroned in the praises of His people (see Ps. 22:3).

The prime biblical example is David who, in addition to being a shepherd and a king, was also a prophetic psalmist. Half or more of the psalms in the Bible were written by David. As a young man, he played his harp and sang, causing demons to flee from King Saul. What a combination!

Several examples of the prophetic psalmist in our own generation would be David Ruis, Julie Meyer, Sean Feucht, Matt Redmon, Misty Edwards, and Jeff Deyo. A new breed of radical Salvation Army bands are hurtling forth on the scene. A fresh combination mixing evangelistic and prophetic graces is emerging to impact the lost for Jesus' sake. But many of this new breed of holy warriors will find their expression primarily through music.

Prophetic Intercessors

Under this anointing, a person receives a burden from God that releases intercession that can affect individuals, communities, cities, and even nations. Depending on the measure of sphere and authority granted by the Lord, a prophetic intercessor may move under a particular international burden.

In the Old Testament, Daniel prayed three times a day for the release of the children of Israel from Babylonian captivity. He interceded for their return to their home and for their restoration (see Dan. 6:10, Dan. 9).

The second chapter of Luke tells of Anna, a prophetess and widow who *"never left the temple, serving night and day with fastings and prayers"* (Luke 2:37b).

Although not a single personal prophecy of hers is recorded, the Bible does say that she devoted her time to fasting and prayer. Anna was a prophetic intercessor.

It takes a strong prophetic spirit to endure in prayer before the Lord even when much time goes by with nothing seemingly happening. Without such an anointing, people become hopeless, disappointed, and discouraged to the point of giving up. The anointing for prophetic intercession imparts the grace to endure. You don't just pray to God, but you learn to pray the prayers of God!

For me personally, my anointing seems to be deepest in this area of prophetic intercession. God has given me the faith for it as well as the grace to impart it to others. It is awfully hard to give away something you do not have. Among all the things I do, this has been the strongest anointing upon my life. Cindy Jacobs of Generals International, Beth Alves of Increase International, Chuck Pierce of Global Spheres, Lou Engle of TheCall, Tom Hess, Dick Simmons, and thousands of others make up this army of revelatory prayer warriors.

The next five are expressions of the prophetic anointing that I believe the Holy Spirit wants to release on a wider scale and has even begun to do so.

Spirit-Bearers

John 3:8 says, *"The wind blows where it wishes and you hear the sound of it, but do not know where it comes from and where it is going; so is everyone who is born of the Spirit."* This is a word for every believer. All of us who are born-again are to catch the wind of the Spirit.

There are some people, however, who seem to have an anointing to catch that wind more than others. They wet their finger, stick it up in the air to find out which way the wind is blowing, then set their sails and follow that wind wherever it goes. To others they may appear flighty or even slightly crazy, but they don't care because they are caught up in following the wind of the Holy Spirit in their lives.

Through a love-walk with the Lord they practice the presence of Jesus. God uses these prophetic Spirit-bearers to release unusual manifestations of the Holy Spirit in the midst of a corporate people. There may be people falling in the Spirit, quaking, shaking, ecstatic speech, power encounters, or kingdom clashes of angelic and demonic warfare. Sometimes they will move in the realm of the angelic presence, even perhaps in a realm where they simply blow on people and an activity of God occurs.

The late Jill Austin, who was a dear friend of mine and the leader of Master Potter Ministries, was a modern-day Spirit-bearer. When she showed up, He showed up! Spirit-bearers' main purpose is to be with Jesus and to get up in front of people and say, "Come, Holy Spirit!" They are used to create a connecting point between Heaven and earth and bring Him into the place.

Prophetic Counselors

People with this anointing combine pastoral caring and healing understandings with the prophetic. There is a tremendous need for this kind of ministry today because so many people are so full of hurt and trauma and turmoil. Prophetic counseling often mingles the spirit of counsel and the spirit of understanding as stated in Isaiah 11:2:

> *The Spirit of the Lord will rest on Him, the spirit of wisdom and understanding, the spirit of counsel and strength, the spirit of knowledge and the fear of the Lord.*

Sometimes prophetic counselors also display gifts of healing and discerning of spirits: yet their primary concern is not the big picture, but the wholeness of the internal affairs of men and women on a personal or family basis.

Both compassionate and revelatory, they are able to see into the hurts and wounds of individuals, and they can help release the spirit of understanding. With their prophetic insight and ability to listen, they can help other people quiet their souls and ease their troubled hearts. John and Paula Sandford of the Elijah House Ministries are indeed a father and mother of this sphere. Joan Hunter has picked up the mantle of her parents "the Happy Hunters" and moves in a prophetic healing grace. The global Healing

Rooms Ministries led by Cal Pierce and many others are examples of these prophetic healers in our day and age!

So many people get so excited about all the amazing things that happen in meetings, but so much more happens in little gatherings and one-on-one counseling, as troubled individuals come face-to-face with the love, compassion, and healing power of the Lord through the ministry of sensitive and gifted prophetic counselors.

Prophetic Equippers

This is a prophet/teacher combination. All the offices of the fivefold ministry—apostle, prophet, evangelist, pastor, and teacher—are provided for equipping the Church; but some folks seem to have a special grace for equipping others. Some prophetic equippers may perform their ministries primarily through modeling, without significant involvement in individual people's lives. Others learn by listening to them speak and by watching their lives.

Many other prophetic equippers, however, function most effectively through direct interaction with other people in a teaching setting. They possess the teaching grace with a prophetic flare, which enables them to explain to others the ways of the Spirit taking the bizarre and making it practical, relatable, and understandable. Their call and desire is for the discipling of other believers with a particular burden for multiplication through mentoring, which is much-needed today.

The late John Wimber, former leader of the Vineyard Movement, was one of the most profound equippers I ever met. While his seminars where full of the power and presence of God, students were always given detailed notes and training sessions to help them learn "to do the stuff."

Dr. Bill Hamon, through his schools and prophetic training, has activated and equipped thousands of prophets and prophetic ministers located on every continent of the world. He has raised up many men and women, such as Sharon Stone, Jane Hamon and so many others. Thank the Lord for these activists and equippers!

Kris Vallonton and the Bethel School of Supernatural Ministry, in Redding, California, might just have the highest level of impartation today! Thank the Lord that new leaders are emerging and coming forth!

Prophetic Writers

Prophecy is not limited to the verbal and the visual; it may also come forth in written form. Although not as common, perhaps, as the spoken forms of prophecy, prophetic writing is just as valid. People with this anointing are just as prophetic as anyone else. The difference is that they have the gift and bent to communicate more powerfully and effectively through the written word than through the spoken word.

Over the years, I have seen many prophetic people who were awkward in front of people, but give them a pen and paper or a computer and watch out! On the other hand, I have also seen many powerful speakers with incredible charisma and "stage presence" who could hardly jot down two sentences together coherently, much less write a book. The written word and the spoken word are quite different, and there is a prophetic anointing for each.

Prophetic writers write with revelatory anointing, expressing in printed form God's heart to contemporary society. Gene Edwards is marvelously used in this manner to poetically paint pictures that draw the reader into His Majesty's courts.

Graham Cooke, of Vacaville, California, is probably one of the best examples of this convergence in recent years. His works are filled with wisdom, jewels of the journey with great prophetic insight.

Another past example of a revelatory piercing writer is the late Francis Schaeffer, founder of L'Abri Fellowship. Dr. Schaeffer was a powerful communicator through the written word, a true prophetic writer and statesman whose books and other writings continue to convict and challenge the Church worldwide 25 years after his death.

There are many other voices today, older and younger, who walk in this anointing. Yes, trendsetters like Rick Joyner of MorningStar Ministries, Dutch Sheets, Julia Loren, Sister Gwen Shaw of the End-Time Handmaidens, and

Servants and so many others. New voices with the pen of the ready writer are upon us!

Prophetic Evangelists

These are the ones who take the revelatory gifts to the streets, stadiums, neighborhoods, health clubs, executive places—anywhere and everywhere. How desperately our society needs people who move in the anointing of the prophetic evangelist! This anointing does not necessarily mean getting up in front of hundreds or thousands of people and preaching. Some prophetic evangelists will do that, of course, but most will operate in a smaller and more intimate sphere. One of the real needs is for evangelists in the ordinary, day-to-day places that we all know: the elevator, the grocery store, the bus, the ball field, the gas station, the doctor's office, the campus, the boardroom—anyplace where people interact.

Mahesh and Bonnie Chavda rattled my world. Through the prophetic and apostolic giftings upon their lives, they have seen hundreds of thousands come to faith in the Lord Jesus Christ. But other such champions are also arising on the scene today, like Patricia King, Mickey Robinson, Jeff Jansen, Munday Martin and scores of others who are breaking down the Church's walls and thrusting a people forth to take action.

How eager the Lord is to release Holy Spirit activity in the everyday world through the lives and words of faithful prophets who carry the prophetic evangelist anointing!

POISON AND ANTIDOTE

Clearly then, the prophetic anointing manifests in many diverse ways. All arise from the same Holy Spirit, who gives as He wills. With this in mind, a warning is in order. There is a deadly poison that can kill our ministry and our ability to walk in our anointing, whatever it may be: the poison of covetousness. Comparing ourselves to someone else and wanting what they have produces death. We should never judge or evaluate our anointing by someone else's anointing. It is vitally important to avoid jealousy and insecurity. God has plenty of anointing to go around. Let's be satisfied to seek our own calling and walk in our own anointing.

The antidote to this poison is to learn to walk in accountability with others, cultivating faithfulness, while giving ourselves to the unique expression of grace that God has imparted to each of us. Sometimes we are prone to allow ourselves to be hindered by rejection, criticism, legalistic traditions, and the restrictive yokes and molds of others' unrealistic and erroneous expectations.

The Holy Spirit will help us and liberate us to be unique and varied expressions of His wonderful prophetic presence and yet walk circumspectly with integrity within the Church. God has never been in a box. We are the ones in boxes! It is time to let the Holy Spirit take the lid off so that, in gratitude *to* Him, we can become all that we can be *in* Him. Let's let His anointing break the yoke. Instead of wishing we were somebody else or had what somebody else has, let's be faithful and accountable to walk in the unique expression of grace that God has given to each of us.

Chapter Three

VISION:
THE POWER THAT SUSTAINS

M oses had ascended Mount Sinai to meet with God. He had been gone over a month. In the valley below, the people of Israel, newly freed from slavery, began to wonder about his fate. Perhaps they believed a wild animal had killed him or that he had fallen from a cliff and died. In any case, the people came to Aaron, Moses' brother and spokesman, and induced him to make for them a "god," a golden image to go before them. They said to Aaron, *"This Moses, the man who brought us up from the land of Egypt, we do not know what has become of him"* (Exod. 32:1b).

Aaron took gold from the people and fashioned from it a molten calf, which the Israelites installed as their god, the one who had brought them out of Egypt. Then the people began to worship the calf and to celebrate with dancing and singing. They offered burnt sacrifices to the calf and indulged themselves in licentious play and behavior, perhaps like what they had seen in Egypt (see Ex. 32:2-6).

On the mountain, God saw what the people were doing and was prepared to destroy them, but Moses interceded on their behalf. The Lord relented and spared the people. Moses came down from the mountain, confronted the people, and in a symbolic gesture illustrating their disobedience, broke the tablets of the law at the foot of the mountain. He then destroyed the golden calf.

Seeing that the people were *"out of control"* (Exod. 32:25), Moses called out, *"Whoever is for the Lord, come to me!"* (Exod. 32:26). When *"all the sons of Levi"* gathered to Moses' side, he sent them out to put to death the instigators and leaders of the rebellion. In the end, 3,000 Israelites died that day.

This incident from the Book of Exodus illustrates perfectly the truth of Proverbs 29:18: *"Where there is no vision, the people are unrestrained, but happy is he who keeps the law."* This verse in the New International Version reads: *"Where there is no **revelation**, the people cast off restraint; but blessed is he who keeps the law."* Some other translations, such as the New Revised Standard Version, use the word *prophecy* instead of *vision* or *revelation*. The point is clear: without prophecy, without divine revelation or vision, people will cast off all restraint. They will run wild because they have no guidance—no *vision*. The Word of God— His *law*—provides vision and guidance for living, and those who follow it are blessed. All people need a vision to sustain them in life.

William Blake, the noted British artist and poet of the eighteenth and early nineteenth centuries, was also a visionary. He first began seeing visions as a child and continued to do so throughout his life. This visionary capacity profoundly influenced his life and work:

> In later years Blake habitually talked about the supernatural subjects of his pictures as being actually present in his studio when he was drawing them. A visitor once surprised him hard at work on a picture of an invisible sitter. He looked and drew, drew and looked, apparently intent on capturing a likeness. "Do not disturb me, I have one sitting to me," he said. "But there's no one here," exclaimed the visitor. "But I see him, sir," replied Blake haughtily. "There he is—his name is Lot—you may read of him in the Scriptures. He is sitting for his portrait."[1]

Some of Blake's best work, both artistically and poetically, was inspired by the visions that sustained him.

In the year AD 312, Constantine and Maxentius were rivals in the fight over who would be emperor of the Roman Empire. Both men and the forces under their commands drew up battle lines at the Milvian Bridge over the Tiber River. On the day before the battle, Constantine had a vision of a flaming cross outlined against the sun. On the cross were the Greek words *En touto nika,* which mean, "In this [sign] you shall conquer." The next morning, Constantine had a dream in which a voice commanded him to have his soldiers mark on their shields the *chi ro*—the monogram for Christ. Constantine obeyed, fought Maxentius, and won,[2] becoming emperor of Rome—and the first Roman emperor to embrace the Christian faith. Constantine had a vision that sustained him, led him to victory, and changed his life.

"Where there is no vision, the people perish" (Prov. 29:18a KJV). Unrestrained behavior leads eventually to destruction. People who have no vision also have no goal or purpose—nothing to shoot for. They have nowhere to go in life and, therefore, go nowhere.

As Christians, we are called to be a people of vision. We must learn to set a goal or target in front of our eyes to gaze upon. It is only when we aim at something that we have any chance of hitting it! The apostle Paul set his sights on knowing Christ, which he acknowledged was a lifelong process:

> *Brethren, I do not regard myself as having laid hold of it yet; but one thing I do: forgetting what lies behind and reaching forward to what lies ahead, I press on toward the goal for the prize of the upward call of God in Christ Jesus. Let us therefore, as many as are perfect, have this attitude* (Philippians 3:13-15a).

Like Paul, we need to be a people of vision. Let us set our sights on the Lord and aim at His goals.

THE VISION THAT SUSTAINED ELISHA

Elisha, who succeeded Elijah in prophetic ministry, was a man of vision. Even as a young man, Elisha hungered for more of God, and his hunger made him tenacious in pursuit of his goal. He kept before his eyes a vision of the

Lord that sustained him through a life of ministry even greater and more miracle-filled than Elijah's.

When the time drew near for Elijah to leave and be taken up into Heaven, Elisha would not leave his side. Three times the Lord instructed Elijah to go to a specific place—Bethel, Jericho, and the Jordan. Three times Elijah requested that Elisha stay behind, but Elisha refused each time. At the Jordan, Elijah struck the waters with his folded cloak, the waters parted, and the two men crossed over on dry ground.

Impressed and encouraged by Elisha's tenacity, Elijah wanted to find out what he was really after:

> When they had crossed over, Elijah said to Elisha, "Ask what I shall do for you before I am taken from you." And Elisha said, "Please, let a double portion of your spirit be upon me." He said, "You have asked a hard thing. Nevertheless, if you see me when I am taken from you, it shall be so for you; but if not, it shall not be so." As they were going along and talking, behold, there appeared a chariot of fire and horses of fire which separated the two of them. And Elijah went up by a whirlwind to heaven. Elisha saw it and cried out, "My father, my father, the chariots of Israel and its horsemen!" And he saw Elijah no more... (2 Kings 2:9-12a).

What exactly did Elisha see? Obviously, he saw Elijah being taken up to Heaven, because the verses that follow these make it clear that Elisha *did* receive a double portion of the spirit that had been upon Elijah. However, Elisha's own words make it clear that he saw more than this: *"My father, my father, the chariots of Israel and its horsemen!"* The words *"my father"* may refer to Elijah, whom Elisha certainly regarded as a mentor and father figure. It is also possible that Elisha, at the moment of his anointing, caught a glimpse of God the Father Himself—or at least of the glory that surrounds Him, since Exodus 33:20 says that no one can *see* God and live.

As for *"the chariots of Israel and its horsemen,"* this may be a reference to the innumerable company of the army of the heavenly host. Whatever Elisha saw, he was profoundly and deeply affected by the vision, and that vision sustained him throughout the rest of his life.

If you remember from Chapter One, this was not the only time Elisha saw a heavenly army of chariots and horsemen. When the king of Aram sent his army to surround Dothan and capture Elisha, Elisha's servant was terrified until Elisha prayed for his eyes to be opened. That is when the servant saw what Elisha saw: chariots of fire and horses surrounding them. Once the servant saw the divine army that was invisible to natural vision, his fear went away.

Elisha was a man of vision, a man of revelation, and he never let go of it. What about you? I don't know what prophetic promise the Lord may have spoken to you. As Christians, we have the biblical promises as well as the current-day revelatory words that are spoken into each of our lives, which come in a multiplicity of manners. Sometimes they come by the quiet, still witness of the Spirit; at other times, through dreams or visions. They may come from God directly to you or through someone speaking to you what they have received from God.

Whatever the case, don't cast away your dream, for it will have a great reward. Don't take off your dream coat in the presence of your enemy. Keep the vision God has given you before your eyes. Vision is a power that sustains a people.

THE VISION THAT SUSTAINED JACOB

Jacob is another Old Testament character who was sustained by a vision. Having fled his home to escape the murderous wrath of his brother, Esau, Jacob lay down to sleep in the wilderness.

> *He had a dream, and behold, a ladder was set on the earth with its top reaching to heaven; and behold, the angels of God were ascending and descending on it. And behold, the Lord stood above it and said, "I am the Lord, the God of your father Abraham and the God of Isaac; the land on which you lie, I will give it to you and to your descendants. Your descendants will also be like the dust of the earth, and you*

will spread out to the west and to the east and to the north and to the south; and in you and in your descendants shall all the families of the earth be blessed. Behold, I am with you and will keep you wherever you go, and will bring you back to this land; for I will not leave you until I have done what I have promised you"(Genesis 28:12-15).

For the next 21 years, Jacob worked for his uncle Laban, who also became his father-in-law when Jacob married his daughters Leah and Rachel. Laban was somewhat of a trickster and deceiver, just as Jacob was. Jacob worked seven years to get Rachel as his wife, only to end up with Leah, who was the older. He got Rachel as well, but had to work another seven years in return. Jacob labored an additional seven years in order to build up his own flocks and herds in preparation for returning to his homeland. In the process, Laban changed Jacob's wages ten times and tried in other ways to cheat him, but God was always at work behind the scenes, keeping His promise to Jacob.

Finally, when Jacob was preparing to leave, Laban tried to get him to stay by offering to pay whatever Jacob asked for as wages. Jacob replied that the only wages he desired were all the striped, speckled, and spotted sheep and goats in Laban's herds, as well as all the black lambs. Laban readily agreed, then hastened to place all the animals that fit that description into the care of his sons and sent them on a three-days' journey away. It seemed as though Laban had cheated Jacob again.

Jacob was undeterred:

> *Then Jacob took fresh rods of poplar and almond and plane trees, and peeled white stripes in them, exposing the white which was in the rods. He set the rods which he had peeled in front of the flocks in the gutters, even in the watering troughs, where the flocks came to drink; and they mated when they came to drink. So the flocks mated by the rods, and the flocks brought forth striped, speckled, and spotted. Jacob separated the lambs, and made the flocks face toward the striped and all the black in the flock of Laban; and he put his own herds apart, and did not put them with Laban's flock. Moreover, whenever the stronger of the flock were mating, Jacob would place the rods in the*

sight of the flock in the gutters, so that they might mate by the rods; but when the flock was feeble, he did not put them in; so the feebler were Laban's and the stronger Jacob's. So the man became exceedingly prosperous, and had large flocks and female and male servants and camels and donkeys (Genesis 30:37-43).

Jacob took fresh rods from poplar and almond trees (trees symbolize authority), peeled white stripes in them, and placed them in the watering troughs for the sheep and the goats. When the animals came to drink, they also mated (symbolizing intimacy) in front of the peeled rods. The resulting offspring were striped, speckled, and spotted. Jacob did this only when the stronger animals were mating, so he ended up with the strongest and healthiest flocks, while Laban's animals were weaker.

Jacob prospered greatly because the sheep and goats brought forth the right kind of offspring. They produced the desired result because there was a vision that was put in front of their eyes, and they begat what was put in front of them. This illustrates the principle that *vision is the power that sustains*. Whatever we keep in front of our eyes is what will determine our outcome!

THE VISION THAT SUSTAINED ZECHARIAH

Like the Books of Daniel and Revelation, the Book of Zechariah contains many visions and apocalyptic images. Zechariah was a visionary prophet whose visions related specifically to the time after the Babylonian exile and the beginning of the Messianic period in Israel's history.

One of Zechariah's visions is the context for one of the most-quoted verses in the Old Testament:

Then the angel who was speaking with me returned and roused me, as a man who is awakened from his sleep. He said to me, "What do you see?" And I said, "I see, and behold, a lampstand all of gold with its bowl on the top of it, and its seven lamps on it with seven spouts belonging to each of the lamps which are on the top of it; also two olive trees by it, one on the right side of the bowl and the other on its left side."Then I said to the angel who was speaking with me saying, "What are these, my lord?" So the angel who was speaking with me answered and said to me, "Do you not know what these are?" And I said, "No, my lord."Then he said to me, "This is the word of the Lord to Zerubbabel saying, 'Not by might nor by power, but by My Spirit,' says the Lord of hosts. 'What are you, O great mountain? Before Zerubbabel you will become a plain; and he will bring forth the top stone with shouts of "Grace, grace to it!"''" (Zechariah 4:1-7)

An angel came and roused Zechariah as if from a deep sleep. Have you ever been startled or awakened in the middle of the night and felt as though a spiritual presence was in the room? Perhaps you sensed the presence of God or His holiness, or you simply had a conscious awareness that God was there. It may have been exactly that way with Zechariah. One of God's *"ministering spirits"* (see Heb. 1:14) woke Zechariah in order to show him the vision and explain its meaning. This is the same way the Lord works with many of His seer vessels today as well.

In his vision, Zechariah saw an elaborate golden lampstand with two olive trees on either side of it. His first response was very intelligent. He asked the angel, "What are these, my lord?" Asking a question is a wise course of action whenever visionary revelation occurs. That is a lesson I learned from Zechariah. No matter what I see or how many times I think I may have seen it before, I always ask, "What is this, Lord?" I am confident that the same God who gives me the revelation can also interpret it for me.

Even when the angel asks him specifically, "Do you not know what these are?" Zechariah answers with humility, "No, my lord." Had Zechariah not responded with humility and openness, he probably would not have gained much from the whole experience. People who think they know it all already cut themselves off from learning anything new.

Years ago, when I was younger in these ways of God, I and a few others would spend some time with the parabolic seer, Bob Jones, in his home. He would tell us some pretty awesome and unusual things he had "seen." He would always ask us one last question. "Did you get that?" We would stay poker-faced, nod our heads and say, "Sure, we got that!" Then we would get in our vehicles and chatter, "Did you understand that?" I probably missed a lot I could have learned by not responding in humility. But I have since changed a few of my ways! I now respond a lot more like Zechariah!

As it turns out, Zechariah's vision had to do with a message for Zerubbabel, the civic official of the returning exiles under whose leadership the temple in Jerusalem would be rebuilt. The word of the Lord to Zerubbabel was, *"Not by might nor by power, but by My Spirit"* (Zech. 4:6). This was meant as an encouragement to Zerubbabel and the rest of the returning exiles that a new era was beginning, an era characterized by the working of God's Spirit in power and the coming day of the Messiah.

A new epoch of the Spirit was at hand. This was the vision that sustained Zechariah and, by extension, Zerubbabel and all of the returning exiles. It encouraged and motivated them to rebuild the temple in Jerusalem, as well as the walls of the city and the city itself, which had been destroyed by the Babylonians. Vision sustains a people, and humility is a key that releases understanding!

THE VISION THAT SUSTAINED DANIEL

Daniel was a prophet who regularly moved in the visionary realm. Essentially, visions can be classified into two varieties: *internal* and *external*. An internal vision is the kind that we sometimes call an impression or a mental picture. We see the picture with our mind's eye, but the picture itself comes from the Lord. An external vision is what we also sometimes call an open vision, where we see the vision with our natural eyes, but it's often superimposed over whatever is going on in the natural world around us. Daniel moved in both.

In the seventh chapter of the Book of Daniel, the prophet records his summary of a graphic and powerful vision he received while in bed one night:

> *Daniel said, "I was looking in my vision by night, and behold, the four winds of heaven were stirring up the great sea. And four great beasts*

were coming up from the sea, different from one another. The first was like a lion and had the wings of an eagle. I kept looking until its wings were plucked, and it was lifted up from the ground and made to stand on two feet like a man; a human mind also was given to it" (Daniel 7:2-4).

These verses contain two important phrases that help explain Daniel's success as a visionary prophet: *"I was looking"* and *"I kept looking."* As soon as the vision began, Daniel was looking for its meaning and kept looking until the end. One of the dangers I have become aware of in walking in the prophetic seer capacity is what I call *revelation fixation*: becoming so impressed with what we see that we quit looking. We get hung up on the images themselves to the point where we stop seeing and never press on to understand their meaning. It is as though we think the vision is an end in itself rather than an instrument God wants to use to teach us something.

Daniel did not let himself get caught up in revelation fixation. Throughout the course of the vision he said, *"I kept looking."* He was determined to stay alert to the end so he could understand what God was fully showing him.

In his vision, Daniel saw a succession of four beasts rise from the sea. The first was like a lion with eagle's wings. The wings were plucked off, the lion stood on two feet like a man, and a human mind was given to it. Next came a beast like a bear, which was told to *"devour much meat."* The third beast was like a leopard with four bird's wings and four heads, and which was given dominion. Daniel *"kept looking"* and saw the fourth beast, *"dreadful and terrifying and extremely strong; and it had large iron teeth. It devoured and crushed and trampled down the remainder with its feet..."* (Dan. 7:7b). It also had ten horns. As Daniel continued to watch, another, smaller horn grew and ripped out three of the other horns and took their place. This horn *"possessed eyes like a man and a mouth uttering great boasts"* (Dan. 7:8b).

What Daniel was witnessing was a vision of the revival of evil. He did not let it rest there, however, as he *"kept looking."* Because it is vision that sustains a people, Daniel wanted to look beyond the revival of evil to see the Lord's response to it. He was not disappointed:

I kept looking until thrones were set up, and the Ancient of Days took His seat; His vesture was like white snow and the hair of His head like pure wool. His throne was ablaze with flames, its wheels were a burning fire. A river of fire was flowing and coming out from before Him; thousands upon thousands were attending Him, and myriads upon myriads were standing before Him; the court sat, and the books were opened. Then I kept looking because of the sound of the boastful words which the horn was speaking; I kept looking until the beast was slain, and its body was destroyed and given to the burning fire. As for the rest of the beasts, their dominion was taken away, but an extension of life was granted to them for an appointed period of time. I kept looking in the night visions, and behold, with the clouds of heaven One like a Son of Man was coming, and He came up to the Ancient of Days and was presented before Him. And to Him was given dominion, glory and a kingdom, that all the peoples, nations and men of every language might serve Him. His dominion is an everlasting dominion which will not pass away; and His kingdom is one which will not be destroyed (Daniel 7:9-14).

Unimpressed with the visionary revelation concerning what the evil one was going to do, Daniel kept looking for something higher, an even greater revelation. He did not give in to revelation fixation. Daniel did not stop looking until he had seen a vision of the Son of man and His Kingdom being extended throughout the earth.

Like Daniel, we live today in the midst of a revival of evil, so we need a vision to sustain us as a people—a vision that shows us clearly how the promises of God are more than all the power of evil. Let us then be a people of vision who will not perish, but will walk together in hot pursuit of the Lord, so that we too will be able to hold before our eyes an all-consuming vision of the conquering Son of Man and the Ancient of Days sitting upon His throne. Keeping our vision of the Lord clear before us will sustain us through the many labors of our lives and ministries.

SEEKING THE VISION THAT SUSTAINS US

Over the years, I have become convinced that in the Christian life at least two things are certain: God *never* changes, and we are *always* changing. Our lives as Christians are a continual transition from one place to another, one level to another, one understanding to another. The purpose of spiritual light is to bring us into change and growth. The more light we have, the more change we experience; and the more we change (for the better), the more we are brought into higher levels of glory. Unless we are in constant transition, we will stop somewhere along the way and settle down. The Christian life is a frontier. God did not call us to be settlers, but to be pilgrims and pioneers.

This is the point of Paul's prayer in the first chapter of Ephesians:

> *That the God of our Lord Jesus Christ, the Father of glory, may give to you a spirit of wisdom and of revelation in the knowledge of Him... that the eyes of your heart may be enlightened, so that you will know what is the hope of His calling, what are the riches of the glory of His inheritance in the saints, and what is the surpassing greatness of His power toward us who believe* (Ephesians 1:17-19a).

The more enlightenment we have, the more wisdom and revelation we are open to receive, and the greater understanding we can develop of the hope of His calling, the glory of His inheritance, and the surpassing greatness of His power as they apply to our lives.

Once, years ago, I was in a particularly troubling time of transition and was seeking the Lord's guidance. Different voices and different people were speaking to me, wanting me to join this team or do that ministry or whatever, and I was confused. I simply did not know what the Lord wanted me to do.

As I was up early one morning seeking the Lord, I had an experience. Although I love experiences, they are not the foundation of my life. My life is founded on the Word of God, prayer, and Jesus—the rock of my salvation. Experiences are simply the icing on the cake, but what delicious icing!

While praying on the living room couch early that morning, I watched through the sliding glass door as the sun rose. For one short moment, a beam of sunlight coming through the venetian blinds lit across my forehead, and the thought came to me, "I will give you a shaft of revelation light." In that moment all my confusion dissipated. I did not hear anything or have any internal knowing of what my decision was to be. My spirit was simply at rest in the confident knowledge that the Lord was revealing it to me.

What is the hope of the Lord's calling on *your* life? Ask Him to give you a vision of it, and don't stop asking. Keep on looking until you see it. Don't look just for a project or for something to do; look for a vision of *Him*! Pray that the eyes of your heart will be enlightened and your spiritual vision enhanced. Ask that a revelatory shaft of light would enter your spirit so that you would know the hope and the expectation of good for your life. Remember that what you keep in front of your eyes is what you will become. Present your eyes, your mind, your heart—your whole self—to the Lord and ask Him to grant you the spirit of revelation. *Ask Him for the vision that will sustain you.*

Chapter Four

THE DIVERSITY OF VISIONARY STATES

There is only one Holy Spirit, but He works in a multiplicity of ways. There are many spiritual gifts, but only one gift-giver: the Holy Spirit of God. The prophetic anointing manifests itself in many diverse ways, but they all derive from the same Spirit. As Paul wrote to the Corinthians:

> *Now there are varieties of gifts, but the same Spirit. And there are varieties of ministries, and the same Lord. There are varieties of effects, but the same God who works all things in all persons. But to each one is given the manifestation of the Spirit for the common good. For to one is given the word of wisdom through the Spirit, and to another the word of knowledge according to the same Spirit; to another faith by the same Spirit, and to another gifts of healing by the one Spirit, and to another the effecting of miracles, and to another prophecy, and to another the distinguishing of spirits, to another various kinds of tongues, and to another the interpretation of tongues. But one and the same Spirit works all these things, distributing to each one individually just as He wills* (1 Corinthians 12:4-11).

This same diversity by the one Spirit applies also to visionary states and experiences. In fact, the New Testament uses a variety of Greek words to express different visionary states. None of these states are "higher" or "better" than any of the others. They are simply different, and the Holy Spirit uses them with different people for different purposes.

Let's take a closer look at some of these visionary states. Examining each one in turn will give us a better understanding of, and appreciation for, the wide diversity of this form of the prophetic seer anointing. Let's investigate eight different words that will unfold eight complementary expressions.

1. ONAR

According to *Vine's Expository Dictionary*, *onar* in Greek is the common word for "dream." It refers simply to the kind of dreaming we all do when we sleep. Everyday dreams are themselves visionary in nature, because our minds generate images that we "see" while we are asleep. As the Bible makes clear, God can and does use these common dreams to communicate with ordinary people. Let's look at three examples.

According to Matthew, God spoke to Joseph, the earthly father of Jesus, through a dream—not once, but three times:

> But when he had considered this, behold, an angel of the Lord appeared to him in a dream, [onar] saying, "Joseph, son of David, do not be afraid to take Mary as your wife; for the Child who has been conceived in her is of the Holy Spirit."...And Joseph awoke from his sleep and did as the angel of the Lord commanded him, and took Mary as his wife, but kept her a virgin until she gave birth to a Son; and he called His name Jesus (Matthew 1:20, 24-25).

> Now when they had gone, behold, an angel of the Lord appeared to Joseph in a dream [onar] and said, "Get up! Take the Child and His mother and flee to Egypt, and remain there until I tell you; for Herod is going to search for the Child to destroy Him." So Joseph got up and

took the Child and His mother while it was still night, and left for Egypt (Matthew 2:13-14).

But when Herod died, behold, an angel of the Lord appeared in a dream [onar] *to Joseph in Egypt, and said, "Get up, take the Child and His mother, and go into the land of Israel; for those who sought the Child's life are dead." So Joseph got up, took the Child and His mother, and came into the land of Israel* (Matthew 2:19-21).

Notice on these occasions that even though Joseph experienced dreams during normal sleep, he recognized that the dreams were from the Lord, and was quick to obey their messages.

After finding and worshiping the infant Jesus in Bethlehem, the wise men also received a word from the Lord through a common dream:

And having been warned by God in a dream [onar] *not to return to Herod, the magi left for their own country by another way* (Matthew 2:12).

In this case, a common dream was involved, but the uncommon element was that apparently all of the magi had the same dream! Let us pray for that to occur today!

On occasion, God even speaks to unbelievers through an *onar* dream:

While he was sitting on the judgment seat, his wife sent him a message, saying, "Have nothing to do with that righteous Man; for last night I suffered greatly in a dream [onar] *because of Him"*(Matthew 27:19).

Pontius Pilate was sitting in judgment over Jesus when his own wife warned him of the dream about Jesus that had troubled her the night before. Here is biblical proof of God passing along "secret information" in the form of a warning dream to an unbeliever, a woman who was not even part of the covenant people of God. The Lord is absolutely sovereign, and He can speak to anyone He wishes, any way He wishes, any time He wishes. Many times He does so through a common dream, an *onar*.

2. ENUPNION

Like *onar*, *Vine's Expository Dictionary* relates the word e*nupnion* to a vision or dream received while asleep. The difference with *enupnion* is that it stresses a surprise quality that is contained in that dream. One example of the word is found in the Book of Jude:

> Yet in the same way these men, also by dreaming [enupnion], *defile the flesh, and reject authority, and revile angelic majesties. But Michael the archangel, when he disputed with the devil and argued about the body of Moses, did not dare pronounce against him a railing judgment, but said, "The Lord rebuke you!"* (Jude 8-9)

The phrase *"these men"* refers to certain *"ungodly persons"* who have *"crept in unnoticed"* (Jude 4) seeking to corrupt the Church and deny Christ. In context, Jude likens them to the angels who rebelled against God and to the people of Sodom and Gomorrah, who were destroyed because of their great sinfulness and immorality. In the same way, *"these men"* in Jude 8 have given themselves over to sensuous dreamings that defile the flesh and, just like Sodom and Gomorrah, are setting themselves up for a sudden and shocking surprise when God's judgment falls on them.

Another instance of the word *enupnion* is found in the second chapter of Acts:

> *"And it shall be in the last days," God says, "that I will pour forth of My Spirit on all mankind; and your sons and your daughters shall prophesy, and your young men shall see visions, and your old men shall dream dreams* [enupnion]" (Acts 2:17).

Literally, the phrase "shall dream dreams" means *"shall be given up to dream by dreams."* This is the kind of dream that really sticks with you after you wake up. Something about it startled you and made your senses alert, perhaps some kind of shocking quality to the dream that caused you to remember it vividly.

I have had several of this type of encounter. Once, when I was ministering in Argentina, I dreamed that an angel was in my room. In the middle of the night, I awoke suddenly to find my room permeated with an atmosphere of awe, surprise, and amazement. Before I knew what was happening, I was catapulted into an open vision of this very same angel manifesting itself at the end of my bed and declaring to me, "Seize the moment!" Immediately I found myself supernaturally filled with the energy of God and the power for my appointment. Yes, sometimes a "surprise element" is released through these seer encounters. Watch out: ready or not, here He comes!

3. HORAMA

According to *Vine's Expository Dictionary*, *horama* is another general term for vision, meaning "that which is seen." It carries the particular sense of a "spectacle, sight, or appearance." New Testament examples commonly associate this word with *waking visions*.

Matthew uses *horama* to describe the vision Peter, James, and John saw at the Transfiguration of Jesus:

> As they were coming down from the mountain, Jesus commanded them, saying, "Tell the vision [horama] to no one until the Son of Man has risen from the dead" (Matthew 17:9).

In the Book of Acts, Ananias received his instructions to go to Saul through a *horama*. The Lord used the same means to let Saul know that Ananias was coming:

> Now there was a disciple at Damascus named Ananias; and the Lord said to him in a vision [horama], "Ananias." And he said, "Here I am, Lord." And the Lord said to him, "Get up and go to the street called Straight, and inquire at the house of Judas for a man from Tarsus named Saul, for he is praying, and he has seen in a vision [horama]

a man named Ananias come in and lay his hands on him, so that he might regain his sight" (Acts 9:10-12).

The tenth chapter of Acts tells the story of Cornelius, the Roman centurion, and Simon Peter, and how the Lord used visions to bring the two men together. Cornelius, a God-fearing man, was praying one day when an angel appeared to him:

> *About the ninth hour of the day he clearly saw in a vision* [horama] *an angel of God who had just come in and said to him, "Cornelius!" And fixing his gaze on him and being much alarmed, he said, "What is it, Lord?" And he said to him, "Your prayers and alms have ascended as a memorial before God"* (Acts 10:3-4).

Following the angel's instructions, Cornelius sent for Simon Peter, who was in Joppa. The next day, while Peter was on the roof of the house where he was staying, he had a vision (see Acts 10:9-16). In these verses, the Greek word used to describe Peter's vision is *ekstasis*, which means "trance" (see below). Afterward, when Peter was trying to understand what he had seen, the word *horama* is used. As Peter pondered the meaning of his vision, the men sent by Cornelius arrived.

> *While Peter was reflecting on the vision* [horama], *the Spirit said to him, "Behold, three men are looking for you. But get up, go downstairs and accompany them without misgivings, for I have sent them Myself"* (Acts 10:19-20).

The apostle Paul also was no stranger to visions. There were times when Paul received direction for his ministry while in a visionary state. One such instance led to the Gospel entering eastern Europe for the very first time:

> *A vision* [horama] *appeared to Paul in the night: a man of Macedonia was standing and appealing to him, and saying, "Come over to Macedonia and help us." When he had seen the vision* [horama], *immediately we sought to go into Macedonia, concluding that God had called us to preach the gospel to them* (Acts 16:9-10).

On another occasion, God used a vision to encourage Paul and to instruct him to settle and preach in the city of Corinth for a while:

> *And the Lord said to Paul in the night by a vision* [horama], *"Do not be afraid any longer, but go on speaking and do not be silent; for I am with you, and no man will attack you in order to harm you, for I have many people in this city." And he settled there a year and six months, teaching the word of God among them* (Acts 18:9-11).

You can be a candidate for *horama* visions as well. Just tell the Lord of your desire to be a person who receives the spirit of revelation and sees visions. It is in His Word. It is for today. It is there for the asking!

4. HORASIS

As *Vine's Expository Dictionary* shows, this word *horasis*, which occurs only twice in the Greek New Testament, refers to sight or vision in *either* an external or internal sense. The Greek language makes no distinction between the perception of the physical eye and the non-physical eye; both external and internal "seeing" are regarded as genuine perception.

We all have two sets of eyes: our physical or natural eyes and the "eyes" of our heart, with which we "see" into the spiritual realm. It was this second set of eyes that the apostle Paul was referring to in Ephesians 1:18 when he said, *"I pray that the eyes of your heart may be enlightened..."* Those are the "eyes" through which we see and understand spiritual truth. The Bible says that our bodies are temples for the Holy Spirit. Every temple has windows and doors. When the Lord comes to dwell in our "temples," He likes to be able to look out His "windows." Our eyes—physical and spiritual—are the windows to our soul.

The first occurrence of *horasis* in the New Testament is found in Acts 2:17 in the phrase, *"your young men shall see visions...."* Revelation 4:3 contains the only other instance of this Greek word:

And He who was sitting was like a jasper stone and a sardius in appearance [horasis]; and there was a rainbow around the throne, like an emerald in appearance [horasis].

In this case, the word is used in its external sense of the *aspect* of one's appearance.

Stated simply, a vision—a *horasis*—occurs when the Spirit who lives within us looks out through the "windows" of our eyes and allows us to see what He sees. Are we seeing in the natural or in the spiritual realm? Sometimes it is hard to tell, and sometimes it is *both*. When our spiritual eyes are open, sometimes our natural eyes can see into the spiritual realm. We may see dual images as visionary spiritual pictures are superimposed over the images we are seeing with our physical eyes.

Some years ago when we lived in another home, I was standing on the deck in our backyard watching our children play on the swing set. At one end of the swing set was a small slide. As I stood watching my children, my spiritual eyes opened up for just a few moments. Although I continued to see the natural image of the swing set, my children, and the slide, with my spiritual vision, I now saw also a small, round swimming pool at the bottom of the slide. While I watched, a full-grown adult man slid down the slide headfirst on his back into the pool.

My first reaction was to ask, "What is that?" To my wonderful amazement, a response came immediately. I heard a voice speak in my spirit, "I will restore the backslidden man into the pool of My purpose." I knew then that the Holy Spirit had given me the interpretation of the vision. It was very encouraging to me. In the years since, I have used that phrase many times in intercession, calling for the backslidden man to be restored into the pool of God's purpose. That revelation came to me through a *horasis* vision in which I saw with both my natural eyes and my spiritual eyes simultaneously.

5. OPTASIA

Another visionary state found in the New Testament is denoted by the word *optasia*—which, according to *Vine's Expository Dictionary*, literally means "visuality," or in concrete form, "apparition." *Optasia* has the very specific connotation of self-disclosure or of letting oneself be seen. The word occurs three times in the New Testament, always in the context of someone seeing a divine or spiritual personage.

For example, in the first chapter of Luke, Zechariah the priest sees a vision of the archangel Gabriel while performing his duties in the temple. Gabriel informs Zechariah that he and his wife, Elizabeth, will have a son, whom they are to name John. Their son would grow up to become John the Baptist. Because Zechariah has trouble believing Gabriel's word, the angel tells him that he will be unable to speak until everything comes to pass. Undoubtedly, Zechariah was profoundly moved by his vision:

> But when he came out, he was unable to speak to them; and they realized that he had seen a vision [optasia] in the temple; and he kept making signs to them, and remained mute (Luke 1:22).

The second instance of the use of *optasia* is in connection with Luke's account of the Resurrection of Jesus. Two of Jesus' disciples are on the road to Emmaus, conversing with the risen Jesus, although they do not recognize Him. One of them says to Jesus:

> But also some women among us amazed us. When they were at the tomb early in the morning, and did not find His body, they came, saying that they had also seen a vision [optasia] of angels who said that He was alive (Luke 24:22-23).

Paul also used *optasia* in the twelfth chapter of Second Corinthians to describe in the third person a visionary experience of his own:

> Boasting is necessary, though it is not profitable; but I will go on to visions [optasia] and revelations of the Lord. I know a man in Christ who fourteen years ago—whether in the body I do not know, or out of the body I do not know, God knows—such a man was caught up to the third heaven. And I know how such a man—whether in the body or apart from the body I do not know, God knows—was caught

up into Paradise and heard inexpressible words, which a man is not permitted to speak (2 Corinthians 12:1-4).

Paul's description reveals another dimension of *optasia*: not only does the vision involve seeing a divine or angelic personage, but the person experiencing the vision may see himself or herself participating in it as if from a third-person perspective. This is the self-disclosure aspect of an *optasia*-type vision.

After my father, Wayne Goll, had passed away to be with the Lord, I was ministering in Atlanta, Georgia, at a prophetic conference. I had spoken that night on "Gate Keepers of His Presence." At the close of the service, I fell on my knees on the platform and was overwhelmed with the beauty of the Lord. Several people were prostrate on the floor seeking the Lord's face.

All of a sudden, as I wept openly, I saw an external picture of my father's face looking right at me. I was stunned by the vision that I saw. I continued to weep, and the Holy Spirit spoke to me, "I have a word to give to you from your father." Again, my father's face appeared right before me. He had passed away from a sickness that had left him as a shell of the strong man he had been. In this open-eyed vision, he appeared healed, strong, and vibrant. I then heard words spoken straight into my heart a second time, "I have a word to give to you from your father." Simple, clear words proceeded as I looked at the vision of my father's face smiling right at me: "I understand you now!" Healing flowed into my being. What an experience! What a blessing! It touched my heart deeply in a way that only God could do. What a personal God!

6. EKSTASIS

Next we come to the word *ekstasis*, from which our English word *ecstasy* is derived. *Ekstasis* occurs seven times in the New Testament according to *Vine's Expository Dictionary*, and, depending on how it is used, means amazement, astonishment, or a trance. Literally, *ekstasis* means "a displacement of the mind," or "bewilderment." When translated as "trance," *ekstasis* refers to one being caught up in the Spirit so as to receive those revelations that God intends. This is very likely the state that John was referring to in Revelation

1:10 when he wrote, *"I was in the Spirit on the Lord's day, and I heard behind me a loud voice like the sound of a trumpet."*

A good example of the first meaning of *ekstasis* is found in Luke 5:26: *"They were all struck with astonishment [ekstasis] and began glorifying God; and they were filled with fear, saying, 'We have seen remarkable things today.'"* This verse describes the response of the crowd who witnessed Jesus' healing of a paralyzed man whose friends had lowered him through the roof in order to get him to Jesus.

The third chapter of Acts records a similar situation where Peter heals a beggar who was born lame:

> *And all the people saw him walking and praising God; and they were taking note of him as being the one who used to sit at the Beautiful Gate of the temple to beg alms, and they were filled with wonder and amazement [ekstasis] at what had happened to him* (Acts 3:9-10).

In both of these cases, the people who witnessed these miracles were so astonished that they were caught up in some form of an ecstatic experience.

On the morning of Jesus' Resurrection, three of the women who had followed Him came to His tomb to anoint His body. Instead, they found the tomb empty and saw an angel of God, who told them that He had risen from the dead and would meet with them again in Galilee. How did they respond to this angelic visitation? *"They went out and fled from the tomb, for trembling and astonishment [ekstasis] had gripped them; and they said nothing to anyone, for they were afraid"* (Mark 16:8).

Ekstasis also means "trance," as in Acts 10:10 when Peter has his vision on the rooftop in Joppa before his visit to Cornelius: *"But he became hungry and was desiring to eat; but while they were making preparations, he fell into a trance [ekstasis]."* A similar thing happened to Paul one day when he was praying at the temple in Jerusalem:

> *It happened when I returned to Jerusalem and was praying in the temple, that I fell into a trance [ekstasis], and I saw Him saying to*

*me, "Make haste, and get out of Jerusalem quickly, because they will
not accept your testimony about Me"*(Acts 22:17-18).

A trance is a form of ecstatic experience. In our day and age, trances
have gotten a bad name because of their association with the New Age movement and the occult. The experiences of Peter and Paul reveal that a trance,
although perhaps not as common as some other types of visions, is nonetheless a legitimate and biblical form of a visionary state that God may choose
to use in imparting revelation to His people. I will deal more with trances in
Chapter Nine.

7. APOKALUPSIS

With *apokalupsis*, we come to the most frequently used word in the New
Testament to describe a visionary state. The word occurs 18 times—once
in Luke, once in Revelation, three times in First Peter, and the rest in six of
Paul's letters. Usually translated "revelation," *apokalupsis,* according to *Vine's
Expository Dictionary,* literally means "disclosure," an "appearing," "coming," or
a "manifestation." It carries specifically the sense of something hidden that has
now been uncovered or revealed.

This sense of the word is clear in the sixteenth chapter of Romans, where
Paul writes:

> *Now to Him who is able to establish you according to my gospel and
> the preaching of Jesus Christ, according to the revelation* [apokalup-
> sis] *of the mystery which has been kept secret for long ages past, but
> now is manifested, and by the Scriptures of the prophets, according to
> the commandment of the eternal God, has been made known to all the
> nations, leading to obedience of faith; to the only wise God, through
> Jesus Christ, be the glory forever. Amen* (Romans 16:25-27).

Paul uses the same word in Ephesians 1:17 when he prays *"that the God
of our Lord Jesus Christ, the Father of glory, may give to you a spirit of wisdom and of
revelation* [apokalupsis] *in the knowledge of Him."*

In several instances, *apokalupsis* appears in connection with the "revelation" or "appearing" of Christ at His return. Peter especially uses the word in this context:

> *In this you greatly rejoice, even though now for a little while, if necessary, you have been distressed by various trials, so that the proof of your faith, being more precious than gold which is perishable, even though tested by fire, may be found to result in praise and glory and honor at the revelation [apokalupsis] of Jesus Christ;... Therefore, prepare your minds for action, keep sober in spirit, fix your hope completely on the grace to be brought to you at the revelation [apokalupsis] of Jesus Christ (1 Peter 1:6-7,13).*

Have you ever had an experience where you suddenly felt like a little light went on inside? You may not necessarily have had an actual vision, but just a sense that something that you did not understand, something that was hidden from you, was now revealed. That is an *apokalupsis*-type experience.

Of course, the most familiar use of the word *apokalupsis* is Revelation 1:1:

> *The Revelation [apokalupsis] of Jesus Christ, which God gave Him to show to His bond-servants, the things which must soon take place; and He sent and communicated it by His angel to His bond-servant John.*

This is where our English word *apocalypse* comes from.

Because of its association with the Book of Revelation, with all of its graphic depictions of disaster and symbolic imagery, *apocalypse* has come to mean for many people the idea of catastrophic events, particularly related to the end of the world. For many people, the Book of Revelation is full of cryptic puzzles and tantalizing mysteries that are hard to grasp. It is important, therefore, to remember that *apocalypse* or *apokalupsis* does not mean "hidden," but "revelation," or an "unveiling." Expect the Holy Spirit to reveal mysteries to you from the Word of God and through supernatural encounters of a heavenly kind!

8. Egenomehn ehn pneumati

Finally, I want to examine one Greek phrase that has significance to the whole scope of the prophetic visionary state. I mentioned earlier that John, the writer of Revelation, may have been in a trance state—*ekstasis*—during the time he received his revelation from the Lord. Although John himself does not use that word to describe his state, he does use the phrase *egenomehn ehn pneumati*, which means "I was in the Spirit":

> *I, John, your brother and fellow partaker in the tribulation and kingdom and perseverance which are in Jesus, was on the island called Patmos because of the word of God and the testimony of Jesus. I was in the Spirit* [egenomehn ehn pneumati] *on the Lord's day, and I heard behind me a loud voice like the sound of a trumpet...* (Revelation 1:9-10).

The phrase *egenomehn ehn pneumati* literally means "to *become* in the Spirit," a state in which one could see visions and be informed or spoken directly to by the Spirit of God. Therein lies the secret to how we get revelation. How do we receive insight? How do we see visions? We do it by first getting in the Spirit. The more we are filled with the Spirit and walk in the Spirit, the more we become one with the Spirit, and the more our eyes will be opened to see in the Spirit. He will give us the perception to look into the spiritual realm.

Luke uses a similar phrase when he writes:

> *Jesus, full of the Holy Spirit* [plere pneumato hagiou], *returned from the Jordan and was led around by the Spirit in the wilderness for forty days, being tempted by the devil. And He ate nothing during those days, and when they had ended, He became hungry* (Luke 4:1-2).

Notice that the Holy Spirit *led* Jesus into the wilderness, where He was tempted by the devil. That fact opens up a whole new dimension for us. The Spirit can bring us into the realm of the Spirit for the purpose not only of seeing into the heavenly realms or discerning the intentions and motives that lie in the hearts of people, but also of seeing into the demonic realm in preparation for doing battle with the kingdom of darkness.

This leads to a principle that is important for all of us, whether or not we are moving under a particular seer or visionary anointing at any given time: *we should always engage the devil on God's terms, not ours, and never interact with the devil on his terms.* As always, Jesus is our example. In the wilderness, Jesus was full of the Spirit and led by the Spirit, and from that place He had victory over the devil. The only way we can ever hope to engage satan and come out victorious is to be filled with and led by the Holy Spirit. This means that we should not *seek out* encounters with the enemy. We are to seek God. If we are faithfully seeking to live for Christ, those encounters will come to us because the devil will seek us out. We are a threat to the kingdom of darkness. We can enter the fray in the fullness and power of the Spirit, and then together we overcome the enemy. Remember that victory is *"'not by might nor by power, but by My Spirit,' says the Lord of hosts"* (Zech. 4:6b).

Filled and led by the Spirit, we have the power, as Jesus did, to encounter and defeat the enemy. It is only under the Lord's umbrella of protection that we are safe. Realize that each one of us has a distinct gift and calling in God. We are all called to the battle, but some are called as warriors with a gift of faith or other gift mix that enables them in their assignment.

Cindy Jacobs, co-founder of Generals of Intercession and a prophetess of the Lord, walks in the keen gift of discerning of spirits. This enables her to distinguish evil spirits that hinder God's purposes and also to sense, see, or perceive the angelic presence assigned by the Lord over a given region. I have seen her get in the Spirit (*egenomehn ehn pneumati*) and then be used by the Lord in this wonderful dimension. Demonic forces are pushed back as this temporary present darkness is pierced through by God's light.

There is much to learn in all of these facets and spheres of the revelatory anointings. We need the wisdom, enlightenment, and knowledge of the Holy Spirit in order to wisely judge the revelation we receive. But He promises He will give it. He will not give us experiences or gifts without teaching us how to properly use them!

Section Two

SPIRITUAL DISCERNMENT

The great harm of dispensational theology is that it deceives people into thinking that God no longer speaks to His people except through the Bible. This theology mutes God at a time when we are desperate to see Him and hear from Him. Entire segments of the Body of Christ live in fear of being deceived or led astray by supernatural experiences. Even though there have been excesses and abuses, we have no reason to write off these revelatory encounters. God still speaks today! He does speak to us through visions, dreams, and angelic visitations. There is no reason to fear these spiritual experiences. God is capable of protecting His people from deception and misuse.

When it comes to the realm of supernatural events, God has provided resources that will create a structure of safety for us. These resources will assist us in discerning the validity of our spiritual experiences. This safety net is composed of the confirming voice of the Holy Spirit, the confirmation of the Holy Scriptures, and our relationships in a Bible-believing fellowship.

It is important to understand that there are three sources of spiritual revelation: the Holy Spirit, the human soul, and evil spirits. Since it is possible that all of us can be deceived, it is important to know how to test our revelations and experiences. Besides applying the nine scriptural tests to ensure the accuracy, authority, and validity of our revelations, we should also learn and apply the 15 wisdom issues.

Exercising wisdom in judging revelatory activity is absolutely vital to the health and integrity of all ministry, whether that of the everyday believer or a visionary prophet. Nowhere is this truer than in the area of the discerning of spirits. The gift of discerning spirits is critical to a healthy spiritual life, for it is through this gifted ability that we are able to discern the source of all spiritual things that pass through our lives.

Chapter Five

WISELY JUDGING
REVELATORY ENCOUNTERS

W hat would you think if you had a spiritual experience that made your hair stand on end? Would you write it off as absolutely satanic or "off the wall" because it didn't fit your theological code? Many people would and do. Supernatural encounters are real. The seer dimension into the spirit world is not something relegated to yesterday—it exists today and is on the rise! The question we must answer is: Do all such revelatory encounters come from the one true God, or can there be other sources? How can we tell the source or nature of the spirit beings we encounter? What are the marks of a truly God-initiated encounter or revelatory experience?

There is only one dependable, unshakable guide through the minefield of supernatural encounters. In a world filled with spiritual voices of the New Age and every other type and description, Christians need to know how to make their way through a spiritual field littered with hidden (and deadly) weapons of the enemy designed to wound or destroy the unwary and the undiscerning.

Entire segments of the Body of Christ have "written off" the supernatural aspects of God's Kingdom and His workings in the Church today because of fears about being deceived and led astray. Others have written them off due to excess, abuse, and the bad testimony left behind by lone rangers who are not accountable to anyone in the Body of Christ. The prophetic has been given a bad rap at times, but some of the wounds have been self-inflicted. Nonetheless, God *does speak* to His people today and He is very capable of preserving us from harm and deception.

> [Jesus said] *"For everyone who asks, receives; and he who seeks, finds; and to him who knocks, it will be opened. Now suppose one of you fathers is asked by his son for a fish; he will not give him a snake instead of a fish, will he? Or if he is asked for an egg, he will not give him a scorpion, will he? If you then, being evil, know how to give good gifts to your children, how much more shall your heavenly Father give the Holy Spirit to those who ask Him?"* (Luke 11:10-13)

What about it—can we trust our Father? Believe it or not, God wants us to hear His voice even more than we want to hear it! He is a gracious Father who gives good gifts to His children. What is the foundation that we must lay? Stick close to Jesus, seek Him, and love Him! Give our all to Him. James 4:8a says it this way: *"Draw near to God and He will draw near to you."* We could never overemphasize this point: Cultivate intimacy with God through a relationship with His only Son, Jesus Christ.

God is a Father, and He can be trusted. If we ask Him for the things of the Holy Spirit in the name of Christ, He will give us the real thing, not a counterfeit. Nonetheless, there are many issues that we must consider when approaching this valuable subject of wisely judging revelatory encounters.

SAFETY IN THE FAMILY

Let's backtrack for a moment and re-examine some basics. God still speaks today through many different avenues, including visions, dreams, and angelic visitations. Another one of these ways of the Holy Spirit is called "inner knowings." We simply know that we know that we know! He also speaks to us through His inner voice, external audible voice, by journaling, through

His Creation, and other awesome ways and means. Yet our most important source of revelation is the *logos* canon of Scripture. The only way we can accurately and safely interpret supernatural revelation of *any kind* is to ask God for the spirit of wisdom and understanding and to seek the counsel of the Lord.

Since the Bible is our absolute standard against which we must test *all* spiritual experiences, it should be obvious that we need to know and study God's Word. It is our only absolute, infallible, unchanging standard of truth. Just as we must learn to crawl before we learn to walk in the natural, so we must learn the ways of the *logos*, the written Word of God, before we can learn to safely work with *rhema*, the revealed "now" word of God. A solid and balanced working knowledge of the New Testament is the very minimum requirement as we begin to investigate *rhema* revelation in depth. Otherwise, we have no plumb line of measurement.

God has also ordained that we find safety in our relationship to a Bible-believing fellowship. Paul wrote to the Ephesians to, "submit to one another," and he described many of the areas of covering that God has placed in our lives. The Bible says, *"In the multitude of counsellors there is safety"* (Prov. 11:14b KJV). In an age of lawlessness, we find safety under the umbrella-like covering of the Lord, of His Word, and of the local church. We are not called to be proud religious rebels "doing our own thing." God has called us to be humble servants committed to a local expression of Christ's Body, diligently studying the Scriptures, praying daily, and being led by the Spirit of truth into His purposes and individual will for our lives.

Though I am involved in many councils at national and international levels and have a somewhat recognized prophetic and intercessory voice, my family and I are regular members of a local, Spirit-filled fellowship. So what I put before you is not theory to me. It is walking in a form of simplicity and purity unto Christ. We never outgrow the ABCs! With this in mind, we should all ask ourselves five basic questions in our quest to discern God's voice in the spirit realm:

1. Am I regularly studying the Scriptures?

2. Am I maintaining a life of prayer?

3. Am I seeking purity, cleansing, and holiness in my life?

4. Am I a worshipful member of a local Christian congregation?

5. Am I committed to a few peer relationships that can speak into my life?

These building blocks must be firmly in place before we begin to investigate the principles of testing spiritual experiences. With these ABCs in place, our next step is to *"examine everything carefully; hold fast to that which is good"* (1 Thess. 5:21).

SOURCES OF REVELATION

The Scriptures indicate that spiritual revelation or communication comes from any one of three sources: the Holy Spirit, the human soul, and the realm of evil spirits. The need for discernment in this area is obvious.

The Holy Spirit is the only true source of revelation (see 2 Pet. 1:21). It was the Holy Spirit who "moved" the prophets of the Old Testament and the witnesses of the New Testament. The Greek word for "moved," *phero*, means "to be borne along" or even "to be driven along as a wind."[1]

The human soul is capable of voicing thoughts, ideas, and inspirations out of the unsanctified portion of our emotions (see Ezek. 13:1-6; Jer. 23:16). These human inspirations are not necessarily born of God. As Ezekiel the prophet said, they are prophecies *"out of their own hearts…Woe unto the foolish prophets, that follow their own spirit, and have seen nothing"* (Ezek. 13:2-3 KJV).

Evil spirits operate with two characteristics common to their master. They can appear as "angels of light" (or as "good voices"), and they always speak lies, because they serve the chief liar and the father of lies, satan. Messages delivered through evil spirits are often especially dangerous to people ignorant of God's Word or inexperienced, in discernment because satan loves to mix just enough "truth" or factual statements in with his lies to trick gullible people. Just think of it as tasty bait carefully placed in the middle of a deadly trap. Acts 16:16-18 tells about a slave girl with a spirit of divination who *spoke the truth* about the disciples, but got it from a satanic source. When the apostle Paul eventually had heard enough and was irritated within, he commanded the spirit of divination to leave her.

In a world of imperfect people, God-given revelation can be mixed with competing information from sources that are *not* of God. People functioning as prophetic mouthpieces or visionaries are imperfect instruments, though vital to the Church today. None of us are immune to the effects of outward influences on our lives. Even though God's Spirit is in union with our spirits, we can be strongly affected in our spirits and souls by such things as the circumstances of life, our physical or bodily circumstances, by satan or his agents, and very often by other people around us (see 1 Sam. 1:1-15; John 13:2; 1 Cor. 15:33). The solution is to "test" every source and aspect of the revelation—whether it is a dream, apparition, spoken word, or other type. First we should test ourselves with a series of self-diagnostic questions.

THE SELF TEST

1. Is there any evidence of influences other than the Spirit of God in my life?

2. What is the essence of the "vision" or revelation? (How does it compare to God's written Word?)

3. Was I under the control of the Holy Spirit when I received the vision?

4. Have I presented my life to Jesus Christ as a living sacrifice?

5. Have I been obedient to His Word?

6. Am I being enlightened with His inspiration?

7. Am I committed to doing His will, no matter what it is?

8. Am I yielding my life to the praises of God or to critical speech?

9. Am I waiting quietly and expectantly before Him?

THE SOURCE TEST

The next step is to test whether the image, prophetic message, or vision received is from our own soulish arena, from satan's realm, or from God. Dr. Mark and Patti Virkler, founders of the Christian Leadership University in Buffalo, New York, offer some excellent guidelines in this area in their landmark work, *Communion With God*. They teach that "the eyes of your heart can be filled by self or satan or God."[2] The following guidelines are adapted from a table in the Virklers' study guide.[3] First are three general instructions:

1. I am to cut off all pictures put before my mind's eye by satan (see Matt. 5:28; 2 Cor. 10:5) using the blood of Jesus.

2. I am to present the eyes of my heart to the Lord for Him to fill. In this way, I prepare myself to receive (see Rev. 4:1).

3. The Holy Spirit will then project on the inner screen of my heart the flow of vision that He desires (see Rev. 4:2).

TESTING WHETHER AN IMAGE IS FROM SELF, SATAN, OR GOD

1. Find its origin (test the spirit; see 1 John 4:1).

   SELF: Was it primarily born in the *mind?* Does it feed my ego or exalt Jesus? What does it resemble?

   SATAN: Does the image seem destructive? Does it lure me away from the Lord?

   GOD: Is it a "living flow of pictures" coming from my innermost being? Was my inner being quietly focused on Jesus?

2. Examine its content (test the ideas; see 1 John 4:5).

   SELF: Does it have ego appeal? Is self the centerpiece, or is Jesus the one lifted up?

   SATAN: Is it negative, destructive, pushy, fearful, and accusative? Is it a violation of the nature of God? Does it violate the Word of God? Is the image "afraid to be tested"?

GOD: Is it instructive, uplifting, and comforting? Does it accept testing? Does it encourage me to continue in my walk with God?

3. Check its fruit (test the fruit; see Matt. 7:16).

    SELF: The fruits here are variable, but eventually they elevate the place of people in contrast to the centrality of Christ.

    SATAN: Am I fearful, compulsive, in bondage, anxious, confused, or possessing an inflated ego as a result of the encounter?

    GOD: Do I sense quickened faith, power, peace, good fruit, enlightenment, knowledge, or humility?

NINE SCRIPTURAL TESTS

Here is a list of nine scriptural tests by which we can test every revelation that we receive for accuracy, authority, and validity. The following truths are for all of us—whether you are an acknowledged seer prophet or everyday believer in the Lord Jesus Christ. Let's drop the plumb line of God's Word in our lives!

1. ***Does the revelation edify, exhort, or console?*** *"But one who prophesies speaks to men for* **edification** *and* **exhortation** *and* **consolation"** (1 Cor. 14:3). The end purpose of all true prophetic revelation is to build up, to admonish, and to encourage the people of God. Anything that is not directed to this end is not true prophecy. Jeremiah the prophet had to fulfill a negative commission, but even his difficult message contained a powerful and positive promise of God for those who were obedient (see Jer. 1:5,10). First Corinthians 14:26c sums it up best: *"Let all things be done for edification."*

2. ***Is it in agreement with God's Word?*** *"All scripture is given by inspiration of God"* (2 Tim. 3:16a KJV). True revelation always agrees with the letter and the spirit of the Scriptures (see 2 Cor.

1:17-20). Where the Holy Spirit says "yea and amen" in Scripture, He also says yea and amen in revelation. He never, ever, contradicts Himself.

3. **Does it exalt Jesus Christ?** *"He will glorify Me; for He will take of Mine, and will disclose it to you"* (John 16:14). All true revelation ultimately centers on Jesus Christ and exalts and glorifies Him (see Rev. 19:10).

4. **Does it have good fruit?** *"Beware of the false prophets, who come to you in sheep's clothing, but inwardly are ravenous wolves. You will know them by their fruits..."* (Matt. 7:15-16). True revelatory activity produces fruit in character and conduct that agrees with the fruit of the Holy Spirit (see Eph. 5:9; Gal. 5:22-23). Some of the aspects of character or conduct that clearly are not the fruit of the Holy Spirit include pride, arrogance, boastfulness, exaggeration, dishonesty, covetousness, financial irresponsibility, licentiousness, immorality, addictive appetites, broken marriage vows, and broken homes. Normally, any revelation that is responsible for these kinds of results is from a source other than the Holy Spirit.

5. **If it predicts a future event, does it come to pass?** (See Deuteronomy 18:20-22.) Any revelation that contains a prediction concerning the future should come to pass. If it does not, then, with a few exceptions, the revelation is not from God. Exceptions may include the following issues:

- Will of the person involved.

- National repentance—Nineveh repented, so Jonah's word of judgment did not occur.

- Messianic predictions (they took hundreds of years to be fulfilled).

- There is a different standard for New Testament prophets than for Old Testament prophets, whose predictions played into God's Messianic plan of deliverance.

6. ***Does the prophetic prediction turn people toward God or away from Him?*** (See Deuteronomy 13:1-5.) The fact that a person makes a prediction concerning the future that is *fulfilled* does not necessarily prove that that person is moving by Holy Spirit-inspired revelation. If such a person, by his own ministry, turns others away from obedience to the one true God, then that person's ministry is false—even if he makes correct predictions concerning the future.

7. ***Does it produce liberty or bondage?*** *"For you have not received a spirit of slavery leading to fear again, but you have received a spirit of adoption as sons by which we cry out, 'Abba! Father'"* (Rom. 8:15). True revelation given by the Holy Spirit produces liberty, not bondage (see 1 Cor. 14:33; 2 Tim. 1:7). The Holy Spirit never causes God's children to act like slaves, nor does He ever motivate us by fear or legalistic compulsion.

8. ***Does it produce life or death?*** *"Who also made us adequate as servants of a new covenant, not of the letter, but of the Spirit; for the letter kills, but the Spirit gives life"* (2 Cor. 3:6). True revelation from the Holy Spirit always produces life, not death.

9. ***Does the Holy Spirit bear witness that it is true?*** *"As for you, the anointing which you received from Him abides in you, and you have no need for anyone to teach you; but as His anointing teaches you about all things and is true and is not a lie, and just as it has taught you, you abide in Him"* (1 John 2:27). The Holy Spirit within the believer always confirms true revelation from the Holy Spirit. The Holy Spirit is "the Spirit of truth" (see John 16:13). He *bears witness* to that which is true, but He rejects that which is false. This ninth test is the *most subjective* test of all the tests we've presented here. For that reason, it must be used in conjunction with the previous eight objective standards.

Testing the Spirits

Discernment is desperately needed in the Body of Christ. We need a clear, clean stream of prophetic grace to flow in our day. The apostle John warns believers of every age:

> Beloved, do not believe every spirit, but test the spirits to see whether they are from God, because many false prophets have gone out into the world. By this you know the Spirit of God: every spirit that confesses that Jesus Christ has come in the flesh is from God; and every spirit that does not confess Jesus is not from God; this is the spirit of the antichrist, of which you have heard that it is coming, and now it is already in the world (1 John 4:1-3).

As we noted earlier, we have to test the spirits because prophecy, like the other gifts of the Spirit, is delivered through imperfect people. God has chosen to deliver the prophetic to the Church through the flawed and often immature vessels of humanity. Although "scriptural revelation" was perfect and inerrant, "prophetic revelation" in the Church of Jesus Christ does not function on this level of inspiration. This is because prophecy is not our only source or way to hear God's voice. We have the living God dwelling in our hearts and the Holy Spirit leading and guiding each of us daily. Perhaps most importantly, since Calvary, the seer and the prophet serve in a supportive and secondary role to the Bible, which is God's *"more sure word of prophecy"* (see 2 Pet. 1:19 KJV), and to the indwelling Spirit of Christ in the heart of each believer.

Another reason discernment is needed is because God has chosen to speak through many people prophetically instead of using just one or two "perfected" people in a generation. Thus there is always the possibility of mixture in the revelatory word, because He chooses to use wounded people with clay feet (see 1 Cor. 14:29). At the same time, all believers have the basic tools to discern truth from falsehood for themselves. The fact that revelation is open for judgment in this age proves its present, imperfect state. But remember, the imperfect state of prophecy is directly linked to the imperfect state of the people who deliver it—not to an imperfect God!

Evil and deceived false prophets are not the major source of erroneous revelation to God's people today. Though this is on the rise, the vast majority of "diluted stuff" comes from sincere people who are simply adding their own insights to what started out as authentic, God-given revelation. They "add" to the nugget of God's prophetic message by drawing from things in their own human psyche, heart, emotions, concern, or sympathy. We need to learn to discern when God has stopped talking and people have continued on. Some of us over the years have called this "hamburger helper"! Whenever we share a revelation or vision that God has given us for someone else, we must be very careful to give what God has given and then to clearly label or preface anything else we say as our own interpretations and views concerning that revelation or vision.

God's Word tells us that we must prove all things and hold fast to that which is good (see 1 Thess. 5:21). At all times we must seek the Lord's wisdom while refusing to use "wisdom" as an excuse for fear. We must be careful not to become offended at the genuine things that the Holy Spirit is doing, no matter how strange they may appear to us. Divine revelation and visionary experiences come in many different forms, and it is vital that we understand how to discern the true from the false.

With this in mind, let me share with you briefly five tests to apply to a prophetic message or ministry to help in discerning whether or not it is valid. These tests were suggested by Roger Olson of Bethel College, a scholar with strong ties to the Open Bible Standard Churches; they were included in an editorial by David Neff in *Christianity Today*:

1. The Christ Touchstone. If a prophecy promotes Christ and not the prophet, it may be valid.

2. The Apostolic Norm. If it is consistent with the message of the gospel as found in the didactic writings of the New Testament, it may be valid.

3. **The Unity Criterion.** If a prophecy does not promote spiritual elitism or schism, it may be valid.

4. **The Sanity Check.** If it does not require the sacrifice of intellect and the mindless acceptance of newly revealed teachings, it may be valid.

5. **The Messiah Test.** If it does not exalt some individual into an object of veneration, it may be valid.[4]

Now I know that some of you are waiting for me to dish out "some of the deeper things" to you by this point. But from my perspective, I would be remiss not to make sure these foundational truths are laid well before taking us further on our "mystical journey." With this in mind, we would do well to study the 15 "wisdom issues" listed below. They will help us learn how to wisely judge the various forms of revelation we will encounter in our adventure with Christ.

FIFTEEN WISDOM ISSUES

1. *Search for proper exegesis and scriptural context.* One of the most important issues concerning wisdom is our interpretation of Scriptures—or proper exegesis. Many times, "prophetically gifted" people seem predominantly to take a type of loose symbolic interpretation of the Scriptures. Although there are different schools and methodologies of interpretation, we should look for the historical context from which the Scripture is speaking. Wisdom suggests that individuals with revelatory gifts should consult teachers, apostles, and pastors for additional clarity on scriptural interpretation. *"Study to shew thyself approved unto God..."* (2 Tim. 2:15 KJV). Walk with others!

2. *Focus on Jesus.* Manifestations of the Holy Spirit should not take center stage—*Jesus* is our central focus. While giving ourselves to the purposes of God, the movements of the Holy Spirit, and revelatory experiences from Heaven, let us not jump on just any bandwagon. Sometimes people will jump into anything that's moving because

they lack security and a proper biblical foundation. Remember the simple test: "Does this experience lead me closer to Jesus Christ?"

3. *Major on the "main and plain" things.* Manifestations are not our primary message. In the mainstream of evangelical orthodoxy, our emphasis is to be on the "main and plain" things of the Scriptures: salvation, justification by faith, sanctification, and so forth; these are followed by the consequential experiences revealed in people's testimonies of how they are advancing in their relationship with God and the community of believers.

4. *Follow biblical principles—not the rigid letter of the law.* Some things fall into a "non biblical" category. This does not mean that they are wrong, "of the devil," or contrary to the Scriptures. It just means that there is no sure "biblical proof text" to validate the phenomena. (There was no "proof text" to justify Jesus' spitting in the dirt and anointing a man's eyes with mud either—but it was obviously "right.") Don't stretch something to try to make it fit. Realize there will not be a Scripture for every activity. What is important is making sure that we follow the clear *principles* of the Word of God.

5. *Build bridges.* In "times of refreshing and supernatural experiences," keep in focus the reality that there are other sincere believers who are not as excited about it as we are. This is normal and to be expected. Some of the disciples, such as Thomas, were less excited about the Resurrection than others, but they all stood for Christ in the end. We must be careful to keep ourselves clean from spiritual pride and arrogance and to devote ourselves to building bridges to our "more cautious" brethren through love, forgiveness, understanding, and kindness.

6. *Honor and pray for leaders.* Realize that every leadership team of a local congregation or ministry has the privilege and responsibility to set the tone or the expression of the release of the Spirit in their gatherings. God works through delegated authority! Pray for those in authority with a heart and attitude

THE SEER EXPANDED EDITION

clean before God. Ask that they be given God's timing, wisdom, and proper game plan. (Be careful and hesitant to apply the label of "controlling spirit" or similar titles to leaders! Most leaders are sincere believers who simply want to do what's best for the overall good of their particular flock—and remember, they are God's appointed and anointed.)

7. **Be aware of times and seasons.** Is anything and everything supposed to happen all the time? Apart from a sovereign move of God, I think not. Ecclesiastes 3:1 KJV tells us, *"To every thing there is a season, and a time to every purpose under the heaven."* The Scriptures vividly depict "Pentecost meetings," but also include clear admonitions from Paul on how to walk with those who are the "ungifted" or the unbeliever as well. We should never use our freedom to purposefully offend others. I personally believe that it is in line with God's Word to have specific meetings for predetermined purposes. The leading of the Spirit works both ways. We can predetermine by His guidance that certain gatherings or sessions are oriented as "prophetic or life in the Spirit gatherings." But also be hungry for and welcome those spontaneous occurrences when His manifest presence is ushered in even when we don't expect or plan it.

8. **Let love rule.** The "unusual and rare" is not to be our consistent diet, nor will it ever replace the daily Christian spiritual disciplines. If all a person does is "bark like a dog" and quits reading the Scriptures and relating properly to other members of the local church, then most likely some other spirit is at work. Perhaps the individual has simply lost focus and needs a word spoken in love to help him or her maintain spiritual equilibrium in the midst of a mighty outpouring. Whatever the case, let love always be the rule.

9. **Maintain balance.** There is no exact science for figuring out all the manifestations of the Holy Spirit. When something is unclear, we should not over-define what we do not understand.

There is a godly tightrope of dynamic tension between the reality of subjective experience and biblical doctrine. Let us strive to maintain our balance! There is a tension—it is supposed to be there!

10. ***Understand the relationship of divine initiation and human response.*** Is all this demonstrative activity (laughter, crying, shaking, falling, and so forth) necessarily from God? I specifically call these "manifestations of and to the Holy Spirit" for a very good reason. Although some of these external, visible, and audible signs are divinely initiated, we must admit that some of them are human responses and reactions to the Holy Spirit's movement upon us or upon others close by. Divine initiative is followed by human response. This is normal. We must also make room for ethnic and different cultural displays of our affection to God. Every gift comes from God, but becomes expressed through a variety of clay pots!

11. ***Be known by your fruits.*** Although we want to bless what we see the Father doing, let us also direct this blessing into fruitful works. If we have been truly activated by the Holy Spirit, then we must channel it into *practical works* that express our faith. Let us channel this energy from a "bless me club" into a "bless others" focus that feeds the hungry and ministers to the poor, the widow, the orphan, and the single parent. Channel God's river of revelatory blessing into a life of evangelism, intercession, worship, and other things that display the passion and compassion of Jesus for people.

12. ***Perceive the works of God and the motives of people.*** Although the phenomena of manifestations and prophetic encounters have occurred in revivals throughout Church history, I doubt that we can make a case for any of these individuals *willing* these things into being. These experiences were equated with receiving an anointing for power in ministry and as tools of radical means whereby God brought personal transformation.

13. ***Control your flesh and cooperate with God.*** Self-control is one of the fruits of the Spirit (see Gal. 5:22-23). Too many of us have forgotten it or thrown it out the window! Nowhere in the Scriptures are we told that we are to "control God"—we are told to control "self." The fruit of self-control is to conquer the deeds of the flesh—lust, immorality, greed, and so forth. We are to *cooperate* with and yield to the presence of God and *control* the deeds of the flesh.

14. ***Be alert and aware.*** Let us search the Scriptures, review church history, seek the Lord, and receive input from those who are wiser and more experienced than us. Seasoned believers know that the enemy always tries to "club" Christians over the head after they have had an encounter or experience, in hopes that they will become confused, discouraged, and bewildered. We must continually arm ourselves for battle. This is a real war. These radical, revelatory visitations are not just "fun and games." They come to lead us into greater effectiveness for our Master!

15. ***Avoid spiritual ditches.*** There are two deep ditches we should avoid. First, we should watch out for *analytical skepticism*, which will cause us to be offended by what we do not understand. The other deadly ditch is *fear* (of people, rejection, fanaticism, and so forth). Both of these "ditches" have a common fruit: criticism. Consider this nugget of wisdom spoken to me some years ago: "If you can't jump in the middle of it, bless it. If you can't bless it, then patiently observe it. If you can't patiently observe it, then just don't criticize it! Do not stretch out the rod of your tongue against those things you do not understand!"

FEAR GOD, NOT THE DEVIL

Unfortunately, some churches have taught people to be afraid of the devil instead of emphasizing the completed work of the Cross and the authority of the believer. Although we need to have a healthy respect for the powers of darkness, we are never taught in the Scriptures to fear the devil. Let us turn on the light of truth and expose the deception of the evil one. The next chapter on "Discerning of Spirits" will help us learn more about this arena.

Let's keep our focus clear—the Scriptures teaches us to *"fear God and keep His commandments"* (Eccles. 12:13). Let us trust our Father, ask for the gifts of the Holy Spirit in Jesus' name, and expect authentic supernatural encounters of the heavenly kind to come down. Let us fear God, not the devil, and believe that our Father will give us good gifts.

Chapter Six

DISCERNING OF SPIRITS

Exercising wisdom in judging revelatory activity is absolutely vital to the health and integrity of all ministry, whether of the everyday believer or a visionary prophet. Nowhere is this truer than in the area of the discerning of spirits. Unless we can consistently and reliably determine the source of the "revelation" and the nature of the spirit from which it comes, we run a high risk of deceiving ourselves and others. The proper use of this gift is important for multiple reasons, which we will investigate.

At the outset, let me clarify that we are talking about two overlapping but different issues here: general discernment, which is a product of experience, discipline, and study; and discerning of spirits, which is a spiritual gift imparted by the Holy Spirit. All of us as believers can grow in discernment by meditating regularly on the Word of God and by spending much time in the Lord's presence. The more we mature in our faith and the more life experience we gain, the more our discernment will grow. We also learn by observing and gleaning from others, particularly people who are more mature and whose wisdom and judgment we respect.

Essentially, discernment is a wisdom issue. Discernment means having a place of perception in our lives—gained through meditation, study, and experience—that enables us to give wise counsel. It is this kind of discernment that Isaiah 11:2 describes as *"the spirit of wisdom and understanding, the spirit of counsel and strength, the spirit of knowledge and the fear of the Lord."*

Discernment or distinguishing of spirits is different because it goes beyond our natural learning abilities. It is a supernatural gift from the Lord; we cannot earn it. No amount of human insight or learning will enable us to discern between spirits. Only God can impart that ability, and He does so by His sovereign choice. General discernment and the discerning of spirits are different, but related. One comes through disciplined study and holy living, while the other comes through direct, divine impartation. The principles for growing in both arenas are the same, however: regular meditation on the Word of God and the crucible of life experience.

DEFINING DISCERNMENT OF SPIRITS

One of the best ways to begin understanding the whole arena of discerning of spirits is by turning to the words of experienced and godly servants of the Lord who have walked in this anointing for many years. The late Derek Prince once stated:

> Discerning of spirits is the supernatural ability to recognize and distinguish between not only good and bad, but various classes of spirits:
>
> - The Holy Spirit
> - Good angels
> - Fallen angels
> - Demons or evil spirits
> - The human spirit
>
> Discernment is a form of direct perception where knowledge is the impartation of fact.[1]

That last statement actually makes a distinction between discerning of spirits and receiving a word of knowledge. Discernment is a perception, a feeling, a sight-oriented thing, whereas a word of knowledge is a fact that is dropped into our thoughts or spirits.

John Wimber, the late Vineyard Ministries International leader, said:

> Discerning of spirits is the supernatural capacity to judge whether the spirit operating has a source that is human, demonic, or divine. It is a supernatural perception in the spiritual realm for the purpose of determining the source of spiritual activity.[2]

Although this is an excellent definition, I personally believe that discerning of spirits goes beyond simply determining the source of the spiritual activity. That is only part of the picture. Discerning the source is the starting place, but there are other purposes as well.

According to apostolic leader Dick Iverson:

> The gift of discerning spirits is the God given ability or enablement to recognize the identity (and very often the personality and condition) of the spirits which are behind different manifestations or activities. To "discern" means to perceive, distinguish, or differentiate. The dividing line between human and divine operation may be obscure to some believers, but one with the faculty of spiritual discernment sees a clear separation.[3]

Sometimes when dealing with the spiritual realm, we can find ourselves facing "gray" areas where things are unclear. That is one time when we need the gift of discerning of spirits to clear away the gray and separate matters into black and white.

The late Kenneth Hagin, father of the Word of Faith movement, expressed a similar idea:

The discerning of spirits gives insight into the spiritual world. It has to do with spirits, both good and bad. It is supernatural insight into the realm of spirits. To discern means to see— whether it be divine spirits, evil spirits, the human spirit or even the discerning of the similitude of God.[4]

Francis Frangipane, author and noted speaker on spiritual warfare, adds:

Spiritual discernment is the grace to see into the unseen. It is a gift *of the Spirit* to perceive what is *in the spirit*. Its purpose is to see into the nature of that which is veiled.[5]

DISCERNMENT AND OUR FIVE SENSES

Discernment is a gift from God. This is true whether we are talking about general discernment between good and evil or discerning of spirits. Only in the rarest of cases does this gift come "full-blown" into a believer's life. For most of us, discernment grows over time as we nurture it carefully from day to day. More often than not, discernment operates through our five senses and becomes strong in us through practice. Consider these words from the Book of Hebrews: *"But solid food is for the mature, who because of practice have their senses trained to discern good and evil"* (Heb. 5:14).

Some things we learn by experience, and some we learn by watching others. We learn discernment by practice. When we submit ourselves to the lordship of Christ, He washes us clean from the defilement of the world, the flesh, and the demonic realm of the spirit. Our five natural senses— sight, smell, taste, touch, and hearing—are free then to be trained in the discernment of good and evil. The more closely we walk with Christ and the more we submit our minds and wills to Him, the more acute our senses will become in discernment. It is a progressive unfolding.

One of the operative principles of the Kingdom of God that applies in every area of life is that our faithfulness in little things leads to being entrusted with greater things. As we prove faithful with what God has given us, He will give us more. For example, our faithfulness in managing natural mammon will lead to our being given rule over what Jesus called true spiritual riches. It is a simple principle: faithfulness in the natural will bring increase in the realm of the spirit.

The more we yield our natural five senses to the Lord, the more the anointing of God can come upon them, making us progressively more sensitive to His promptings. The more we learn to recognize and obey those promptings, the more promptings we will receive. As we prove ourselves faithful with a little, the Lord will entrust us with more.

Basically, discernment is perception, which can come in a variety of ways. Sometimes it is as simple as an inner knowledge, a "gut feeling," that we cannot explain yet somehow know is real. This kind of spiritual perception is often so subtle that we can easily miss it or attribute it to something else, such as a "hunch."

Seeing is another avenue of perception. As we have already observed, seeing can be internal, through images in the mind's eye, or external, through an open vision. Sometimes it may be nothing more than a flash of light that brings a strong sense of a spiritual presence in the room, such as an angel. At other times, we may see an outline form or even a kind of fog of His glory filling the room. This again is a part of the "seer" package—divine perception. As our discernment grows, we may observe a kind of shimmering presence or, eventually, a fully defined vision, whether internal or external.

Sometimes spiritual discernment will come through our sense of smell. Many people have testified to sensing the presence of the Lord accompanied by the smell of roses. It is also possible at times to identify the enemy in the same way. A particular situation may not "smell right," even if we don't quite understand why. All we know is that it smells bad. There may be an actual unpleasant odor associated with the situation, such as the smell of sulfur. If there is no visible, apparent cause for the odor, it may be an indicator that an unclean spirit is present. Often, I have discerned addictions in a person's life through this means. I actually "smell" a type of smoke that comes from a particular form of addiction—I then know in part how to proceed in ministering in that situation.

What about spiritual perception through the sense of taste? Have you ever heard someone say, "I don't know for sure what's going on, but this just leaves a bad taste in my mouth"? That phrase may be literal or figurative. In Ezekiel 3:3, the prophet, during a vision, eats a scroll that represents the Word of the Lord, and it is "sweet as honey" in his mouth. John records a similar experience in Revelation 10:9-10, where he eats a scroll containing God's judgments on the nations. Although the scroll tastes as sweet as honey in John's mouth, it makes his stomach bitter.

As far as the sense of touch is concerned, spiritual discernment may take the form of a tingling feeling, or even pain, particularly in situations where the Lord is revealing areas where He wants to release physical healing or deliverance. At times I receive physical pains in my heart, showing me wounding that has occurred in another's life as a tool to "set the captives free." This feeling arena can also be used to distinguish what spirit is in operation behind a certain activity.

Not long ago, at five o'clock one morning, my bedroom was ice-cold and I could feel this dark presence. I prayed in the Spirit and called on the blood of Jesus. I then fell back to sleep only to awaken from a dream from the Lord. In this dream, believers were proclaiming, "The Jezebel spirit has been bound!" The room was then filled with white light and a warm glowing feeling was now permeating the room. Victory had come, as the enemy had been discerned and flushed out!

Perception through hearing is the realm most of us are probably most familiar with. At times there may be the sound of bells, the telephone ringing, or even music. One of the most common sounds associated with spiritual perception is the sound of wind, such as occurred on the Day of Pentecost. One time, in the middle of the night, a supernatural wind came blowing through a closed bedroom window of our house. My wife, Michal Ann, and I were instantly awakened. Angels were released and messages from God came our way. With the wind came His presence!

No matter which of our senses bring us spiritual perception, we are tapping into a grace gift of God. Consistency and growth in this area calls for us to have our hearts set toward the Lord Jesus Christ. We cannot be living in open rebellion to Him. All of our affections must be focused on Him. We must be bathed in the blood of Jesus and have submitted ourselves to Him spirit, soul, and body.

DISCERNING OF THE HOLY SPIRIT

Essentially, there are four categories of discerning spirits. The most important of these is the ability to discern the presence and work of the Holy Spirit. Two prominent biblical examples demonstrate this discernment in operation.

> *John testified saying, "I have seen the Spirit descending as a dove out of heaven, and He remained upon Him. I did not recognize Him, but He who sent me to baptize in water said to me, 'He upon whom you see the Spirit descending and remaining upon Him, this is the One who baptizes in the Holy Spirit.' I myself have seen, and have testified that this is the Son of God"* (John 1:32-34).

After John baptized Jesus, he saw a dove descend and rest on Jesus. This was God's sign to John identifying Jesus as the Son of God. Whether John saw a dove in the natural realm or the spiritual realm is not clear in the text. Either way, however, John knew it to be the Holy Spirit descending and remaining on Jesus. The only way he could know this was through the gift of discernment. Such knowledge was beyond normal human faculties.

> *When the day of Pentecost had come, they were all together in one place. And suddenly there came from heaven a noise like a violent rushing wind, and it filled the whole house where they were sitting. And there appeared to them tongues as of fire distributing themselves, and they rested on each one of them. And they were all filled with the Holy Spirit and began to speak with other tongues, as the Spirit was giving them utterance* (Acts 2:1-4).

The believers in the upper room were waiting for the fulfillment of Jesus' promise made at the time of His ascension ten days earlier, that He would send the Holy Spirit to clothe them with *"power from on high"* (Luke 24:49). When the Spirit came on that Day of Pentecost, He appeared in two forms: wind and fire. There is no indication that these believers knew beforehand *how* the Spirit would appear, but when He came, they knew He was there. Once again, only the gift of discernment could impart this knowledge.

At times, my spiritual eyes have been opened, and I have seen a flame of fire over a person's head or a flash of fire appear in front of an individual. This has been a helpful tool in knowing whom to minister to prophetically or for healing. I recall a time a large flame of fire stoked right up in front of a person. As I blessed what I saw the Father doing, this person was overwhelmed by the power of the Spirit and healed of chronic pain from head to foot. Thank the Lord—it works!

DISCERNING OF ANGELS

Discerning of spirits also involves discerning of angels, because they are spiritual beings. Jesus saw an angel while He was praying in the Garden of Gethsemane:

> He knelt down and began to pray, saying, "Father, if You are willing, remove this cup from Me; yet not My will, but Yours be done." Now an angel from heaven appeared to Him, strengthening Him (Luke 22:41-43).

The text does not say *how* Jesus saw the angel, whether in the spiritual realm alone or in full bodily appearance, but He was strengthened by the angel's presence. No one can see angels unless God enables it through the seer dimension of the gift of discernment. He does not release things without a purpose. If God enables us to see—whether angels or anything else—it is for a reason, and we need to search out that reason.

On the day of Jesus' Resurrection, Mary Magdalene saw two angels when she visited the empty tomb:

But Mary was standing outside the tomb weeping; and so, as she wept, she stooped and looked into the tomb; and she saw two angels in white sitting, one at the head and one at the feet, where the body of Jesus had been lying. And they said to her, "Woman, why are you weeping?" (John 20:11-13a)

Did Mary see these angels with her natural eyes or in the realm of the spirit? How did she know they were angels? The text does not say. Let it suffice that Mary had a spiritual experience in which she discerned the presence of angels.

These angels came to point Mary in a new direction. She came looking for Jesus' body. They came to prepare her to meet her risen Lord, which she did immediately after this encounter. Seeing Jesus in the garden, Mary thought at first that He was the gardener. Upon recognizing Him at last, she fell at His feet in worship. Later, she went to the disciples and proclaimed, *"I have seen the Lord"* (John 20:18).

God sent angels to direct Mary to see Jesus as He really was rather than as she thought He was. Sometimes, if needed, He will do the same for us: to correct our vision so that we can get rid of false impressions and see our Lord as He really is.

Paul also saw an angel. In the middle of a great storm at sea, an angelic envoy delivered a message of hope and encouragement for the apostle and all who were on the ship with him. The next day, Paul shared his vision with the others:

"Yet now I urge you to keep up your courage, for there will be no loss of life among you, but only of the ship. For this very night an angel of the God to whom I belong and whom I serve stood before me, saying, 'Do not be afraid, Paul; you must stand before Caesar; and behold, God has granted you all those who are sailing with you'" (Acts 27:22-24).

Was Paul dreaming, or did he have an open vision? No one really knows. The important thing is that the message the angel brought was fulfilled just as promised. In the end, the ship ran aground and was beaten apart by the waves, but everyone aboard made it safely to land.

DISCERNING OF HUMAN SPIRITS

Another area of discernment is the ability to discern the human spirit—the true character or motive behind a person's words or actions—even if hidden from casual view. Jesus possessed this ability to an exceptional degree. One example is His first meeting with Nathanael, one of His disciples.

> Philip found Nathanael and said to him, "We have found Him of whom Moses in the Law and also the Prophets wrote—Jesus of Nazareth, the son of Joseph." Nathanael said to him, "Can any good thing come out of Nazareth?" Philip said to him, "Come and see." Jesus saw Nathanael coming to Him, and said of him, "Behold, an Israelite indeed, in whom there is no deceit!" Nathanael said to Him, "How do You know me?" Jesus answered and said to him, "Before Philip called you, when you were under the fig tree, I saw you." Nathanael answered Him, "Rabbi, You are the Son of God; You are the King of Israel" (John 1:45-49).

Jesus was in one geographical location and Nathanael was in another, but in the realm of discerning of spirits, Jesus not only *saw* Nathanael, but He knew His inner character. Nathanael's question about Nazareth sounds brazen and sarcastic, but Jesus saw a man who was transparent, a man who was not being outwardly religious and putting up all kinds of veneer, but who instead spoke his mind. When it came to matters of integrity and the truth, Nathanael did not play games. He did not think one thing and speak another. He had no hidden agenda.

Simon Peter demonstrated the ability to discern the condition of the human spirit when he encountered a sorcerer who was also named Simon. A resident of the city of Samaria, Simon the sorcerer professed faith in Christ after hearing the preaching and witnessing the miracles of Philip. So did many others in the city. After the church in Jerusalem sent Peter and John to

Samaria to pray for the new believers to receive the Holy Spirit, Simon was amazed to see the power of the Spirit on display:

> *Then* [Peter and John] *began laying their hands on them, and they were receiving the Holy Spirit. Now when Simon saw that the Spirit was bestowed through the laying on of the apostles' hands, he offered them money, saying, "Give this authority to me as well, so that everyone on whom I lay my hands may receive the Holy Spirit." But Peter said to him, "May your silver perish with you, because you thought you could obtain the gift of God with money! You have no part or portion in this matter, for your heart is not right before God. Therefore repent of this wickedness of yours, and pray the Lord that, if possible, the intention of your heart may be forgiven you. For I see that you are in the gall of bitterness and in the bondage of iniquity." But Simon answered and said, "Pray to the Lord for me yourselves, so that nothing of what you have said may come upon me"* (Acts 8:17-24).

Peter had the ability to discern the true spirit and motivation that were in Simon's heart. Once Peter exposed Simon's duplicity, Simon may have had his own eyes opened to his sin, leading perhaps to his repentance.

The Book of Acts tells how Paul was able to discern faith for healing on the part of another person:

> *At Lystra a man was sitting who had no strength in his feet, lame from his mother's womb, who had never walked. This man was listening to Paul as he spoke, who, when he had fixed his gaze on him and had seen that he had faith to be made well, said with a loud voice, "Stand upright on your feet." And he leaped up and began to walk* (Acts 14:8-10).

No one can "see" faith. We can observe faith in action as it is demonstrated, but only the Spirit of God can impart the ability to discern faith in another. As for me and my house, I want this capacity!

DISCERNING OF EVIL SPIRITS

One area of discernment where we must exercise care, caution, and maturity is in the discerning of evil spirits. (Now remember our earlier chapter that presented "Nine Scriptural Tests for Wisely Judging Revelation"—the subjective is submitted to the objective!) Having reinforced that foundation, this kind of discernment can come through any one or more of the five senses. Have you ever been in a place or situation where you simply felt the presence of evil? What about a time, as I said before, where a rotten or unpleasant odor was present with no identifiable natural source? These are only two examples of how discernment of evil spirits *may* occur, but great sensitivity is necessary in walking in this arena.

In Luke 13:11-17, Jesus discerns an evil spirit as the cause of a woman's physical affliction:

> *And there was a woman who for eighteen years had had a sickness caused by a spirit; and she was bent double, and could not straighten up at all. When Jesus saw her, He called her over and said to her, "Woman, you are freed from your sickness." And He laid His hands on her; and immediately she was made erect again and began glorifying God* (Luke 13:11-13).

This woman's spinal curvature was caused by a spirit of infirmity, which is why she had never been able to find healing by natural means. When the synagogue leader criticized Jesus for healing on the Sabbath, Jesus replied:

> *"You hypocrites, does not each of you on the Sabbath untie his ox or his donkey from the stall and lead him away to water him? And this woman, a daughter of Abraham as she is, whom Satan has bound for eighteen long years, should she not have been released from this bond on the Sabbath day?"* (Luke 13:15b-16)

Not every illness Jesus encountered was caused by an evil spirit, but this one was, and He discerned it and dealt with it. In the same way, we find some people today who are not healed immediately through prayer or laying on of hands. In some of these cases, a spirit of infirmity may be at work, which must be taken care of before healing will occur. In a visionary sense, such a spirit may be revealed as appearing like a leech on a person, sucking the strength out of whatever part of the body is afflicted.

Another biblical example is the account discussed earlier from the sixteenth chapter of Acts where Paul cast a spirit of divination out of a slave girl:

> It happened that as we were going to the place of prayer, a slave-girl having a spirit of divination met us, who was bringing her masters much profit by fortune-telling. Following after Paul and us, she kept crying out, saying, "These men are bond-servants of the Most High God, who are proclaiming to you the way of salvation." She continued doing this for many days. But Paul was greatly annoyed, and turned and said to the spirit, "I command you in the name of Jesus Christ to come out of her!" And it came out at that very moment (Acts 16:16-18).

In this case, a sort of "double" discernment was at work. The spirit of divination *(python)* gave the slave girl the ability to discern the Holy Spirit in Paul and his companions. Paul, on the other hand, obviously recognized an evil spirit at work in the girl's ability as a fortune-teller. Her description of Paul and his colleagues was accurate, but came from an evil source. The presence of such a spirit was quenching and hindering the work of the Holy Spirit, so Paul addressed the spirit of divination and cast it out of her.

Some of the common "symptoms" of the possible presence of evil spirits in a place are an oppressive atmosphere, a sense of confusion, a pervading sense of loneliness or sadness, a feeling of pressure, and depression. These are just a few examples; there are many more.

THE PURPOSE OF THE GIFT OF DISCERNMENT

God never gives gifts or imparts spiritual abilities for no reason. Why is the gift of discernment, and the discerning of spirits in particular, so important? There is a sixfold purpose for this gift in the life of the Church:

1. ***Deliverance from demons.*** Demons must be discerned and exposed before they can be dealt with. Mark 5:1-19 tells the story of a man possessed by a "legion" of demons who was delivered from them at the command of the Lord. The New Testament contains numerous other accounts of demon-possessed people being delivered by Jesus or His followers. This ministry is essential today. Let Jesus' prayer be answered, *"Deliver us from evil!"*

2. ***Reveal the servants of satan.*** Once, when Paul was sharing the Word of God with a Roman proconsul, he was opposed by a magician named Elymas:

   But Elymas the magician (for so his name is translated) was opposing them, seeking to turn the proconsul away from the faith. But Saul, who was also known as Paul, filled with the Holy Spirit, fixed his gaze on him, and said, "You who are full of all deceit and fraud, you son of the devil, you enemy of all righteousness, will you not cease to make crooked the straight ways of the Lord? Now, behold, the hand of the Lord is upon you, and you will be blind and not see the sun for a time." And immediately a mist and a darkness fell upon him, and he went about seeking those who would lead him by the hand. Then the proconsul believed when he saw what had happened, being amazed at the teaching of the Lord (Acts 13:8-12).

3. ***Expose and defeat the work and utterance of demons.*** This is clearly illustrated in Acts 16:16-18 when Paul casts the spirit of divination out of the slave girl. Word curses can be discerned and these hindrances broken in the name of Jesus. I have seen the whole atmosphere of a place change as authority is taken over demonic word curses and the power of God's blessing is invoked. Greater is the power of the blessing than the power of the curse!

4. ***Expose error.*** Discerning of spirits reveals not only the workers of satan, but the errors of their teachings as well: *"But the Spirit explicitly says that in later times some will fall away from the faith, paying attention to deceitful spirits and doctrines of demons"* (1 Tim. 4:1). This

operation of the Holy Spirit is especially needed in "religious" cities. God have mercy on us and deliver us from the slumbering effects of religious spirits. Where the Spirit of the Lord is, there is freedom!

5. **Acknowledge and confess Christ.** *"Therefore I make known to you that no one speaking by the Spirit of God says, 'Jesus is accursed'; and no one can say, 'Jesus is Lord,' except by the Holy Spirit"* (1 Cor. 12:3). It takes God to know God. Welcome the manifested presence of the Holy Spirit and watch the conviction of sin fall upon people. As the spirit of prophecy is poured out, people will fall on their faces and declare that Jesus is Lord (see 1 Cor. 14:24-25).

6. **Know the moving of the Holy Spirit so as to cooperate with Him.** *"The wind blows where it wishes and you hear the sound of it, but do not know where it comes from and where it is going; so is everyone who is born of the Spirit"* (John 3:8). Unless we recognize (discern) where and how the Holy Spirit is moving, we could find ourselves unintentionally working at cross-purposes to Him. Sensitivity at this point can help ensure that we always act in league with the Spirit. Declare with me, "Come, Holy Spirit—reveal Jesus!"

The late Jill Austin, a dear friend of mine and the founder of Master Potter Ministries, moved tremendously in this manner. I was with her often when she discerned the corporate move of God and, like John Wimber of Vineyard in the past, she declared, "Come, Holy Spirit," and sure enough, power encounters happened all over the room!

Today a new group of believers are arising, like Joshua Mills, Ryan Wyatt, Steven Springer, Matt Sorger, Ryan Pena, Shawn Bolz and so many others. The baton has been passed and it is time for the faceless generation to arise!

GUIDELINES FOR OPERATING IN THE GIFT OF DISCERNMENT

Just as there is a sixfold purpose for the gift of discerning of spirits, I want to share six guidelines for walking uprightly and effectively in that gift.

1. ***Cultivate the gift.*** We can cultivate the gift of discernment by regularly exercising our spiritual senses, learning to give a spiritual interpretation of what our normal senses perceive during a visionary experience. Remember Hebrews 5:14: *"But solid food is for the mature,* **who because of practice have their senses trained to discern good and evil.***"*

2. ***Test the spirits.*** Don't automatically assume that every vision or spiritual presence is from God. He commands us to test the spirits in order to distinguish the true from the false:

   Beloved, do not believe every spirit, but test the spirits to see whether they are from God, because many false prophets have gone out into the world. By this you know the Spirit of God: every spirit that confesses that Jesus Christ has come in the flesh is from God; and every spirit that does not confess Jesus is not from God; this is the spirit of the antichrist, of which you have heard that it is coming, and now it is already in the world (1 John 4:1-3).

3. ***Examine the fruit.*** One of the best ways to test the spirits is to look at the results, keeping in mind that fruit takes time to develop. That is why we should be careful not to enter into a quick judgment concerning whether or not something is of God, but take a little bit of time to watch. At the same time, however, we need to be sensitive to the "smell" of rotten fruit, so we can nip it in the bud. Does the activity draw people to Christ or pull them away from Him? Does it encourage them in righteousness or lead them into unrighteousness? Jesus said:

   You will know them by their fruits. Grapes are not gathered from thorn bushes nor figs from thistles, are they? So every good tree bears

good fruit, but the bad tree bears bad fruit. A good tree cannot pro-
duce bad fruit, nor can a bad tree produce good fruit. Every tree that
does not bear good fruit is cut down and thrown into the fire. So then,
you will know them by their fruits (Matthew 7:16-20).

4. ***Discerning of spirits is* not *the gift of suspicion.*** It is easy to fall into the trap of using this gift to "see" things about other people and "report" what we see in a way that hurts or damages them. Like all spiritual gifts, this one should never be used for the purpose of gossip, slander, or manipulation, but rather for the edification and healing of those who are of the Body of Christ.

5. ***Wisdom, wisdom, wisdom!*** Wisdom is an *absolute* necessity in exercising the gift of discernment. In order for this explosive gift to be a boon and blessing for us and others in the Body of Christ, we must seek wisdom from above—a wisdom that is beyond our years and beyond our human faculties alone. Such wisdom comes only from God.

6. ***Intercede!*** Along with the gift of discernment may come faith to act or pray with authority. This is usually true of all the revelatory gifts. First, we should pray our revelation back to the Father and seek His application. Afterward, we may choose or be guided by the Spirit to release a command to rebuke the enemy. The key, however, is to *always* pray first for discernment so that we will know what to do in any specific situation.

The gift of distinguishing of spirits is needed today. Deliverance is needed today. Supernatural strength and aid are needed today! Though the term *seer* is used in the Old Testament, technically it is not used in the New. It is my view that the gift of discerning of spirits encompasses these seer perceptive capacities. Let's call them forth and welcome them for the edifying of the Body of Christ.

DREAMS, VISIONS, AND OTHER HEAVENLY REALMS

The Holy Spirit uses three different avenues of visionary revelation to speak to us: dreams, visions, and trances. Dreams occur during the hours of sleep, while visions usually take place while one is fully awake or conscious. A trance is a supernaturally incited excitement of the physical body.

Dreams are the language of emotions and often contain much symbolism. The Bible is a great resource for us in the interpretation of the symbolic language of these dreams. I have discovered seven categories of biblical symbols, and the study of these symbols will assist us in the interpretation of dreams.

Let me offer a word of caution. Dreams and visions excite us on our spiritual journey, but we must never forget the goal of all spiritual experiences. That goal is to enhance our love for Jesus and a furthering of our understanding of His purposes.

Another form of prophetic visualization comes in the form of visions. Visions come to us as a spiritual light that creates a mental snapshot engrained in our memory that can be reviewed and studied. Supernatural visions are recorded throughout the Bible. Within the pages of the Scriptures, we can identify at least 12 different types or levels of visionary supernatural experience.

One of these supernatural visionary experiences is the trance. A trance brings us into the "ecstatic" realm of the Spirit. When properly understood and when initiated by the Spirit of God, a trance is an exciting, fabulous, wonderful thing—another powerful visionary experience that brings a person into the heavenly realm.

Biblically and historically, the trance has been a legitimate method God sometimes has used to impart visionary revelation, and it continues to be so today. My purpose here is not to promote trances. My purpose is to promote the Kingdom of God.

Chapter Seven

DREAM LANGUAGE

As mentioned above, the Holy Spirit uses three different avenues of visionary revelation to speak into our lives: dreams, visions, and trances. In this chapter and the two that follow, we will look more closely at each of these in turn.

Dreams are closely associated with visions. The primary difference is that dreams occur during the hours of sleep, while visions usually take place while one is fully awake or conscious. Both means of visual revelation have solid biblical precedent: *"If there is a prophet among you, I, the Lord, shall make Myself known to him in a vision. I shall speak with him in a dream"* (Num. 12:6).

The Lord spoke these words to Miriam and Aaron when they challenged Moses' position as God's sole spokesman to the Israelites. He went on to say that His relationship with Moses was different, because He spoke to Moses face-to-face or, literally, "mouth-to-mouth" (see Num. 12:8). For our purpose, the pertinent point is that God clearly states here that dreams and visions are avenues He will use to speak to His prophets—in the past, the present, and the future.

While dreams are a specific portion of the prophetic ministry, they are not limited only to the prophetically gifted. Joel 2:28 says,

It will come about after this that I will pour out My Spirit on all man-kind; and your sons and daughters will prophesy, your old men will dream dreams, your young men will see visions.

This Scripture was fulfilled on the Day of Pentecost and continues to be fulfilled in our own day. It is time for the Church to return to a biblical under-standing of dreams as an avenue of discerning God's voice.

BIBLICAL EXAMPLES OF GODLY DREAMS

As stated in Numbers 12:6, God sometimes speaks to His prophets through dreams. There are many occurrences of this in the Scriptures. For example, in Genesis 15:12-17, God speaks to Abraham in a dream regard-ing the centuries of slavery his descendants will endure in Egypt, as well as their eventual deliverance and settlement in the Promised Land. The occa-sion of this dream is the cutting of the covenant between Abraham and God. Although most people think of Abraham as a patriarch, Genesis 20:7 also refers to him as a prophet, the first person in the Bible so designated.

God also used dreams to speak to Jacob, Abraham's grandson who was also a patriarch and, according to Psalm 105:15, a prophet as well. In the first of these dreams, Jacob saw a ladder extending into Heaven with angels ascending and descending it. At the top stood the Lord, who promised to be with Jacob, to prosper him, to make of his descendants a great nation, and to bring them into a land of their own (see Gen. 28:12-15). This was a reitera-tion of the promise God had made to Abraham. Interestingly enough, this passage in Genesis 28 also unfolds for us the understanding of "open heavens." Is this not what we each want in our lives, congregations, and cities?

Daniel is another Old Testament prophet who received dreams from the Lord. The seventh chapter of the Book of Daniel relates his dream of four great and fearsome creatures, representing earthly kingdoms, and their even-tual defeat by the Son of Man. With the possible exception of Ezekiel, no Old Testament prophet was more visionary than Daniel.

Prophets were not the only people in the Bible to receive dreams from God. The Scriptures record numerous instances when God used dreams to speak to heathens—people who did not know or fear Him. His purpose always was to protect His people and bring glory to His name. Here are a few examples:

1. ***Abimelech.*** This pagan king took Sarah, Abraham's wife, into his own harem, believing her to be Abraham's sister. God intervened: *"But God came to Abimelech in a dream of the night, and said to him, 'Behold, you are a dead man because of the woman whom you have taken, for she is married'"* (Gen. 20:3). Abimelech rightly professed his innocent intent.

   Then God said to him in the dream, "Yes, I know that in the integrity of your heart you have done this, and I also kept you from sinning against Me; therefore I did not let you touch her. Now therefore, restore the man's wife, for he is a prophet, and he will pray for you and you will live. But if you do not restore her, know that you shall surely die, you and all who are yours" (Genesis 20:6-7).

   Abimelech did as he was told, and all was well.

2. ***Laban.*** Jacob's father-in-law pursued Jacob after he fled with his wives, children, and flocks. Apparently, Laban intended to harm, even perhaps kill, his son-in-law. As with Abimelech, God intervened: *"God came to Laban the Aramean in a dream of the night and said to him, 'Be careful that you do not speak to Jacob either good or bad'"* (Gen. 31:24). As a result, Jacob and Laban met in peace and departed on good terms.

3. ***A Midianite soldier.*** God had called Gideon to command a band of 300 men to deliver his land from the Midianite invaders. When Gideon needed encouragement, God sent him by night to eavesdrop at the Midianite camp:

   When Gideon came, behold, a man was relating a dream to his friend. And he said, "Behold, I had a dream; a loaf of barley bread was tumbling into the camp of Midian, and it came to the tent and struck it so that it fell, and turned it upside down so that the tent lay flat." His friend replied, "This is nothing less than the sword of Gideon the son of Joash, a man of Israel; God has given Midian and all the camp into his hand." When Gideon heard the account of the dream and its interpretation, he bowed in worship. He returned to the camp of Israel and said, "Arise, for the Lord has given the camp of Midian into your hands" (Judges 7:13-15).

Not only did God give a dream to one pagan soldier, He gave its interpretation to another!

4. ***Pharaoh's butler and baker.*** When Joseph was in prison in Egypt, he interpreted two dreams: one from Pharaoh's butler and another from his baker. Both dreams had to do with the future. Just as Joseph interpreted, three days later the butler was released and restored to Pharaoh's service, while the baker was hanged (see Gen. 40:1-23). God gave dreams to two non-believing Egyptians, and Joseph's interpretations of them set the stage for his release, his interpretation of Pharaoh's dream, and his rise to power as second-in-command in Egypt.

5. ***Pharaoh.*** Genesis chapter 41 tells of Pharaoh's dream from God predicting seven years of plenty followed by seven years of famine. Joseph alone is able to interpret Pharaoh's dream. In recognition of Joseph's wisdom and insight, Pharaoh elevates him to prime minister and places him in charge of running the country and preparing for the years of famine. All of this served God's greater purpose of bringing Joseph's family to Egypt, where they would grow into a great nation, to be led out by Moses 400 years later.

6. ***Nebuchadnezzar.*** One of the most evil rulers of the ancient world, Nebuchadnezzar nevertheless received a dream from God, a dream so profound and powerful that he was obsessed with understanding its meaning. Of all his sages and officials, only Daniel was able to interpret the king's dream (see Dan. 2:1-49).

As a result, Nebuchadnezzar promoted Daniel to rule over the province of Babylon and all the other wise men in the kingdom. Furthermore, Nebuchadnezzar came to recognize the power and glory of the God of Israel, who had given the dream and its interpretation.

7. ***The wise men.*** These magi or astrologers from the east who came to worship the newborn Christ were warned by God in a dream not to return to Herod (see Matt. 2:12). This was part of God's plan to protect His Son from Herod's murderous jealousy.

8. ***Pilate's wife.*** During Jesus' trial before Pilate, the Roman governor received a warning from his wife: While he was sitting on the judgment seat, his wife sent him a message, saying, *"Have nothing to do with that righteous Man; for last night I suffered greatly in a dream because of Him"* (Matt. 27:19). How did she know Jesus was a "righteous Man"? God revealed it to her in her dream.

The Bible also tells of godly people who, although not regarded as prophets, nevertheless received dreams from God. Joseph, son of Jacob, is one of these. In Genesis 37:5-11, Joseph relates to his parents and brothers a dream he had that symbolized his ruling over them and their bowing before him. This event leads directly to the incident where Joseph's jealous brothers sell him into slavery in Egypt. Joseph's dream comes true many years later, after he has risen to be prime minister of Egypt; and his brothers, not recognizing him, bow before him seeking food for their families because of the great famine. May the Lord raise up men and women of revelation and excellence once again to give the timely counsel of God to those in authority.

King Solomon, son of David, was another non-prophet who had a dream from God. *"In Gibeon the Lord appeared to Solomon in a dream at night; and God said, 'Ask what you wish me to give you'"* (1 Kings 3:5). What an open-ended offer! Solomon could have asked for anything! In the end, the king asked only for wisdom to rule his people well. Greatly pleased with the king's request, God made Solomon the wisest man who ever lived—and gave him great riches and honor as well, which he hadn't even asked for!

Joseph, the earthly father of Jesus, received three dreams related to Jesus' birth and early life. The first dream revealed that he should not fear to take Mary as his wife because the child she carried was of the Holy Spirit (see Matt. 1:20). After Jesus was born, an angel warned Joseph in a dream to take Mary and Jesus and flee to Egypt to escape Herod's clutches (see Matt. 2:13). Joseph's third dream came after Herod died. An angel instructed Joseph to return to Israel with his family because conditions were now safe (see Matt. 2:19-20).

THE SYMBOLIC LANGUAGE OF DREAMS[1]

Dreams are the language of emotions and often contain much symbolism. When dealing with the visionary prophetic realm, we must learn to take our interpretations first from the Scriptures and then from our own lives. Just a casual overview of the dreams in the Bible will make it clear that they are full of symbolic images and elements. One important point to remember in trying to understand dream language is that God is consistent with His symbolic language. How He speaks in Genesis is similar to how He speaks in Revelation. Throughout the Bible, the types and symbols remain very much the same. This same consistency of symbolism holds true in our own lives as well.

Generally speaking, biblical symbols can be classified into seven different categories:

1. **Symbolic actions.** In Ephesians 2:4-6, Paul says that *"God...made us alive together with Christ...and raised us up with Him, and seated us with Him in the heavenly places in Christ Jesus."* Two symbolic actions—raising and seating—describe what God has done for us spiritually through Christ. *Raised* refers to the Resurrection, and *seated* symbolizes a place of ruling. As Christians, we have been raised to new life in Christ and seated by His side to rule with Him.

2. **Symbolic colors.** In prophetic dreams, specific colors often symbolize specific things. This is particularly true for the seer. We will look more closely at the symbolism of colors a little later.

3. ***Symbolic creatures.*** Two quick examples should suffice here.

   And the great dragon was thrown down, the serpent of old who is called the devil and Satan, who deceives the whole world; he was thrown down to the earth, and his angels were thrown down with him (Revelation 12:9).

   Two symbolic creatures—the dragon and the serpent—are used to represent satan.

   And I saw coming out of the mouth of the dragon and out of the mouth of the beast and out of the mouth of the false prophet, three unclean spirits like frogs; for they are spirits of demons (Revelation 16:13-14a).

   In this instance, John uses the frog as a symbolic creature for an unclean spirit.

4. ***Symbolic directions.*** For example, *up* often means toward God or toward righteousness, while *down* means the opposite. *"And you, Capernaum, will not be exalted to heaven, will you? You will be brought **down** to Hades"* (Luke 10:15). In Genesis 12:10, Abram went *down* to Egypt (away from the land where God had directed him) to escape a famine; in Genesis 13:1, he went up from Egypt, returning to his home.

5. ***Symbolic names.*** One common characteristic of names in the Bible is that they often reflect the character of the individual.

   Please do not let my lord pay attention to this worthless man, Nabal, for as his name is, so is he. Nabal is his name and folly is with him; but I your maidservant did not see the young men of my lord whom you sent (1 Samuel 25:25).

   This is Nabal's wife, Abigail, speaking to David about her husband, and she should know! The name *Nabal* literally means "dolt." By his foolish and inconsiderate actions toward David and his men, Nabal lived up to his name. My father's middle name was Wayne. My middle name is Wayne. Wayne means wagon-builder or burden-bearer. My earthly father was a carpenter, ran a lumberyard, and worked with wagons. Though I am not a carpenter, I am a builder—but of a spiritual house. Indeed, one of the greatest passions in my life is being a burden-bearer in prophetic intercession. Names carry weight in the spirit. Often their meaning is more than just symbolic.

6. **Symbolic numbers.** Numbers have great symbolic meaning throughout the Bible. Humanity was created on the sixth day, and God finished His work and rested on the seventh. The introduction and the interpretation of these numbers are consistent throughout the Scriptures. We will examine symbolic numbers more closely later as well.

7. **Symbolic objects.** *"I also say to you that you are Peter, and upon this rock I will build My church; and the gates of Hades will not overpower it"* (Matt. 16:18). In this verse, Jesus uses two symbolic objects: a rock, symbolizing Peter (and perhaps Himself, in a play on words) and a gate, symbolizing the entrance to the realm of darkness. A rock as a symbol for the Lord is quite common in the Bible (see Ps. 18:2; 1 Cor. 10:4). Many other common objects are used in a similar way, such as shields, bowls, harps, candlesticks, and so forth.

THE MEANING OF SYMBOLIC COLORS

The use of symbolic colors in prophetic dreams calls for a little closer examination. Colors often are highly symbolic in the Scriptures with specific colors representing specific things, qualities, or characteristics. Here are several of the most common:

1. **Amber**—the glory or presence of God.

   And I looked, and, behold, a whirlwind came out of the north, a great cloud, and a fire infolding itself, and a brightness was about it, and out of the midst thereof as the color of amber, out of the midst of the fire (Ezekiel 1:4 KJV).

Amber is not gold, but more of a brilliant, shining, fire-like color—a very appropriate color to represent God's glory. By the seer grace, one time I experienced the "beauty realm" of God where I saw an amber substance that appeared to be full of life. In this interactive vision, as I reached my hand into this glowing material, I was touched in a deep way by the Lord's brilliant presence. I encountered the glory of God and was changed.

2. **Black**—sin, death, or famine.

When He broke the third seal, I heard the third living creature saying, "Come." I looked, and behold, a black horse; and he who sat on it had a pair of scales in his hand. And I heard something like a voice in the center of the four living creatures saying, "A quart of wheat for a denarius, and three quarts of barley for a denarius; and do not damage the oil and the wine" (Revelation 6:5-6).

3. **Blue**—Heaven or the Holy Spirit.

Speak to the sons of Israel, and tell them that they shall make for themselves tassels on the corners of their garments throughout their generations, and that they shall put on the tassel of each corner a cord of blue (Numbers 15:38).

Blue is also often interpreted as the promises of God and/or the prophetic activity of the Holy Spirit.

4. **Crimson / scarlet**—blood atonement; sacrifice.

"Come now, and let us reason together," says the Lord, "though your sins are as scarlet, they will be as white as snow; though they are red like crimson, they will be like wool" (Isaiah 1:18).

5. **Purple**—kingship; royalty. *"And the soldiers twisted together a crown of thorns and put it on His head, and put a purple robe on Him"* (John 19:2).

6. **Red**—bloodshed; war.

   And another, a red horse, went out; and to him who sat on it, it was granted to take peace from the earth, and that men would slay one another; and a great sword was given to him (Revelation 6:4).

7. **White**—purity, light, righteousness. *"I looked, and behold, a white horse, and he who sat on it had a bow; and a crown was given to him, and he went out conquering and to conquer"* (Rev. 6:2). The late Derek Prince interpreted the white horse as the horse of the Gospel of peace that Jesus rides, which goes forth to conquer the nations. Historically, times of war (the red horse) have been preceded by times of spiritual awakening and renewal (the white horse). God has a testimony of witness that goes forth into a land before a war breaks out. Historically, I have seen this occur time after time.

8. **Green**—life; the Levites; intercession.

   Blessed is the man who trusts in the Lord and whose trust is the Lord. For he will be like a tree planted by the water, that extends its roots by a stream and will not fear when the heat comes; but its leaves will be green, and it will not be anxious in a year of drought nor cease to yield fruit (Jeremiah 17:7-8).

THE INTERPRETATION AND MEANING OF SYMBOLIC NUMBERS

Numbers are highly symbolic in the Bible, as well as in prophetic dreams, and great care must be exercised in properly interpreting their meaning. Here are six basic principles for interpreting symbolic numbers that will help prevent error or going to extremes.

1. The simple numbers 1-13 often have spiritual significance.

2. Multiples of these numbers, or doubling or tripling them carry basically the same meaning, only they intensify the truth. The number 100, for example, would have the same meaning as the number ten (law or government; see below), but to a greatly magnified degree.

3. The first use of a number in the Scriptures generally conveys its spiritual meaning.

4. Numbers should be interpreted consistently throughout the Scriptures. God is consistent, and what a number means in Genesis, it means through all Scriptures through Revelation.

5. The spiritual significance is not always stated, but may be veiled, hidden, or seen by comparison with other Scriptures.

6. Generally, there are good and evil, true and counterfeit, and godly and satanic aspects of numbers.

With these six principles in mind, let's consider the symbolic meaning of individual numbers:

*   ***One***—God, beginning, source. *"In the beginning God* [who is One] *created the heavens and the earth"* (Gen. 1:1). *"But seek first* [number one priority] *His kingdom and His righteousness, and all these things will be added to you"* (Matt. 6:33).

*   ***Two***—witness, testimony. *"On the evidence of two witnesses or three witnesses, he who is to die shall be put to death; he shall not be put to death on the evidence of one witness"* (Deut. 17:6). *"Even in your law it has been written that the testimony of two men is true"* (John 8:17).

*   ***Three***—godhead, divine completeness. *Go therefore and make disciples of all the nations, baptizing them in the name of the Father and the Son and the Holy Spirit* [three-in-one], *teaching them to observe all that I commanded you; and lo, I am with you always, even to the end of the age* (Matthew 28:19-20).

*   ***Four***—the earth, Creation, winds, seasons. *"All flesh is not the same flesh, but there is one flesh of men, and another flesh of beasts,*

and another flesh of birds, and another of fish" [four kinds of flesh in Creation] (1 Cor. 15:39). *Then He said to me, "Prophesy to the breath, prophesy, son of man, and say to the breath, 'Thus says the Lord God, "Come from the four winds, O breath, and breathe on these slain, that they come to life"'"* (Ezekiel 37:9).

- **Five**—cross, grace, atonement. This could include, for example, the fivefold ministry gifts: *And He gave some as apostles, and some as prophets, and some as evangelists, and some as pastors and teachers, for the equipping of the saints for the work of service, to the building up of the body of Christ; until we all attain to the unity of the faith, and of the knowledge of the Son of God, to a mature man, to the measure of the stature which belongs to the fullness of Christ* (Ephesians 4:11-13).

- **Six**—humanity, beast, satan. The number of the beast in Revelation is 666 (see Rev. 13:18). As stated earlier, humanity was created on the sixth day of Creation (see Gen. 1:26-31).

- **Seven**—perfection, completeness. God completed His creative work on the seventh day and rested (see Gen. 2:1-2). In the sixth chapter of Joshua, the Israelites march around Jericho once a day for six days and on the seventh day, seven times. When their march was *completed*, they blew trumpets and shouted, and the walls of Jericho fell.

- **Eight**—new beginning. As a sign of God's covenant with Israel, every male was to be circumcised when he was eight days old (see Gen. 17:10-12). When the Lord sent a great flood on the earth, He saved eight people (Noah and his family) in an ark to make a new beginning (see 1 Pet. 3:20). Many agree that the modern prophetic movement had its origins in 1988. This was a birthing time of a new beginning for the Body of Christ.

- **Nine**—finality, fullness. Galatians 5:22-23 lists nine fruits of the Spirit: *But the fruit of the Spirit is love, joy, peace, patience, kindness, goodness, faithfulness, gentleness, self-control; against such things there is no law.* First Corinthians 12:8-10 lists nine gifts of the Spirit:

word of wisdom, word of knowledge, faith, healing, miracles, prophecy, distinguishing of spirits, tongues, and interpretation of tongues.

- *Ten*—law, government. The most obvious example of this is the Ten Commandments in the twentieth chapter of Exodus.

- *Eleven*—disorganization, lawlessness, antichrist. *As for the ten horns, out of this kingdom ten kings will arise; and another* [the eleventh] *will arise after them, and he will be different from the previous ones and will subdue three kings. He will speak out against the Most High and wear down the saints of the Highest One, and he will intend to make alterations in times and in law; and they will be given into his hand for a time, times, and half a time. But the court will sit for judgment, and his dominion will be taken away, annihilated and destroyed forever* (Daniel 7:24-26).

- *Twelve*—divine government, apostolic fullness. There were 12 tribes of Israel (see Exod. 28:21), and Jesus chose 12 disciples (see Matt. 10:2-4).

- *Thirteen*—rebellion, backsliding, apostasy. *"Twelve years they had served Chedorlaomer, but the thirteenth year they rebelled"* (Gen. 14:4). This is the first appearance in Scripture of the number 13, which sets the standard for its interpretation.

WISDOM POINTS TO REMEMBER

Dreams and visions can be exciting and wonderful as a means of receiving insight and revelation, as long as they come from the right source. Remember that dreams and visions can arise from three places: the demonic realm, the soulish realm (our own human mind and spirit), and the Holy Spirit. In order to be effective in either giving or receiving visionary revelation, we must be able to distinguish the source. This is where the gift and discipline of discernment is so important.

Another important factor is giving careful attention to our environment. There may be occasions, for example, when we will have to remove from our homes some things that should not be there, such as certain cultic, occultic, or even soulish-tie objects, before our sleep will be sweet and clean, and our environment ready to receive pure revelation. We must be careful to identify and close off all potential demonic entrances to our home in Jesus' name.

I travel out of the country quite frequently and like to collect flags and dolls in each nation that I visit. Over the years, I have built up quite a beautiful collection. At times I have to be very careful, however, especially when I travel to countries that have a lot of demonic activity. In those places, certain objects, particularly dolls, may be used for purposes other than providing souvenirs—witchcraft, for instance. These are the kinds of things we need to look closely at through our eyes of discernment and, through prayer, determine whether something is safe or needs to be disposed of.

Deuteronomy 13:1-5 contains a precautionary warning to all who would either receive or share visionary revelation:

> *If a prophet or a dreamer of dreams arises among you and gives you a sign or a wonder, and the sign or the wonder comes true, concerning which he spoke to you, saying, "Let us go after other gods (whom you have not known) and let us serve them," you shall not listen to the words of that prophet or that dreamer of dreams; for the Lord your God is testing you to find out if you love the Lord your God with all your heart and with all your soul. You shall follow the Lord your God and fear Him; and you shall keep His commandments, listen to His voice, serve Him, and cling to Him. But that prophet or that dreamer of dreams shall be put to death, because he has counseled rebellion against the Lord your God who brought you from the land of Egypt and redeemed you from the house of slavery, to seduce you from the way in which the Lord your God commanded you to walk. So you shall purge the evil from among you (Deuteronomy 13:1-5).*

Here is the main point: Dreams and visions are wonderful, but our lives are more than just dreams and visions. Our lives are in our Master, Jesus

Christ. Someone may reveal true and accurate information and still be a deceptive tool of the enemy to seduce us and draw us in by fascination, and lead us away from Christ.

Don't simply get caught up in the glitter and glamour of revelatory seers. Examine their message. Look at their lifestyle. What is their conduct? What actions are they calling for? If they call for something that is contrary to the principles found in the written Word of God, then they are deceived, immature at best, or even false prophets, no matter how genuine their visions seem to be or how powerful the messages.

We must always be on guard not to be deceived. After all, we are not following gifts alone; we are following Jesus. Dreams and visions are wonderful, but they must direct us to Jesus. It is Jesus we really want. Let Him be our goal. In all our getting, let's be sure to get Jesus. In all our "seeing," let's see Jesus! If we get Jesus, we will get God, His Father, and if we get God, we get the Author of all authentic dreams and visions. Let us be like John the Beloved on the Isle of Patmos: in the Spirit on the Lord's day and seeing Jesus!

Chapter Eight

LEVELS OF
SUPERNATURAL VISIONS

H ow do visions "happen"?

For me, they began as what I would call mental pictures. After I was filled with the Holy Spirit in 1972, I began receiving "flashes" of light—mental images or pictures that lasted a second or less. At the time I did not know that they were legitimate "visions." I did not know what to call them. In those days, there were no seminars or conferences and very little writing or teaching on the subject of visions, let alone *The Seer*! Through a slow process of growth, I gradually learned that these mental "snapshots" were visual insights from the Holy Spirit. The more I grew and matured in the visionary arena, the more sustained the images became.

A mental "snapshot" is a good way to describe how visions can happen. Think of how an instant camera works. The shutter opens, allowing light to enter through the lens, imprinting on the film the image that is in front of the lens. The film develops "instantly" so the image can be viewed and analyzed. In a vision, "light" from the Lord enters the "lens" of our spiritual eyes and imprints an image on the "film" of our hearts and our minds. As the image "develops," we gain a better understanding of what it means. Most visions are internal in nature. An image is ingrained in our memory, and we can take it out, look at it, and study it any time we need to.

Another way to explain in simple language how visions happen is to think of each believer in Christ as a house or temple. First Corinthians 6:19 says that our bodies are temples of the Holy Spirit. As Christians, we have Jesus in the power of the Holy Spirit living in us; He dwells inside our "houses." Houses generally have windows that let in light. Our eyes are the windows of our soul. Sometimes Jesus, who lives in our houses, likes to look out of His windows and share with us what He sees. That is when a vision occurs—we see what Jesus sees when He looks out the windows of His house.

Whether we see it internally or externally, as if on a large projection screen, is not of primary importance. Our first priority is to be sensitive to the Spirit's desire to let us see what He sees. Just look through the eyes of Jesus—He wants to share with you what He is seeing!

Supernatural visions are recorded throughout the Bible. Within the pages of the Scriptures we can identify at least 12 different types or levels of visionary supernatural experience. Let us examine each one briefly, moving progressively from the simplest to the most profound.

Spiritual Perception

I speak the things which I have seen with My Father (John 8:38a).

As the lowest level of supernatural vision, spiritual perception may or may not involve a literal "seeing." Perception is not limited to the visual. Spiritual perception is the realm of knowing, of *impression*. In this type of vision, *people* may "see" something in *their* spirits, but *their* minds see no image. The Holy Spirit often reveals things to us by an *unction* or, to use a more familiar word, an *anointing*. Yet we may not be able to describe those things pictorially. Often, a hunch, a prompting, or a "gut feeling" we have is due to a perception in our inner *self* receiving nudges from the Holy Spirit.

Jesus walked by faith and always pleased His Father (see John 8:29). He discerned (saw) His Father's acts and acted accordingly: *"I speak the things which I have seen with My Father"* (John 8:38a). He also knew (perceived the innermost heart of) all people:

> *But Jesus, on His part, was not entrusting Himself to them, for He knew all men, and because He did not need anyone to testify concerning man, for He Himself knew what was in man* (John 2:24-25.)

It seems that in the life of Jesus, His spiritual eyes perceived things that His mind did not always visualize. Such spiritual perceptions could be the operation of the gift of a word of wisdom, word of knowledge, discerning of spirits, the gift of faith or even the gift of prophecy. Often, the higher the level of spiritual vision, the higher the dimension of spiritual sight that occurs. I, like you, want to follow Jesus' example and "do what we see the Father doing."

PICTORIAL VISION

> *If there is a prophet among you, I, the Lord, shall make Myself known to him in a vision. I shall speak with him in a dream* (Numbers 12:6b).

In a pictorial vision, an image is revealed and can be identified and described in terms of pictures. They are Holy Spirit visual aids! Symbols may or may not be involved. Often, the revelatory gifts come to us in the form of a pictorial vision that we see with our inner sight. However, a pictorial vision also may come in a picture superimposed over the subject. In other words, we might see two things at once: the main scene in the natural, with the object of the pictorial vision placed over or around it. I often see Scriptures written on people's foreheads. This is a useful tool, as it depicts something they are deeply pondering, or serves as medicine from the Lord to help them in their current or future situation. I often have to look up the verse and read it to them. This level of vision begins to enter both the internal and external arenas.

For another example, when praying for the sick, one may "see" an image of a bodily organ, a bone, or another body part flash in his or her mind. This indicates what to pray for or leads to dialogue with the person being ministered to. A pictorial vision is the type that is manifested when a Christian is praying for an individual, and the Holy Spirit starts showing things in "snapshots." This person may say, "The Lord is showing me..." or "I am seeing..." or "Does this picture mean anything to you?" This is because pictorial visions are presenting distinct pictures in his or her mind, and not only in the spirit, as is the case with spiritual perception.

Years ago, when I was pastoring a church in the Midwest, I "saw" an image of an inflamed stomach. I mentioned it from the platform, but no one came forth with that particular ailment. But I could not get away from the vision. After a little while, one woman in the group went downstairs to the nursery in the basement to relieve her daughter, who was tending the children's nursery. When the young lady came up the stairs and through the back door of the sanctuary into the main meeting, a "knowing" went off on the inside of me. I knew she was the one. As it turned out, the daughter had an inflamed stomach, a pre-ulcerous condition. She came forward, and the power of the Holy Spirit came upon her, and the Lord healed her completely that night!

It all began while in worship with a momentary pictorial vision in my mind of the affected organ. That is very often how these visions work.

Panoramic Vision

I have also spoken to the prophets, and I gave numerous visions, and through the prophets I gave parables (Hosea 12:10).

A panoramic vision is one in which a person sees a pictorial vision, not in snapshot form, but in motion in his or her mind. This "motion picture" may last several seconds and may include words heard in the realm of the spirit.

A panorama is a picture that unfolds before the spectators in such a way as to give the impression of a continuous view. Acts 9:10-16 records two panoramic visions. First, Ananias receives a vision that he is to go and lay his hands on Saul (later to be called Paul) so that he may receive his sight back. The second vision is that which Saul himself, although blind, had *"seen in a vision a man named Ananias come in and lay his hands on him, so that he might regain his sight"* (Acts 9:12). In both cases, the Greek word for "vision" is *horama*, one of the roots for our English word *panorama*. It is interesting that this is the term used often for cinema—it is panoramic. Both Ananias and Saul saw a "motion picture" vision of what was going to come about.

I remember when I received my call to the nations after receiving prayer from the healing evangelist Mahesh Chavda. As I was resting on the floor, I could see a list of nations in typed print roll before my eyes. It happened three times (I guess I needed to get the picture!). Over a period of years, I have ministered in all the nations that "panned" before my eyes. It took 20 years, but God has been faithful to fulfill the vision He gave to me that glorious morning.

Dream (Sleeping Vision)

In the first year of Belshazzar king of Babylon Daniel saw a dream and visions in his mind as he lay on his bed; then he wrote the dream down and related the following summary of it (Daniel 7:1).

We looked at dreams and dream language earlier, but let's review them briefly for comparison. A dream is a visionary revelation from the Holy Spirit that one receives while asleep. Supernatural dreams can occur in any level of sleep: light rest, regular sleep, deep sleep, or even in a trance state. Any one of the revelation gifts, or any combination of them, may manifest in a dream. Symbols may or may not be present. In any given situation, an entire scenario may be revealed in the dream.

It says in the Book of Job:

Indeed God speaks once, or twice, yet no one notices it. In a dream, a vision of the night, when sound sleep falls on men, while they slumber

in their beds, then He opens the ears of men, and seals their instruc-
tion (Job 33:14-16).

God wants to speak to us, but often during the day He can hardly get a word in edgewise. When we are asleep, however, our souls become more rested and more inclined to receive from Him. Then He can open our ears and give us instruction on various levels.

We need to be thankful to God for His persistence! After all, He often tries talking to us during the daytime, but we do not listen. Rather than giving up, God waits until we are asleep, then releases His secret service agents—His gifts of revelation—to come upon us in our sleep. God comes in quietly at night and says, "I want to talk to you." That is how supernatural dreams come about.

Dreams do not happen because of the pizza or pickles or anything else we eat. They happen because of God's love. God wants us to watch with Him. He wants us to see and hear more than we want to see and hear. If He has trouble getting in through the front door, He will come in through the rear—through dreams.

AUDIBLE MESSAGES

And behold, a voice out of the heavens said, "This is My beloved Son,
in whom I am well-pleased" (Matthew 3:17).

Often, visions include a voice speaking a message along with a visual image. Sometimes a message is declared apart from any visual pictures. Audible messages in the spiritual realm can involve people speaking words or objects making sounds. We can perceive such messages inside of us by our inner ears or outside of us by our physical ears.

Voices or sounds we hear internally can indeed be messages from the Lord. That which we hear outside of us—a message from above and beyond the natural mind and ears—is called a supernatural audible message. Audible messages from the Lord come in many ways: the Holy Spirit, Jesus, the

Father, angels of the Lord of various realms, and numerous other sounds He uses.

Audible voices that are unfamiliar to us may bring doubt and confusion or even fear. Deceiving or seducing spirits are usually the ones who behave mysteriously, as though they have something to hide. The word *occult* means "hidden." The enemy tries to hide, but we can flush satan and his cohorts out through the blood of Jesus. Just test the spirits to determine if they are from God.

God is not the author of doubt, confusion, or fear. When God releases His message to us, even through one of His angels, we should sense purity and holiness, a reverence to the Lord, and openness, because they have nothing to hide. The Spirit of God is not afraid to be tested. We should never fear offending God by testing the spirits. On the contrary, God is honored when we do because He told us in His Word to do so (see 1 John 4:1-3).

The infamous morning of 9/11/01, the voice of the Holy Spirit came to me in an external audible manner. He said, "The hunters have just been released!" I was familiar with this term from my history in prayer and carrying God's heart for the Jewish people. I then sensed an urgency to turn on the television. Sure enough—like millions of others—I saw the footage of the World Trade Towers being destroyed by terrorists. The Holy Spirit was giving a portion of God's interpretation to the events of our time by warning me, "The hunters have just been released." Indeed, we are living in days when the spirits of terror, antichrist, and anti-Semitism are increasing.

The Bible is full of examples where individuals heard God or an angel speak in an audible voice:

- God speaks from Heaven when Jesus is baptized (see Matt. 3:17).

- God speaks to Peter, James, and John on the Mount of Transfiguration (see Luke 9:28-36).

- An angel speaks to Philip (see Acts 8:26).

- The Lord Jesus speaks to Saul on the road to Damascus (see Acts 9:3-7).

- The Holy Spirit speaks to the prophets, teachers, and other believers at Antioch (see Acts 13:1-3).

We should not be afraid of the possibility of hearing an audible voice from the Lord. Rest assured! Jesus said that His sheep know His voice (see John 10:27). He is a great teacher—the greatest teacher in all of history. He is *the* Teacher, and He wants us to hear His voice even more than we want to hear it!

AN APPEARANCE (APPARITION)

And an angel of the Lord appeared to him, standing to the right of the altar of incense (Luke 1:11).

At this level of supernatural vision, people see beings that literally appear to them seemingly "out of thin air." This appearance may be observed with the natural eyes, either open or closed, and may even be a tangible experience. In some cases, it may be perceived physically—the being's presence may be felt—without being obviously seen. It is an appearing, a visiting, but not necessarily a sighting.

An appearance or apparition is different from a pictorial vision in that it is an actual—perhaps tangible and audible—visitation occurring outside of the person. Pictorial visions, by themselves, are basically symbolic revelations with images shown to the mind by the Holy Spirit. These images may be of a person, a place, a thing, or any combination of these. In an apparition, an object, a place, a person, an angel, or Jesus Himself might actually appear. These appearances can be "interactive" as well.

As with the audible voice, the Bible contains many examples of people seeing apparitions. Here are just a few:

- Jacob physically wrestled with an angel (see Gen. 32:24-31).

- Joshua saw Jesus (in His pre incarnate form), the captain of the Lord's army (see Josh. 5:13-15).

- Zacharias saw the archangel Gabriel (see Luke 1:11).

- Mary also saw the archangel Gabriel (see Luke 1:26-38).

- The risen Christ appeared to His followers on numerous occasions for 40 days after His Resurrection (see Acts 1:3).

- The disciples saw the Holy Spirit appear on the Day of Pentecost as "tongues of fire" (see Acts 2:3).

- An angel appeared to Cornelius with a message from God (see Acts 10:1-6).

I will never forget the fall of 1993 when God's angels came and invaded our home with the presence of God. It started with a lightning bolt crash in our backyard as electric white light pierced through our bedroom window at 11:59 at night. As I was suddenly awakened, I saw a man standing in our room addressing me, "Watch your wife. I am about to speak to her!" This began a nine-week period of visitations of fire, the angels of Heaven, and the glorious intrusion of His presence that consumed my wife. Heaven invaded our home and my wife was "changed and rearranged" by the power and presence of God. This arena is real—as my wife, Michal Ann, testified often during her lifetime!

DIVINE SIGHT

So Moses said, "I must turn aside now and see this marvelous sight, why the bush is not burned up" (Exodus 3:3).

More than just a spiritual vision, a divine sight is an actual disclosing of a supernatural event. It is like an appearance or apparition, in that it is an actual occurrence outside of the person or persons experiencing it. With divine sight, however, the vision is not of a being, but of an object or activity in the spiritual realm being disclosed to the natural realm.

When Moses was near Mount Sinai, he actually saw a bush burning without it being consumed. This great sight and the penetrating voice he heard from within it were divine manifestations of God. On that holy ground, the

Lord conversed with Moses and commissioned and anointed him to deliver His people, Israel, from Egyptian bondage.

Other biblical accounts of divine sight include:

- At the time God gave the law to Moses on Mount Sinai, He descended upon the mountain in the form of thunder, lightning, fire, and smoke (see Exod. 19:16-18).

- Moses and the elders saw the Lord with a sapphire pavement under His feet (see Exod. 24:9-10).

- When the temple that Solomon built was dedicated in Jerusalem, the glory cloud of the Lord descended and filled the temple (see 2 Chron. 5:13-14).

- While Saul was on the road to Damascus, a light from the sky, which was disclosed in the first heaven, shone around him, and he saw Jesus (see Acts 26:13-19).

OPEN HEAVEN

Now it came about in the thirtieth year, on the fifth day of the fourth month, while I was by the river Chebar among the exiles, the heavens were opened and I saw visions of God (Ezekiel 1:1).

An open Heaven is a vision where a hole seems to appear in the immediate sky, the celestial realm is disclosed, and heavenly sights of God become seeable. The term *open Heaven* originated in historic revivals to describe those times when the manifested presence of God seems to come down in a tangible manner as conviction of sin, conversions, and healings take place. We are now moving from an era of prophetic renewal into a new epoch of the Holy Spirit. We are crossing a threshold into a period of apostolic open Heavens for whole cities and regions to be visited by the presence of the Almighty.

Examples of an open Heaven are found throughout the Scriptures. Here are four instances:

- Ezekiel states that *"the heavens were opened."* He then describes a great cloud sent by God to protect Ezekiel from His brightness. Then he sees flashing lightning, brilliant light, angels, and other details (see Ezek. 1:1-4).

- At Jesus' baptism, the *"heavens were opened"* and the Holy Spirit descended upon Him in the form of a dove. Then the Father spoke audibly, *"This is My beloved Son, in whom I am well pleased"* (see Matt. 3:16-17).

- As Stephen was being stoned for preaching the Gospel, he looked up into Heaven and saw *"the sky loosened and the clouds rolled back"* and Jesus standing to receive him (see Acts 7:55-56).

- The apostle John was about 80 years old and in exile on the island of Patmos when, while meditating on the Lord's day, he heard a voice and saw *"a door opened in heaven."* He is then shown the One who walks among the lampstands and receives many detailed messages from the Lord (see Rev. 1).

The book *The Heavens Opened* by Anna Rountree vividly describes a modern-day account of open Heavens. In a similar manner to that of John the Beloved, on the eve of Hanukkah, 1994, in a cabin on a lake in Texas, the Heavens opened. Anna was caught up in a tremendous vision of satan's brutal attack on the Church. Suddenly, the revelation led her to a stairway into the actual realm of Heaven, by which she escaped the terrible attack. There Anna was met and taught by the angels and by the Lord Jesus Himself. At the end of the encounter, she stood trembling before God the Father as He ordered her to release what she had seen and heard. He commissioned her to compose "letters from home to the homesick" and to share His heart of unbounded love for His children and for the lost.[1]

This is but one example of humble authentic vessels in our day who are receiving open Heavens and other levels of revelatory activity in their lives. These experiences are on the increase. As the last days unfold, such encounters will only multiply!

TRANCE

It happened when I returned to Jerusalem and was praying in the temple, that I fell into a trance (Acts 22:17).

Because it is so easily misunderstood today and is linked in so many people's minds with New Age and the occult, we must be very careful in dealing with the subject of trances. For this reason, the next chapter is devoted to an in-depth look at this type of vision. For now, here is a brief overview.

A trance is more or less a stunned state wherein a person's body is overwhelmed by the Spirit of God, and that person's mind can be arrested and subjected to visions or revelations that God desires to impart. The New Testament Greek word for trance is *ekstasis*, from which our English word *ecstasy* is derived. Basically, a trance is a supernaturally incited excitement of the physical body. Often, a person in a trance is stupefied—held, arrested, and placed in a supernormal (above normal or other-than-normal) state of mind. *Vine's Expository Dictionary of New Testament Words* defines *trance* as "a condition in which ordinary consciousness and the perception of natural circumstances were withheld, and the soul was susceptible only to the vision imparted by God."[2] Another definition of trance is a rapturous state whereby one is caught up into the spiritual realm so as to only receive those things that the Holy Spirit speaks.

Below are eight biblical examples that could be said to describe various forms of a trance-like state:

- Amazement (see Mark 16:8).

- Astonishment (see Mark 5:42).

- Falling as if dead (see Rev. 1:17). The word *ekstasis* is not used here, but the condition of falling as if dead aptly describes a trance-like state.

- A great quaking (see Dan. 10:7).

- A trembling or a shaking (see Job 4:14).

- A sudden power (see Ezek. 8:1; 1 Kings 18:44-46).

- The hand of the Lord (see Ezek. 1:3).

- A deep sleep from the Lord (see Job 33:14-16; Dan. 8:18).

OUT-OF-BODY EXPERIENCE

He stretched out the form of a hand and caught me by a lock of my head; and the Spirit lifted me up between earth and heaven and brought me in the visions of God to Jerusalem (Ezekiel 8:3a).

An out-of-body experience is the actual projecting forth of a person's spirit from his or her body. When God inspires such an experience, He puts a special faith, anointing, and protection around the person's spirit so that that person can perform in the arena where the Lord is leading.

In an out-of-body experience, a person's spirit literally leaves his or her physical body and begins to travel in the spiritual dimension by the Spirit of the Lord. Once out there, the surrounding environment appears different than it does naturally because now the spiritual eyes are seeing, not the natural eyes. The Lord directs the eyes to see what He wants them to see in exactly the way He wants them to see it.

Ezekiel is the prime biblical example of a person who had out-of-body experiences:

- *"The Spirit lifted me up..."* (see Ezek. 3:12-14).

- *"He...caught me by a lock of my head; and the Spirit lifted me up between earth and heaven..."* (see Ezek. 8:1-3).

- *"The Spirit lifted me up and brought me..."* (see Ezek. 11:1-2).

- *"The hand of the Lord was upon me, and He brought me out by the Spirit of the Lord and set me down in the middle of the valley..."* (see Ezek. 37:1-4).

- *"And the Spirit lifted me up and brought me into the inner court"* (see Ezek. 43:5-6).

Paul also apparently had an out-of-body experience. Most scholars believe Paul was referring to himself when he wrote:

> I know a man in Christ who fourteen years ago—whether in the body I do not know, or out of the body I do not know, God knows—such a man was caught up to the third heaven. And I know how such a man—whether in the body or apart from the body I do not know, God knows—was caught up into Paradise and heard inexpressible words, which a man is not permitted to speak (2 Corinthians 12:2-4).

Look at the way Paul speaks of this holy, wonderful realm. He does not make a big deal out of it. Whether he was in or out of his body is not the issue. The issue is what he heard and learned while in the experience. What was the message, and what was its fruit?

As with the trance, this is a visionary experience that we must approach very carefully because of its occultic associations in the minds of many people. Counterfeits of all true Holy Spirit-inspired experiences do exist. Outwardly, there may seem to be little difference, but internally, the difference is great both in fruit and purpose. We are *never* to *will* ourselves into such an experience! This type of experience is *only* to be God-induced and God-initiated!

This is *not* self-projection or some rendition of astral projection. It is *not* "willing" to project us forth; that is of the occult and witchcraft. God, by His initiative and through the Holy Spirit, can, if He desires, lift us up into a spiritual realm, but we are not to project *ourselves* forth into anything.

When spiritists, sorcerers, and yogis practice this without the Holy Spirit and seem to prosper by it, it is because they are not a threat to satan. They are already deceived. Whether they realize it or not, they are already in league with him and are not his enemies.

Do not let the enemy steal what God has ordained. Do not be afraid of these unusual ways of the Holy Spirit, and yet do not enter into some type of self-induced activity.

TRANSLATION

When they came up out of the water, the Spirit of the Lord snatched Philip away; and the eunuch no longer saw him, but went on his way rejoicing (Acts 8:39).

Translation (supernatural transportation or translocation) is more properly defined as an actual physical experience and not just a vision. But when this unusual experience does occur, the individual could be shown various things of the supernatural visionary sort as he or she is being transported. Out of all of these levels of activity mentioned, I have not yet experienced this one. I have friends who have incredible stories of such events. As for me, I am asking the Lord that I might experience all that He has available for me and desires for my life.

Here are a few biblical examples:

- After Jesus was tempted by the devil in the wilderness, He was transported to another place (see Matt. 4:3-5).

- Philip the evangelist was translated after he shared the Gospel with the Ethiopian eunuch (see Acts 8:39).

- Peter was translated out of prison, but while it was happening, he did not realize it. As far as he was concerned, he was having a vision or a dream. Although there is no way to know for sure, this could have been some form of a translation (see Acts 12:8-9).

HEAVENLY VISITATION

I know a man in Christ who fourteen years ago—whether in the body I do not know, or out of the body I do not know, God knows—such a man was caught up to the third heaven (2 Corinthians 12:2).

The Bible refers to three heavens:

1. The lowest heaven, the atmospheric sky that encircles the earth (see Matt. 16:1-3).

2. The second heaven, the stellar heaven that is called outer space, where the sun, moon, stars, and planets reside (see Gen. 1:16-17).

3. The third Heaven, which is the highest one, and the center around which all realms revolve, is Paradise, the abode of God and His angels and saints (see Ps. 11:4; Neh. 9:6).

A heavenly visitation is like an out-of-body experience, except that the person's spirit leaves the earth realm, passes through the second heaven, and goes to the third Heaven. This can occur while the person is praying, while in a trance or a deep sleep from the Lord, or at death.

Some biblical examples include:

- **Moses.** During his 40 days of fasting on Mount Sinai, Moses "saw" the tabernacle in Heaven and was given the "blueprint" for building an earthly version. This may possibly have been a heavenly visitation; we cannot tell for sure. At the very least, it was an open Heaven experience (see Exod. 24:18; 25:1,8-9; Heb. 8:5).

- **Paul.** Again, the apostle was *"caught up to the third heaven,"* where he heard unspeakable words and had a truly paradisiacal experience. Paul seems to have immediately been caught up into this realm (see 2 Cor. 12:2-4).

- **Enoch.** According to Genesis, Enoch *"walked with God"* and God took him. He was caught up into Heaven without dying and never returned to earth (see Heb. 11:5).

In the same way that people can visit the third Heaven by having out-of-body experiences, they can also visit the various regions of hell. If they are sinners, they approach hell by descending—in death or a near-death experience or in a supernatural vision—and are shown where they are destined to spend eternity unless they repent and accept Jesus Christ as their personal Lord and Savior. Then they are brought back to earth into their bodies by the mercy of God.

If people are Christians, the Spirit of the Lord may bring them to hell in such an experience as well, for the purpose of revealing the suffering torments of the damned. They are then sent back to their bodies to testify and warn non-Christians to repent and to receive Jesus as Lord. These experiences are also used as tools of encouragement to the Body of Christ that the unseen world is real. God is a rewarder of those who diligently seek Him (see Heb. 11:6). Heaven and hell are real! Every person is an eternal being, and the final destination is what matters!

I believe heavenly visitations have occurred not only in the Bible but also throughout history. Such experiences will increase as true apostolic ministry emerges in these last days. Join me and express your desire that you might step into all that our Father God has prepared for you.

Chapter Nine

THE ECSTATIC REALMS
OF THE SPIRIT

Ever since November 1972, when I was filled with the Holy Spirit with the release of the gifts of the Spirit in my life, I have had a great love for the things of the Spirit of God. At the same time, however, I harbored for many years a suspicion of phenomena such as trances and out-of-body experiences. So many good things from God have been appropriated by the devil to the point that most people today automatically link such phenomena with New Age philosophies and the occult.

I was the same way until I decided to study the subject in depth and spent time around godly people who had a lot more experience with such things than I did. What I learned is that these kinds of phenomena originated with God; satan merely usurped and corrupted them as he did everything else. *When properly understood and when initiated by the Spirit of God, a trance is an exciting, fabulous, wonderful thing, another powerful visionary experience that brings a person into the heavenly realm.* The *key* is that such an experience *must* be initiated by the Holy Spirit *only*. It must *never* be self-induced.

A trance brings us into the "ecstatic" realm of the Spirit. As we saw in the last chapter, "trance" is one translation of the Greek word *ekstasis*, from which we get our English word *ecstasy.* Literally, an ecstatic trance is a displacement of the mind, a bewilderment that is commonly accompanied by amazement or astonishment. It is a distraction, especially one resulting from great religious fervor, and it often includes feelings of great joy, rapture, and delight that arrest the whole mind.

Ekstasis refers to "any displacement, and especially, with reference to the mind, of that alteration of the normal condition by which the person is thrown into a state of surprise or fear or both; or again, in which a person is so transported out of his natural state that he falls into a trance."[1]

In his book, *Prophetic Gatherings in the Church: The Laying on of Hands and Prophecy*, Dr. David Blomgren writes:

> A trance is a visional state in which revelation is received. This rapturous state is one in which a prophet would perceptively be no longer limited to natural consciousness and volition. He is "in the Spirit" where full consciousness may be temporarily transcended.[2]

David Castro, a dear prophetic brother from Brooklyn, New York, has written some of the most insightful material on this subject. He writes:

> A trance is basically an ecstatic experience wherein one is more-or-less stupefied, stunned. Herein he is susceptible only to the visions God would impart. If a trance (a deep sleep from the Lord) occurs while the person is already asleep, any of the *visual* or *actual* kinds of supernatural dreams may be experienced. One may see visions, hear words (earthly or heavenly) or he may even leave his body and travel in the spirit for a special reason. Of course, these things are *not to be self-induced*, but experienced as the Spirit of God wills it.[3]

There are greater and lesser degrees of ecstatic experiences. The New Testament words *amazed, amazement,* and *astonishment* are also translations of the Greek word *ekstasis.* Hence, we see that both biblically and experientially, there are various degrees of trances.

One can be shocked, amazed, and joyfully "caught up" in one's emotions due to the wondrous activity of the Holy Spirit. In a higher level of trance, one's natural bodily functions are temporarily "put on pause," and the person is caught up in the Spirit (whether in the body or out of the body is not the primary issue), and sees, hears, feels, tastes, touches, or even smells the presence of the Lord in an "otherworldly" or heavenly sort of way.

A brief look at a few scriptural examples of trances will help us better understand this type of visionary experience.

THE TRANCE IN THE SCRIPTURES

One of the most familiar accounts of a Spirit-induced trance is that of Simon Peter in the tenth chapter of Acts. In the early verses of that chapter, Cornelius, a Roman centurion who was *"a devout man…who feared God"* (Acts 10:2), receives a vision of an angel who instructs him to send men to Joppa to summon Peter. Cornelius immediately dispatches two servants and a devout soldier to the task.

> *On the next day, as they were on their way and approaching the city, Peter went up on the housetop about the sixth hour to pray. But he became hungry and was desiring to eat; but while they were making preparations, he fell into a trance; and he saw the sky opened up, and an object like a great sheet coming down, lowered by four corners to the ground, and there were in it all kinds of four-footed animals and crawling creatures of the earth and birds of the air. A voice came to him, "Get up, Peter, kill and eat!" But Peter said, "By no means, Lord, for I have never eaten anything unholy and unclean." Again a voice came to him a second time, "What God has cleansed, no longer consider unholy." This happened three times, and immediately the object was taken up into the sky* (Acts 10:9-16).

During this experience, Peter was temporarily detached from the natural reality around him and saw an open Heaven. The primary purpose of this visionary trance was to prepare Peter for his assignment of entering the home of a Gentile and preaching to the people there. Devout Jews regarded Gentiles as unclean, and Peter needed to overcome his prejudice and learn not to think of other people as unclean just because they were not Jews. He needed to understand that the Gospel of Christ was not for Jews alone, but for all people.

Paul is another apostle who received revelation from God while in a trance. Accosted by a hostile crowd of Jews in Jerusalem and rescued by a band of Roman soldiers, Paul addresses the crowd. After briefly sharing with them his common heritage as a Jew and telling them of his conversion to Christ while on the road to Damascus, Paul then relates the account of his call from God to take the Gospel to the Gentiles:

> And it happened when I returned to Jerusalem and was praying in the temple, that I fell into a trance, and I saw Him saying to me, "Make haste, and get out of Jerusalem quickly, because they will not accept your testimony about Me." And I said, "Lord, they themselves understand that in one synagogue after another I used to imprison and beat those who believed in You. And when the blood of Your witness Stephen was being shed, I also was standing by approving, and watching out for the coats of those who were slaying him." And He said to me, "Go! For I will send you far away to the Gentiles" (Acts 22:17-21).

I find it quite significant that, in both of these cases, the revelation given to Peter and Paul while they were in trances related to their call to preach the Gospel to the Gentiles. Sometimes God chooses unusual and remarkable means to reveal important insights or impart a significant anointing.

There are also numerous examples in the New Testament where people were in an "ecstatic" state that was not described specifically as a trance. Here are just a few:

- "Immediately the girl got up and began to walk, for she was twelve years old. And immediately they were completely astounded [ekstasis]" (Mark 5:42). Jesus raised this young girl from the dead, leaving those who witnessed it (Peter, James, John, and the girl's parents) in a state of ekstasis—profound astonishment.

- *"They went out and fled from the tomb, for trembling and astonishment* [ekstasis] *had gripped them; and they said nothing to anyone, for they were afraid"* (Mark 16:8). Mary Magdalene; Mary, the mother of James; and Salome experienced this ecstatic state of astonishment after seeing an angel in Jesus' tomb who told them that He had risen.

- *"And they were taking note of him as being the one who used to sit at the Beautiful Gate of the temple to beg alms, and they were filled with wonder and amazement* [ekstasis] *at what had happened to him"* (Acts 3:10). An ecstatic state of amazement was the response of those who witnessed Peter's healing of a man lame from birth.

- *"But, so that you may know that the Son of Man has authority on earth to forgive sins,"*—*He said to the paralytic*—*"I say to you, get up, and pick up your stretcher and go home." Immediately he got up before them, and picked up what he had been lying on, and went home glorifying God. They were all struck with astonishment* [ekstasis] *and began glorifying God; and they were filled with fear, saying, "We have seen remarkable things today"* (Luke 5:24-26). This is the story where four men brought their paralyzed friend, dug a hole in the roof, and lowered him down in front of Jesus so that the Lord could heal him.

Concerning this last passage, David Castro writes:

- Of the people present here, some were amazed, others glorified God, and the rest were filled with fear. Those amazed were "en-tranced" into the spiritual realm where they're yielded and inclined to visions of the Lord; although God probably didn't impart visions to all of them. These people were havin' church! They made an effort to come to Jesus' meeting. They came expecting miracles and they were gonna get theirs if they had to break through the wall—and they did! (Talk about bringing down da house!) And as the power of the Lord was present, they got a hold of the realm of the Spirit and went into ecstasy.

God could've easily communicated to them by supernatural revelation if He wanted to. Probably some of them were "slain in the spirit."[4]

Caught Up in the Spirit

The Bible also contains numerous instances of people undergoing possible trance-like experiences even though the word *trance,* or *ekstasis,* is not used. For example, Genesis 15:12 describes a "deep sleep" that fell upon Abram to prepare him for the revelation God was going to give him. God told Abram that his descendants would be slaves in Egypt for 400 years, but afterward would be set free and return to the land where Abram now was. Earlier, at God's direction, Abram had brought a heifer, a goat, a ram, a turtledove, and a pigeon and offered them to the Lord, cutting the three larger animals in half and laying each half opposite the other. It was then that God "cut" His great covenant with Abram:

> It came about when the sun had set, that it was very dark, and behold, there appeared a smoking oven and a flaming torch which passed between these pieces. On that day the Lord made a covenant with Abram, saying, "To your descendants I have given this land, from the river of Egypt as far as the great river, the river Euphrates" (Genesis 15:17-18).

Abram's natural consciousness was put on "pause," and he was brought up into the realm of the Spirit where God spoke His covenantal promises to His friend. This suspension of natural consciousness is a common characteristic of a trance-like state.

The prophet Ezekiel described many of his visionary experiences as being "lifted up" by the Spirit, which can also describe a trance-like condition:

- *"The Spirit lifted me up and took me away..."* (Ezek. 3:14).
- *"The Spirit lifted me up between earth and heaven and brought me in the visions of God to Jerusalem..."* (Ezek. 8:3).

- *"And the Spirit lifted me up and brought me in a vision by the Spirit of God to the exiles in Chaldea"* (Ezek. 11:24).

- *"And the Spirit lifted me up and brought me into the inner court; and behold, the glory of the Lord filled the house"* (Ezek. 43:5).

Daniel, like Abram, often received visionary revelation while in a "deep sleep." After receiving a powerful vision concerning the endtimes, Daniel was trying to understand what he had seen. Gabriel was sent to explain the vision to him. *"Now while he was talking with me, I sank into a deep sleep with my face to the ground; but he touched me and made me stand upright"* (Dan. 8:18). Under the power of the Spirit, Daniel fell to the ground and in a "deep sleep" entered into a prophetic rapturous state.

On another occasion, Daniel saw a "great vision" of the Lord,

> Yet no strength was left in me, for my natural color turned to a deathly
> pallor, and I retained no strength. But I heard the sound of his words; and
> as soon as I heard the sound of his words, I fell into a deep sleep on my
> face, with my face to the ground. Then behold, a hand touched me and set
> me trembling on my hands and knees (Daniel 10:8-10).

We have already looked at Paul's account of being *"caught up to the third heaven"* in such a state that he did not know whether he was *"in the body"* or *"out of the body"* (2 Cor. 12:2). The words *caught up* perfectly describe a trance-like state.

John the Beloved had similar experiences to Paul, which he describes in the Book of Revelation. He was *"in the Spirit on the Lord's day"* when he heard behind him a voice like a trumpet. Turning, he saw *"one like a son of man"* in a long robe with a golden sash. His hair was as white as snow, his eyes blazed like fire, his face shown like the sun, and a two-edged sword came out of His mouth (see Rev. 1:10-16). John's response to this shocking image is understandable:

> When I saw Him, I fell at His feet like a dead man. And He placed
> His right hand on me, saying, "Do not be afraid; I am the first and
> the last, and the living One; and I was dead, and behold, I am alive

forevermore, and I have the keys of death and of Hades"(Revelation 1:17-18).

John was *"in the Spirit,"* saw a revelation of Christ in His glory, and *"fell at His feet like a dead man."* Some people would say he was "slain in the Spirit," and others would say that "the glory came down." However we choose to describe it, John saw Jesus and prostrated himself in worship, perhaps completely overcome with the fear of the Lord and in a trancelike state.

A few chapters later, John describes another visionary experience:

> *After these things I looked, and behold, a door standing open in heaven, and the first voice which I had heard, like the sound of a trumpet speaking with me, said, "Come up here, and I will show you what must take place after these things." Immediately I was in the Spirit; and behold, a throne was standing in heaven, and One sitting on the throne* (Revelation 4:1-2).

This time, instead of a vision of Christ, John saw God the Father, the *"One sitting on the throne."* Once again, John was *"in the Spirit,"* and this state made it possible for him to see into Heaven. This was very possibly a trancelike state that caused John to be receptive to an open Heaven type of experience. Jesus had called John forth into visions of Heaven. As a result, he was able to behold sights in the third Heaven and also on the earth.

It is important to note here that one does not have to be in a trance to be in the Spirit. However, one who has experienced a trance may be properly said to have been in the Spirit.

As I said before, God does nothing without a purpose. His purpose in imparting visionary revelation, whether through a trance or any other means, is not just to give us an "experience," but that we might see and know *Him*. We should not desire or seek visionary experiences for their own sake, but for how they can help us draw closer in deeper intimacy with our Lord.

Lest we think that supernatural trances were limited to biblical days, I want to share several testimonies of such experiences that date more closely to our own day. My desire is to demonstrate that trances from the Holy Spirit can be and are being experienced by "ordinary" Christians today.

"My Little Brother"

Dr. Mahesh Chavda is one of my dearest ministry friends, as his life and testimony have impacted me greatly. The story that follows is from his book, *Only Love Can Make a Miracle*, and tells how he took the final step to receive Christ as his Savior and Lord, becoming the first in his family to embrace Christ. Raised in Kenya by good Hindu parents from India, Mahesh was born into the upper caste—the warrior caste—of India and thus received a fine education while being groomed for leadership in government. This account begins after Mahesh learned about Jesus by reading the Gospels in a Bible given to him by a Baptist missionary.

> In the end, I decided I simply couldn't walk away from it all: my family, my training, my heritage. Part of me wanted Jesus, but I couldn't bring myself to pay the price. And I couldn't take the double-mindedness anymore.
>
> For months now I had lived in agony. I would read the Gospels and find myself so attracted to Jesus that the next step—committing my all to him—seemed obvious and easy. Then the pull would go the other way, as I thought of the heartache I would cause my friends and family.
>
> Finally, I had had enough. It was late one night. I was upstairs in my second-floor bedroom reading my Bible as I usually did. I was sitting at my desk, with a bed sheet wrapped around my body, pulled up over my head, and snuggled around my face, so that my eyes could just peer out. I had to do this because of the mosquitoes swarming around me. The mosquitoes were horrible in that part of Africa, and in those days we had no window screens and, of course, no spray cans of insect repellent.

My moment of decision had arrived at last. "No more," I said to myself. "Enough is enough. I am never going to think about Jesus Christ again." I despaired, thinking about leaving behind the one who I knew loved me so much, but I didn't waver. I slowly, firmly closed the Bible. "I am never going to read this book again," I said. "My mind is made up." And that was that. Or so I thought.

The next thing I knew, I heard my head hit the desk...I seemed to be in a sort of half-sleep, no longer fully awake and in control, but aware of what was going on...

I immediately found myself in a strange and wonderful place. My body was still there at the desk, but in my spirit I was somewhere different, somewhere wonderful, somewhere I had never been before. The thought came into my conscious-ness, very simply and clearly, "I am in heaven."

...The first thing I noticed was that I was walking on a street or pathway of some sort that appeared to be made of gold. It was different from any gold that I'd seen before. It seemed to be clear. You could almost see through it. Years later I read that when scientists purify gold with atomic particles, it becomes translucent. That's what the gold on this pathway was like, as though it had been thoroughly purified.

Along both sides of the path was luxurious grass, like a thick blanket that you could lie down on and fall asleep. There were trees and flowers of every size and description. The colors were fantastic: yellows, greens, golds, blues, pinks—more colors and shades than I could have imagined...

These colors were different. It was as though they provided their own color from within. The light wasn't reflecting off of them, it was pulsating from inside of them, in absolutely pure light...

I became aware that I was hearing music. At least, it was more like music than anything else I had ever experienced. It was as though the grandest symphony orchestra and the most splendid choir ever assembled were performing—though I could not distinguish particular instruments or voices. It was glorious.

I found my whole being dancing in keeping with the music. It was as though every one of my senses was perfectly harmonized with it. In fact, my overall sense was one of complete harmony, of perfection, of the total integration of everything around me...

I was somehow part of it: part of the splendor, part of the harmony, part of the perfection. I wasn't just seeing and hearing and smelling what was around me. I was integrated into it. I didn't just experience joy and love and purity and harmony, I somehow became part of them, and they became part of me.

I felt that I was *home*. This was where I wanted to be, where I was *supposed* to be. This was why I had been created.

...Suddenly, I became aware of a brilliant white light coming toward me. I turned and saw a man walking toward me. I knew immediately who it was. It was Jesus. Now bear in mind that I had never seen a depiction of Jesus...On the natural plane, I had no idea what he looked like. Yet there was not a trace of doubt in my mind that the man now walking toward me was him.

...I was almost blinded by the light that was streaming forth from him. It was bright and pure and alive, as if it contained the fullness of heavenly glory. I could hardly look at Him.

...As he came closer to me, I could see that he was smiling. It was...a smile of utter love and delight...

He came closer still, and I saw his eyes. I will never forget the eyes of Jesus. I could see that those eyes had felt every hurt, every heartache, that had ever been felt. They had shed every tear that had ever been wept on earth. Yet they were not eyes of sadness or gloom. They were eyes of triumph, eyes that seemed to say, "Yes, I know the pain, I know the heartache, I know the tears. I took it all upon myself when I died on the cross. But I have overcome. And you can overcome too."

Then as I stood there gazing into his eyes, he stretched out his hand and placed it upon my shoulder and said to me, simply, "My little brother."

As suddenly as it had begun, it ended. I was once again on the second floor of my house with my bed sheet drawn around my face and my head resting on my Bible—but something strange had happened. When all this had started, when my head had fallen forward onto the desk, my Bible had been closed. I had just made a decision never to open it again. Now, however, it was open. I looked down and I saw that it was opened to chapter eighteen of Luke's Gospel, the story of the rich young ruler.

...I heard a voice within me say to me, "Are you going to turn away from me the same way he did?"

I said, "No, sir."

Then I did something that, to my knowledge, no ancestor of mine had ever done, that no one in all the eight hundred years of our family history could even have imagined doing. I got down on my knees and said, "Jesus, I'm sorry. Please forgive me for all the wrong things I've done. I want you. I want to give my life to you. Please come and live in my heart."[5]

Mahesh's account is an incredibly beautiful and accurate description of how the Holy Spirit brings a person into contact with the love and grace of God. Through the years since that night, Mahesh has been used mightily by God in a worldwide ministry of evangelism and healing and other miracles.

"MY SENSES WERE SUSPENDED"

The life and ministry of Kenneth E. Hagin were profoundly influenced by his visions of Jesus. Here is his account of his third vision, which occurred one evening in December 1952 in Broken Bow, Oklahoma.

> One night after the service, we had returned to the parsonage and were having a sandwich and a glass of milk in the kitchen. As we talked about the things of the Lord, time slipped away from us.
>
> The pastor's little girl was sitting there with us, and finally she became sleepy and said, "Daddy, it's getting late, and I have to get up early in the morning to go to school. Won't you come pray with me now?" It was their custom that he always prayed with her at night and then tucked her into bed.
>
> The pastor looked at his watch and exclaimed, "It's 11:30! Why, I never dreamed it was that late. We have been sitting here talking for two hours." Then he said to his daughter, "Come here honey. We'll just kneel down here and Brother Hagin can have prayer with us. Then you can go to bed."
>
> As we knelt together in that kitchen, each of us beside a chair, I was in the Spirit before my knees ever touched the floor...
>
> On this night in 1952 in the parsonage kitchen, my physical senses were suspended. At that moment I didn't know I was kneeling beside a kitchen chair. It seemed as if I was kneeling in a white cloud that enveloped me.
>
> Immediately I saw Jesus. He seemed to be standing above me, about as high as the ceiling is from the floor. He began to talk to me. "I am going to teach you concerning the devil, demons, and demon possession," He began. "From this night forward, what is known in my Word as the gift of discerning of spirits will operate in your life when you are in the Spirit."[6]

Dr. Hagin then goes on to describe how the gifts of the Spirit and, particularly, the gift of discerning of spirits, were in operation in him *only* when he was in the realm of the Spirit. In other words, it was not at his choice or volition, but only when he was, in his words, "in the anointing."

"A WONDERFUL DISPLAY OF GOD'S POWER"

Maria Woodworth-Etter was a powerful evangelist and revival leader of the late 19th and early 20th centuries. Wherever she went, the power of God fell: people were slain in the Spirit, saw visions, received revelation, and were converted by the thousands. Her book, *Signs and Wonders*, her personal account of the first 40 years of her ministry, contains perhaps some of the most insightful and incredible material that has ever been written on the arena of trances and supernatural manifestations of the Holy Spirit. The account that follows took place in January of 1885, and it is only one of the many amazing displays of God's sovereign power recorded in her book.

> The church was cold and formal, and many of the best citizens had drifted into skepticism. I knew that it would take a wonderful display of God's power to convince the people, so I prayed for God to display His power, that the sinner might know that God still lives, and that there is a reality in religion, and might convict him of a terrible judgment. Five of the leading members of the church said they would unite with me in prayer for the Lord to pour out the power from on high, till the city would be shaken, and the country, for miles around. We prayed that Christians and sinners might fall as dead men; that the slain of the Lord might be many. The Lord answered our prayers in a remarkable manner.
>
> The class leader's little boy fell under the power of God first. He rose up, stepped on the pulpit, and began to talk with the wisdom and power of God. His father began to shout, and to praise the Lord. As the little fellow exhorted and asked the people to come to Christ they began to weep all over the

house. Some shouted; others fell prostrated. Diverse operations of the Spirit were seen. The displays of the power of God continued to increase till we closed the meeting, which lasted about five weeks. The power of the Lord, like the wind, swept all over the city, up one street and down another, sweeping through the places of business, the workshops, saloons and dives, arresting sinners of all classes. The Scriptures were fulfilled. The wicked flee when no man pursueth. Men, women and children were struck down in their homes, in their places of business, on the highways, and lay as dead. They had wonderful visions and rose converted, giving glory to God. When they told what they had seen their faces shown like angels.' The fear of God fell upon the city. The police said they never saw such a change; that they had nothing to do. They said they made no arrest; and that the power of God seemed to preserve the city. A spirit of love rested all over the city. There was no fighting, no swearing on the streets; that the people moved softly, and that there seemed to be a spirit of love and kindness among all the classes, as if they felt they were in the presence of God.

A merchant fell in a trance in his home and lay several hours. Hundreds went in to look at him. He had a vision, and a message for the church. The Lord showed him the condition of many of the members. He told part of his vision, but refused to deliver the message to the church. He was struck dumb. He could not speak a word because he refused to tell what the Lord wanted him to. The Lord showed him he would never speak till he delivered the message. He rose to his feet, weeping, to tell the vision. God loosed his tongue. Those present knew he had been dumb, and when he began to talk and tell his experience it had a wonderful effect on the church and sinners.

One night there was a party seventeen miles from the city. Some of the young ladies thought they would have some fun; they began to mimic and act out the trance. The Lord struck some of them down. They lay there as if they had been shot. Their fun-making was soon turned into a prayer-meeting, and cries of mercy were heard. The people came to the meeting in sleigh loads many miles. One night while a sleigh load of men and women were going to the meeting they were jesting about the trances. They made the remark to each other that they were going in a trance that night. Before the meeting closed all who had been making fun were struck down by the power of God and lay like dead people, and had to be taken home in the sleigh in that condition. Those who came with them were very much frightened when they saw them lying there, and they told how they had been making fun of the power of God on the way to the meeting. Scoffers and mockers were stricken down in all parts of the house.

One man was mocking a woman of whose body God had taken control. She was preaching with gestures. When in that mocking attitude God struck him dumb. He became rigid and remained with his hands up, and his mouth drawn in that mocking way for five hours, a gazing-stock for all in the house. The fear of God fell on all. They saw that it was a fearful thing to mock God or make fun of His work. Surely, the Lord worked in a wonderful way in this meeting. The postmaster was converted. All classes from the roughs and the toughs to the tallest cedars and brightest talents of the city were brought into the fold of Christ. We took the meeting to the opera house and it would not hold the crowds, so great was the awakening among the people.[7]

"Drops of Pure Crystal Light"

Annie is a woman who was brought to Christ out of a life of agnosticism, rebellion, great pain, and suicidal tendencies. Throughout her life as a Christian, Annie has been blessed by God with hundreds of vivid and powerful visions. Many of these have been recorded in a series of books edited by the late R. Edward Miller, the evangelist under whose ministry she found Christ and received a great deliverance. The following account is called "Showers" and is drawn from the book *I Looked and I Saw the Lord*.

> I was before the Lord on the evening of the 8th of July, seeking His face and pouring out my heart before Him, when suddenly I was There. In the Spirit I found myself surrounded by a sweet, powerful force of love. It not only surrounded me but invaded me to the inmost part of my being. At the same time it brought with it such a deep sense of peace, of security, and of well-being. I saw myself encircled by those beautiful angels with their wings folded irradiating light and loving care. Jesus was with me in this angelic circle. His glory shined all around and upon all. He was just like I had last seen Him and He was just loving me. It was just like being inside a dense, transparent, invisible but tangible cloud of pure LOVE. As I was completely covered in this bright cloud of love it began to rain.
>
> It rained, and rained, and rained. But what a strange rain it was. It was not like rain on this earth because it was not wet at all. It was a heavenly rain and it rained all the time I was there. The large drops were like drops of pure crystal lights, or like small diamonds that had light and life inside them. They fell from above so softly and smoothly like little stars. I played and played with the rain drops, catching them in my hands. Although each one gave me such a sense of joy and pleasure, my hands did not get wet. Although of substance, they were still so light and airy and I carried them about in my hand. I laughed and laughed from pure pleasure and the

angels laughed to rejoice with me as if they were enjoying my joy. Jesus showed me that this was His rain of blessing.

Later I was so amazed for in the service that night there was a prophetic word concerning the beautiful showers of rain that He was even now sending upon His people. I felt so joyful for I had been given to see and feel and play with that very rain.[8]

Biblically and historically, the trance has been a legitimate method God sometimes has used to impart visionary revelation, and it continues to be so today. My purpose here is not to promote trances. My purpose is to promote the Kingdom of God. If He wants to use this seer revelation as one of His vehicles to help tune us in to His kind will, then I say, "Bring it on!" Ultimately, God's desire is to bring us close to Himself and impart His will and His ways to us so that we can minister to others in wisdom because we have spent time standing in the council of God.

INTIMACY: THE GOAL OF ALL THINGS

*But who has stood in the **council of the Lord**, that he should* ***see*** *and hear His word? Who has given heed to His word and listened? ...But if they had stood in My council, then they would have **announced** My words to My people, and would have turned them back from their evil way and from the evil of their deeds* (Jeremiah 23:18,22).

The supernatural visionary and audible experiences of the seer are not to be concealed, but to be announced to God's people. The purpose of standing in the council of God is to produce fruit in the lives of God's people: the fruit of holiness, repentance, the fear of the Lord, and a godly lifestyle. God always acts with purpose. He reveals His secret counsel to us because we are His friends, but He also reveals it in order to get a job done—to accomplish His will.

Thus says the Lord of hosts, "If you will walk in My ways and if you will perform My service, then you will also govern My house and also have charge of My courts, and I will grant you free access among these who are standing here" (Zechariah 3:7).

This verse shows us that there are divine conditions for standing in His council: *"walk in My ways and...perform My service."* This involves progressive steps of faithfulness. If we do those things, God promises that we will govern His house, have charge of His courts, and have free access to those who are standing there.

No matter what we do as Christians, our goal—indeed, the goal of all things—should be to grow in intimacy with our loving Father by the power of the Holy Spirit through Jesus Christ our Lord. In my own experience, I have found that the most direct road to greater intimacy with God has come through the practice or discipline of an almost lost art in the fast-paced Church of today—something called contemplative prayer.

I discovered the hidden streams of the prophetic in the writings of the desert fathers and Christian mystics. In their writings, I discovered the truths of the true and false self, centering prayer, recollection, union with God, and spiritual ecstasy. These spiritual disciplines are not the goal. They are the pathway to the goal: union and intimacy with God.

Intimacy is the key to open Heavens. The Heavens open up over those that are radical in their love for Jesus and on those that are wasted on Jesus. If there are true seers in the heartland and beyond today, and there surely are, then we must have our aim and focus clear. We must see Jesus!

Chapter Ten

STANDING IN
THE COUNCIL OF GOD

Across the spectrum of the Christian Church today, many questions arise and much debate occurs concerning the legitimacy of prophetic and visionary ministry. Many Christians hear about others' claims to having angelic visitations or being caught up in the Spirit or being brought up before the throne of God, and they ask, "Are these things biblical?" Sometimes the question comes from a mind-set of doubt, skepticism, and disbelief; at other times, it arises from an attitude of genuine curiosity. More and more believers are beginning to examine these things out of a desire to know and understand more about these mystical ways.

Proverbs 29:18 says, *"Where there is no vision, the people are unrestrained,* [or perish] *but happy is he who keeps the law."* What kind of vision will keep a people from perishing? A vision from the Lord. How do they get such a vision? God imparts vision to people who open their hearts to Him, who are sensitive to His Spirit, and who spend much time in intimate fellowship with Him. The Lord gives vision to those who, in the words of Jeremiah, have *"stood in the council of the Lord":*

But who has stood in the council of the Lord, that he should see and hear His word? Who has given heed to His word and listened?...But if they had stood in My council, then they would have announced My words to My people, and would have turned them back from their evil way and from the evil of their deeds (Jeremiah 23:18,22).

What does it mean to *"stand in the council of the Lord"*? Compare this passage to some verses from the Book of Habakkuk:

The oracle which Habakkuk the prophet saw (Habakkuk 1:1).

I will stand on my guard post and station myself on the rampart; and I will keep watch to see what He will speak to me, and how I may reply when I am reproved (Habakkuk 2:1).

Jeremiah speaks of seeing, hearing, giving heed to, and listening to the Word of God. Habakkuk refers to seeing an oracle and describes himself as a guard on the rampart, keeping watch to see what the Lord will speak to him. These words sound a similar theme to those of Isaiah:

On your walls, O Jerusalem, I have appointed watchmen; all day and all night they will never keep silent. You who remind the Lord, take no rest for yourselves; and give Him no rest until He establishes and makes Jerusalem a praise in the earth (Isaiah 62:6-7).

How can anyone "see" what the Lord "speaks"? The simplest answer is that God has more than one way of "speaking." His speech is not limited to audible words or, indeed, to words of any kind. In the prophetic realm, to stand in the council of God means both to see and to hear the Word of God. But for what purpose? Jeremiah 23:22 gives the answer: to announce God's Word to God's people in order to "[turn] *them back from their evil way and from the evil of their deeds.*" In other words, the purpose of standing in the council of God is to produce fruit in the lives of God's people: the fruit of holiness, repentance, the fear of the Lord, and a godly lifestyle.

In Close Deliberation[1]

The Hebrew word for "council" in Jeremiah 23:18 is *cowd*, which means "a session," or "a company of persons in close deliberation." It implies intimacy, as in secret consultation. By comparison, our English word *council* refers to a group of people called together for discussion or advice. Within the Church at large, a *council* is a formal assembly convened to discuss points of doctrine or theology. Within a business, a *council* is brought together to bring divergent thoughts together to formulate the best plan or way to proceed.

Just as there are earthly councils of men and women who come together to discuss and advise, there is also a council that takes place in Heaven, presided over by Almighty God, where we can hear and receive the *counsel* of the Lord—the wisdom and vision and direction that derive from the council of God. By His sovereign and personal invitation, we can enter God's "hearing room" to listen to the deliberation of His council so as to be able to announce His Word on an issue.

Let's examine some Scriptures that refer in one way or another to this council of God—people joined together with God in close deliberation.

> *Were you the first man to be born, or were you brought forth before the hills? Do you hear the secret counsel of God, and limit wisdom to yourself? What do you know that we do not know? What do you understand that we do not?* (Job 15:7-9)

In these verses, Eliphaz, one of Job's friends, is rebuking Job for standing by his own wisdom while dismissing that of Eliphaz and his companions, Bildad and Zophar. While there certainly is a strong element of resentment and even jealousy in Eliphaz's tone, the important thing to note here is that he *assumes* that there is such a thing as "the secret counsel of God."

The Lord has revelation—secrets, if you will—that He wants to open up to us. Normally, we do not share secrets with just anyone. Most of us confide our deepest and most intimate things only with trusted friends. One of the highest characteristics of a prophetic person is that he or she is supposed to be a trusted friend of God. God has secrets, and He is looking for some friends to share His counsel with. It is an open invitation; we *all* can be friends of God.

> *Who has directed the Spirit of the Lord, or as His counselor has informed Him? With whom did He consult and who gave Him understanding? And who taught Him in the path of justice and taught Him knowledge and informed Him of the way of understanding?* (Isaiah 40:13-14)

> *Also we have obtained an inheritance, having been predestined according to His purpose who works all things after the counsel of His will* (Ephesians 1:11).

The implication in the Isaiah passage is that no one instructs or counsels God; on the contrary, He instructs and counsels us. He is our teacher. Paul's words in Ephesians imply that because of our inheritance from the Lord, we can be brought into the place of *"the counsel of His will."*

The prophet Amos wrote, *"Surely the Lord God does nothing unless He reveals His secret counsel to His servants the prophets"* (Amos 3:7). This verse reveals a very important principle at work in the Kingdom of God: *God's prophetic people are to be His friends.* They are to be the ones to whom He can entrust His word, His message, and His revelation; He often speaks to them beforehand about what He is going to do.

Why does God speak to His servants the prophets before He acts? Is God not sovereign? Can He not do whatever He wants to do without informing any of us? Absolutely, but God has chosen to work this way because at Creation He gave the stewardship of this earth to humanity. He established a chain of command, so to speak. God has never rescinded His original decree giving humankind dominion over the earth. That is why He says, in effect, "Before I do anything, I will let someone—my friends—know what I am about to do."

God always acts with purpose. He reveals His secret counsel to us because we are His friends, but He also reveals it in order to get a job done—to accomplish His will.

It is very important that we recognize and accept our place as *servants* of God. As believers, we *are* God's friends—just as we are co-heirs with Christ—but our friendship with God is characterized by love as well as by faithful obedience and service. We find our identity not in who we are or what our title is, but in Christ and in servanthood. Who we are is not determined by what we do, but to whom we belong. If we are "in Christ," our lives are in Him. He *is* our life.

A prime example of Amos 3:7 in action is found in the twentieth chapter of Genesis. God's intention is to destroy Sodom and Gomorrah because of the sinfulness of the people; but before He does, He reveals His plan to Abraham. Although Abraham intercedes for the cities, God destroys them because fewer than ten righteous people are found there. Abraham's nephew, Lot, his wife, and their two daughters are delivered from Sodom before it is destroyed. Because of Abraham's intercession, several members of his extended family are rescued from destruction.

There are two sides to the coin of standing in the council of God. On one side is the sovereignty of God, and on the other, the initiative of people. One of the amazing truths of the Bible is that the announced intention and counsel of God can be altered by our intercession!

Another important aspect of standing in the council of God is a sense of being in Heaven—in His very throne room. In his book called *The Throne Room Company*, seer Shawn Bolz describes his experience of witnessing the radiance of His glory when the Heavens opened:

> When the heavens opened to me, the atmosphere of Heaven was thick with intense purity in the air. Many spiritual beings surrounded me. An angel guided me into the center of a very large room, which I realized was God's throne room. It had no visible walls; the room seemed as endless as God's awesome presence.
>
> In the center of the room was the glorified Son. His presence was so bright that the pure light coming from His face felt like a walk into the heart of a nuclear explosion. Yet somehow, He gave me grace to be able to walk toward Him.

Although I understood that God dwells in an approachable light, this experience of His glory caused me to become undone. How can those who are unholy come into the very presence of Holiness without shattering into a million particles? God's very covenant of love was my assurance that I was safe. I held on to it as though it were a contract in my hand, because I was so overwhelmed by the fear of the Lord.

This time I wasn't allowed to get very close. However, just being in such nearness to God was overwhelming. I just stared at Him, the King of all glory. I felt like I was crying out of sheer joy, but no tears fell. It was as if my spirit contained the emotion of weeping, but expressed it so much deeper—with a deep sense of astonishment.

Just gazing at God was an act of worship. I didn't have to try to produce words or songs; my whole being was alive in His presence and completely adored Him. It is a natural, automatic response in the midst of His glory.

I was only able to gaze upon Him for a few minutes. I knew if I stayed there much longer, I would not be willing to return to earth. So, the angel interrupted my sweet communion with Jesus. It was the only time my angelic companion felt awkward. We looked at each other with complete understanding and then we both obeyed.[2]

Daniel describes this in the seventh chapter of his book when, after seeing his vision of the four great and terrible beasts, he goes on to speak of a heavenly council:

I kept looking until thrones were set up, and the Ancient of Days took His seat; His vesture was like white snow and the hair of His head like pure wool. His throne was ablaze with flames, its wheels were a burning fire. A river of fire was flowing and coming out from before Him; thousands upon thousands were attending Him, and myriads upon myriads were standing before Him; the court sat, and the books were opened (Daniel 7:9-10).

"The court sat." There was a session, a deliberation in the council room of the Most Holy One. The purpose of a court is to hear a case. In this case, the deliberation resulted in the promise of judgment against the beasts Daniel had seen earlier in his vision. Dominion would be taken from them and given to the Son of Man and His saints forever and ever (see Dan. 7:13-18).

As far as Daniel was concerned, this experience seemed real enough for him to have been present bodily at the heavenly council. Standing in the council equates "being there," as some revelatory people term the experience.

"Being There"

In Second Corinthians 12:1-4, Paul's famous account of being "caught up to the third heaven," the apostle mentions three possible states in which this could have happened: "in the body," "out of the body," and "apart from the body." Paul himself did not know which state he was in when he had this experience, and it really was not important. What was important was what he saw and heard and learned during the experience.

Carlton Kenney, a renowned Bible teacher and a missionary statesman in Japan for many years, has drawn a distinction between the three states of the body that Paul mentions:

1. In the body—a subjective experience where we are spectating. This could relate to various forms of dreams and visions as in Acts 9:10; 10:3; 15:9 and 18:9.

2. Apart from the body—a subjective experience where we not only spectate but also interact or dialogue. Possible examples are trances and other experiences as in Acts 10:10,19; 11:5 and 22:17.

3. Out of the body—a subjective experience where we not only spectate but move about in the spiritual realm. Ezekiel gives us

numerous examples of this as in Ezek. 1:1,3; 3:22; 8:1-11:5,13; 37:1 and 40:1.[3]

An experience of "being there" in the council of God is significant for several reasons. First of all, it is an honor when God grants this kind of audience. Second, the more subjective the experience, the greater the possibility of pure revelation. Finally, our own thoughts are out of the process, and reception in the spirit realm is in clearer focus.

These are important factors to consider because they help us establish the proper mind-set for walking in that realm. After all, if God grants us the privilege of such a supernatural encounter as standing in His council, we had better know how to act when we are there. God gives us instruction for this in His Word. Consider this verse:

> Thus says the Lord of hosts, "If you will walk in My ways and if you will perform My service, then you will also govern My house and also have charge of My courts, and I will grant you free access among these who are standing here" (Zechariah 3:7).

Here are God's conditions for standing in His council: *"walk in My ways and...perform My service."* This involves progressive steps of faithfulness followed by His supernatural enablement. If we do the little things, God will do the big things. He will watch over His promises that we will govern His house, have charge of His courts, and have free access to those who are standing there. I want this in my life! Don't you?

Who are the ones who are "standing here"? Primarily, they are angelic beings, although the Son of God is certainly present as well.

> I saw at night, and behold, a man was riding on a red horse, and he was standing among the myrtle trees which were in the ravine, with red, sorrel and white horses behind him. Then I said, "My lord, what are these?" And the angel who was speaking with me said to me, "I will show you what these are." And the man who was standing among the myrtle trees answered and said, "These are those whom the Lord has sent to patrol the earth." So they answered the angel of the Lord who

*was standing among the myrtle trees and said,"We have patrolled the
earth, and behold, all the earth is peaceful and quiet"* (Zechariah
1:8-11).

Zechariah sees, hears, and speaks to angels, as well as to a man on a red
horse, who is also described as "the angel of the Lord." This phrase is a common Old Testament reference to an appearance of the Son of God, the second
person of the Trinity—Christ in His pre-incarnate form. Notice Zechariah's
humility; he did not know what it was he was seeing, so he asked for an explanation. He did not put on a "know-it-all" air or get caught up in "revelation
fixation." Such humility characterizes Zechariah throughout the book that
bears his name.

Daniel was the same way. Whenever he did not understand part of a
vision, he asked one of those "standing by" to explain it to him. After his powerful vision of the four great beasts and the Son of Man who defeats them,
Daniel was puzzled by what it meant:

> *I approached one of those who were standing by and began asking
> him the exact meaning of all this. So he told me and made known to
> me the interpretation of these things* (Daniel 7:16).

Zechariah and Daniel (as well as all the other prophets and people who
had these kinds of encounters with the Lord) knew they were in the presence
of God, and that realization filled them with a holy fear; and their humility
grew out of that holy fear. One way to identify an authentic encounter with
the Lord is that a holy fear arises in the spirits of all who experience that
encounter.

How then should we walk among those who are standing by in the council of the Lord? What should be our demeanor in His presence? The key—the
only acceptable posture—is a spirit of humility in the holy fear of the Lord.

This leads us to three important guidelines to help protect us from error
during supernatural encounters such as these:

1. Avoid unhealthy familiarity and fascination with their personage.
    In Revelation 19:10, John is tempted to worship the angel who is

speaking to him: *"Then I fell at his feet to worship him. But he said to me, 'Do not do that; I am a fellow servant of yours and your brethren who hold the testimony of Jesus; worship God. For the testimony of Jesus is the spirit of prophecy.'"*

2. Watch out for the issue of "commanding angels" in spiritual warfare encounters. How do we handle such a touchy topic? Let Jesus be our guide. At the time He was betrayed and arrested, Jesus said to His disciples, *"Do you think that I cannot appeal to My Father, and He will at once put at My disposal more than twelve legions of angels?"* (Matt. 26:53) Even the Son of God Himself would seek angelic help not directly, but by appealing to His Father. We should do the same; we should appeal to our Father, the One who sits on the throne.

3. Be careful to use proper discernment in the distinction between the true angelic and the demonic counterfeit. All true spiritual warfare centers on the placement of the Son. Don't be deceived. Remember that both heavenly angels and fallen angels, and especially satan, can appear like lightning. Paul said, *"Even satan disguises himself as an angel of light"* (2 Cor. 11:14). Another key to success in this area is to make sure we have dealt with forgiveness issues so that satan cannot take advantage of us: *"But one whom you forgive anything, I forgive also; for indeed what I have forgiven, if I have forgiven anything, I did it for your sakes in the presence of Christ, so that no advantage would be taken of us by satan, for we are not ignorant of his schemes"* (2 Cor. 2:10-11). Releasing forgiveness is one of the highest tools of spiritual warfare. It nullifies the enemy's ability to gain a foothold in our lives.

THE HINDRANCE OF AN EVIL HEART

No matter how prophetically gifted we may be, our ability to flow in the full power and revelation of the prophetic depends on the purity of our hearts and the closeness of our walks with the Lord. The gifts and calling of

God are without repentance. This means that we may still operate at some level of prophetic revelation even if we are not walking close to the Lord, but we will never reach our full potential as long as we remain in that condition.

Jeremiah the prophet provides us with a good list of the kinds of things we need to watch out for. The entire twenty-third chapter of the Book of Jeremiah is an indictment of the shepherds (spiritual leaders) and prophets in Israel for their failure to honestly and responsibly lead the people in the ways of the Lord. According to Jeremiah, these were the sins of the prophets of Israel:

1. ***Using their power unjustly—***

   *As for the prophets: my heart is broken within me, all my bones tremble; I have become like a drunken man, even like a man overcome with wine, because of the Lord and because of His holy words. For the land is full of adulterers; for the land mourns because of the curse. The pastures of the wilderness have dried up. Their course also is evil **and their might is not right** (Jeremiah 23:9-10).*

   This gets into the issue of manipulation: Why do we want this revelation, and what will we do with it once we have it? God knows the condition of our hearts. A wrong motive hinders revelation.

2. ***Mixing the sources of their message—***

   "Moreover, among the prophets of Samaria I saw an offensive thing: They prophesied by Baal and led My people Israel astray" (Jer. 23:13). This involves mingling the things of the flesh and the world with the things of the Spirit. The result is pollution of the message. We may need some personal cleansing in our lives before we can be fully usable to the Lord.

3. ***Engaging in immorality—***

   Also among the prophets of Jerusalem I have seen a horrible thing: the committing of adultery and walking in falsehood; and they strengthen the hands of evildoers, so that no one has turned back from his wickedness. All of them have become to Me like Sodom, and her inhabitants like Gomorrah (Jeremiah 23:14).

An immoral lifestyle clogs up the channel through which God's revelation and blessings can flow.

4. **Speaking from their own imagination—**

Thus says the Lord of hosts, "Do not listen to the words of the prophets who are prophesying to you. They are leading you into futility; they speak a vision of their own imagination, not from the mouth of the Lord" (Jeremiah 23:16).

We must constantly guard against speaking our own opinions and trying to hang on them the authority of the Lord.

5. **Speaking peace when there is no peace—**

They keep saying to those who despise Me, "The Lord has said, 'You will have peace'"; and as for everyone who walks in the stubbornness of his own heart, they say, "Calamity will not come upon you" (Jeremiah 23:17).

This means they have no backbone; rather than speak the truth, they speak what they think people want to hear.

6. **Giving false reports—**

"Can a man hide himself in hiding places so I do not see him?" declares the Lord. "Do I not fill the heavens and the earth?" declares the Lord. "I have heard what the prophets have said who prophesy falsely in My name, saying, 'I had a dream, I had a dream'" (Jeremiah 23:24-25).

We have an obligation and awesome responsibility to give true reports concerning the Lord. We cannot just present this prophetic stuff as though we know so much more than someone else.

7. **Stealing words from one another—**

"'Therefore behold, I am against the prophets,' declares the Lord, 'who steal My words from each other'" (Jer. 23:30).

If our well is dry, it is very easy to succumb to the temptation to take something we learned at a seminar or heard someone say at a meeting and present it as our own, not so much by claiming it as ours, but by not giving credit where credit is due. Saying "I don't know," or "I don't have a word today" is always better than stealing someone else's word just to save face.

8. *Engaging in reckless boasting—*

> *"Behold, I am against those who have prophesied false dreams," declares the Lord, "and related them and led My people astray by their false-hoods and reckless boasting; yet I did not send them or command them, nor do they furnish this people the slightest benefit," declares the Lord"* (Jeremiah 23:32).

Let's not pretend to be better than we are or to embellish our achievements in front of others.

Another danger is making the mistake of following Balaam's example and allowing ourselves to be bought off for a price (see Num. 22:7; Neh. 13:2; 2 Pet. 2;15.) This again touches on the area of motivation. Why do we do what we do? Hopefully, we do what we do to bring glory, honor, and magnification to Him who is worthy, the Lord Jesus Christ.

Here are a couple of other verses to keep in mind when considering the hindrances of an evil heart:

> *For the devious are an abomination to the Lord; but He is intimate with the upright* (Proverbs 3:32).

> *You adulteresses, do you not know that friendship with the world is hostility toward God? Therefore whoever wishes to be a friend of the world makes himself an enemy of God. Or do you think that the Scripture speaks to no purpose: "He jealously desires the Spirit which He has made to dwell in us"?* (James 4:4-5)

Another word for *devious* in Proverbs 3:32 is *crooked*. To be crooked is to be twisted to some degree. If there is crookedness in our hearts or lives, we cannot be as intimate with the Lord as we would like to be. On the other hand, the Lord is intimate with the upright. This means that He draws near to them and reveals Himself.

On a related theme, James 4:4-5 tells us that we cannot be friends with the world and maintain our friendship with God. The world (unsaved humanity) is an enemy of God, and all who align themselves with the world make themselves God's enemies as well. Jesus said we cannot serve two masters (see Matt. 6:24). Either the Lord is our master or the world is. There is no other option.

CULTIVATE THE FEAR OF THE LORD

One of the main reasons that so many of us as Christians experience so little of the day-to-day reality and presence of God in our lives is because so few of us truly understand what it means to have a holy fear of the Lord. Fear of the Lord is the basis—the starting place—for building intimacy with God.

God already knows us intimately, and He wants us to know Him the same way. Probably no other passage describes God's intimate knowledge of us better than Psalms 139:

> O Lord, You have searched me and known me. You know when I sit down and when I rise up; You understand my thought from afar. You scrutinize my path and my lying down, and are intimately acquainted with all my ways. Even before there is a word on my tongue, behold, O Lord, You know it all... Where can I go from Your Spirit? Or where can I flee from Your presence? If I ascend to heaven, You are there; if I make my bed in Sheol, behold, You are there. If I take the wings of the dawn, if I dwell in the remotest part of the sea, even there Your hand will lead me, and Your right hand will lay hold of me... For You formed my inward parts; You wove me in my mother's womb... Your eyes have seen my unformed substance; and in Your book were all written the days that were ordained for me, when as yet there was not one of them (Psalms 139:1-4,7-10,13,16).

Understanding that God knows us so well should produce the fear of the Lord in our lives; not a frightened fear, but a holy fear of honor, love, and respect for His "God-ness." God is near us and remote from us at the same time—near because He loves us and pursues a personal love relationship with us, and remote because, as God, He is infinitely greater and higher than we are.

Since God is everywhere at all times, and since His all-seeing eyes know everything about us, why don't we simply walk in open, transparent honesty with Him? I believe that is really what the fear of the Lord is all about—being open, honest, and transparent with God.

A transparent walk with God will bear in our lives the wonderful fruit of the genuine joy of the Lord.

> *Arise, shine; for your light has come, and the glory of the Lord has risen upon you. For behold, darkness will cover the earth and deep darkness the peoples; but the Lord will rise upon you and His glory will appear upon you. Nations will come to your light, and kings to the brightness of your rising... Then you will see and be radiant, and your heart will thrill and rejoice..."* (Isaiah 60:1-3,5a).

Remember what happened to Moses. After being in God's presence, his face shone so radiantly that he put a veil over his face to shield it. We who are part of the New Covenant in Christ are to reflect the Lord's brilliance in our lives. When our lives radiate His presence, our hearts will be filled with joy, and that joy will attract others. Basically, Psalms 2:11 says it all: *"Worship the Lord with reverence and rejoice with trembling."* The fear of the Lord brings joy.

It also opens the treasury of God. Isaiah 33:6 says, *"And He will be the stability of your times, a wealth of salvation, wisdom and knowledge; the fear of the Lord is his treasure."* The psalmist writes:

> *Who is the man who fears the Lord? He will instruct him in the way he should choose. His soul will abide in prosperity, and his descendants will inherit the land. The secret of the Lord is for those who fear Him, and He will make them know His covenant* (Psalms 25:12-14).

A great treasure awaits a covenant people who will walk faithfully in the fear of the Lord: a treasure of abundant salvation, spiritual prosperity, and the passion of life—intimacy with God.

GIVING OURSELVES TO THE PROCESS

God is looking for people to share His counsel with. He is looking for people who have a passionate desire for Him. If our passion is for the Lord Himself—not visions or prophecies or manifestations or anything else like that for their own sake—then He will reveal Himself to us in any number of ways. Psalms 37:4 says, *"Delight yourself in the Lord; and He will give you the desires of your heart."* If we seek Him, we will find Him. Jesus promised,

> *Ask, and it will be given to you; seek, and you will find; knock, and it will be opened to you. For everyone who asks receives, and he who seeks finds, and to him who knocks it will be opened* (Matthew 7:7-8).

God rewards all who seek Him with their whole heart:

> *And without faith it is impossible to please Him, for he who comes to God must believe that He is and that He is a rewarder of those who seek Him* (Hebrews 11:6).

> *"For I know the plans that I have for you," declares the Lord, "plans for welfare and not for calamity to give you a future and a hope. Then you will call upon Me and come and pray to Me, and I will listen to you. You will seek Me and find Me when you search for Me with all your heart* (Jeremiah 29:11-13).

For many years, while growing up and as a young adult, my wife prayed earnestly for the Lord to come to her. Some years ago, He answered her prayer in a mighty way. Michal Ann entered a period where she received a series of visitations that were so intense, so strong, that she would cry out, "Hold off, Lord, this is too much!" These visitations usually came at night, and during the day, she would pray, "Lord, don't listen to my prayers at night, but listen to my prayers in the daytime. Oh God, come; oh God, come!"

During one of these encounters, the Lord challenged her: "All your life you have been asking Me to come. Now, do you want Me to come or not?" She answered, "Lord, whether I live or not is not important. If Your presence wants to come so strong that You slay me, then that is Your decision. God, I say this, my God I say, come."

That is the kind of passion God is looking for. If we will call on the name of the Lord and seek Him with all our hearts, He will show us great and mighty things.

Along with our passionate seeking, we must learn how to balance between the *objective* and the *subjective* experience. An objective experience is not determined by impressions, feelings, inner vision or voices, but is based upon convictions concerning God's character—His faithfulness to keep His promises. A subjective experience, on the other hand, is the cry of the soul for a clearer awareness of God, the passionate desire for a distinct hearing of His voice.

Whatever else we do, we must maintain our balance between the subjective and the objective. We must not become so fixated on prophetic or visionary revelation that we throw away the Bible. Let us keep our objectivity. The revelatory word is not a competitor with the written Word, but a complement to it, and *always* subordinate to it. The written Word of God is the unwavering standard by which *all* revelatory word *must* be measured.

Finally, let God be God! Trust Him to lead safely and securely:

> *For the Lord knows the way of the righteous, but the way of the wicked will perish* (Psalms 1:6).

> *Trust in the Lord with all your heart and do not lean on your own understanding. In all your ways acknowledge Him, and He will make your paths straight* (Proverbs 3:5-6).

Who is among you that fears the Lord, that obeys the voice of His servant, that walks in darkness and has no light? Let him trust in the name of the Lord and rely on his God (Isaiah 50:10).

Depending on their background and the teaching they have received in their churches, Christians respond to the phenomena of mystical experiences in different ways. Some are suspicious, while others condemn and reject them outright. There are still others, however, who embrace these experiences, sometimes cautiously at first, then with increasing enthusiasm.

Certainly, great care and understanding are necessary when approaching these things and when trying to relate to other believers who may feel differently about them. Carlton Kenney suggests four parameters or guidelines for us to keep in mind with regard to mystical experiences:

1. We must face up to our prejudices and return to a biblical position concerning mystical experiences. We must not treat them as weird!

2. We must keep our equilibrium. Mystical experiences are merely a means to an end, not something with which to become overly fascinated.

3. These experiences are a genuine part of the prophetic ministry. The Lord wants to grant richer encounters to all who seek Him. May all of God's people be challenged to a more diligent pursuit of God.

4. Let us provide a friendly climate for emerging prophetic people to mature in their gifting. Now abides faith, hope, and love, these three; the greatest of these is love. Love is the greatest way for gifts to happen and for ministry to mature. If the church will cultivate a loving environment, in a few years the church should really get a prophet's reward.[4]

No matter what we do as Christians, our goal—indeed, the goal of all things—should be to grow in intimacy with our loving Father by the power of the Holy Spirit through Jesus Christ our Lord. That is the goal of my life. Want to join me?

Chapter Eleven

HIDDEN STREAMS
OF THE PROPHETIC

In my own experience, I have found that the most direct road to greater intimacy with God has come through the practice or discipline of an almost lost art in the fast-paced Church of today—something called contemplative prayer. Since discovering it well over a decade ago, it has become one of my loves—one of the central features of my walk with God.

But you ask, "What does this have to do with cultivating the seer dimension?" For starters, let me give you one thought that I will develop in this chapter: Prayer brings us into His presence, and in His presence is the spirit of revelation.

One night in 1991, I had a dream that I did not understand (which is not at all unusual for me). A voice from the Lord said to me, "I will reveal to you the hidden streams of the prophetic."

At the time, a young couple was living with Michal and me. Marcus and Alyxius Young were preparing to be sent forth as fourth-generation missionaries to Southeast Asia. Because Marcus grew up on the mission field of the Philippines, his Christian walk was very different from that of most North

American believers. Today their ministry, Divine Inheritance, is rescuing child soldiers in various countries and leading the way in the current-day global justice movement. But Marcus then was largely self-taught, reading basically only the Bible and the writings of the early Christian Church fathers. His literary expertise did not include modern-day Christian writing, charismatic or otherwise.

As I pondered my dream, I thought of Paul Cain, a senior seer statesman at the time, who had re-emerged after almost 25 years of being hidden. Knowing his pilgrimage, I speculated that the words spoken in my dream—"I will reveal to you the hidden streams of the prophetic"—might mean that there were others who were still in hiding. I felt that the Lord was going to bring these hidden vessels out of the closet and reveal them. I was thrilled with the idea that the Lord might allow my path to cross those of others, so that we could cross-pollinate and learn from one another.

When I shared with Marcus my dream and my interpretation of its meaning, he said, "No, that's not what your dream is about. The Lord is going to reveal to you the hidden streams of the prophetic through the desert fathers and the Christian mystics."

When I heard that, my heart leapt inside of me, and I said, "Oh Lord, yes." I have always loved Church history, even though I do not have degrees to show for it. By the Lord's supernatural help, I have often bumped into revelations of significant proportions almost accidentally.

On another similar occasion, I was lying on the floor having some "carpet time" after Mahesh Chavda had prayed for me. As I lay there, I saw a picture of a "kegger," a small round wooden keg. Looking at this in the spirit, I thought, "This can't be from God." Then as I continued looking, I saw that the keg was under the neck of a large dog—a Saint Bernard, in fact. As I continued to watch in this interactive vision, this big dog came up and stared me in the face. "What is this?" I wondered. Just then words entered my mind: "I am going to introduce you to the life of St. Bernard of Clairvaux." I had never heard of him. Only later did I learn that he was a twelfth-century monk who was quite familiar with the ways of contemplative prayer and walking in greater intimacy with God.

These experiences set me on a year-long journey into some of the richest treasures in Christianity, a journey that I would encourage any believer to take. For one full year (I would have loved to do it longer) I read only from the Bible and the writings of the earliest Christian leaders, commonly known as the "desert fathers." I am forever spiritually richer because of this journey. I have since learned a lot and even written the book *The Lost Art of Practicing His Presence* which, incorporates the revelation the Holy Spirit taught me in those formative years.

THE WAY OF CONTEMPLATIVE PRAYER

During that year, the more I read, the more I realized I was on familiar ground. This was a road I was already walking on to some extent. Contemplative prayer was all about the quest for intimacy with God. The Bible is full of references to this quest:

> But we all, **with unveiled face, beholding as in a mirror the glory of the Lord,** are being transformed into the same image from glory to glory, just as from the Lord, the Spirit (2 Corinthians 3:18).

> **Cease striving and know that I am God;** I will be exalted among the nations, I will be exalted in the earth (Psalms 46:10).

> **Fixing our eyes on Jesus,** the author and perfecter of faith, who for the joy set before Him endured the cross, despising the shame, and has sat down at the right hand of the throne of God (Hebrews 12:2).

We are talking about an ancient Christian practice that has not been widely known or practiced in much of the evangelical and charismatic ranks today, but which the Spirit of God is restoring to the broader Body of Christ.

In contemplative prayer, we as Christians do not primarily relate to God as the One who sits upon His throne in Heaven but, through the reality of our new birth in Christ, connect with Him as the One who has taken up residence inside us. We each have a throne in our hearts where He dwells in a very personal way. In contrast, in intercessory prayer, we approach God who is seated on His throne in Heaven. We then, as priestly believers, make our appeal, stand in the gap, and remind God of His Word.

Another phrase that is often used in many circles today is "communion with God." This is commonly understood to mean coming into fellowship with God through the power of the Holy Spirit in Jesus Christ, who dwells in the born-again believer. Communion with God is a way of fellowshipping with the Holy Spirit by learning to quiet the distractions of our soul and of the world, calming the inner chaos and noise from outside that tends to vie so strongly for our attention. In this wonderful form of prayer, we come, as it were, into the heart, or "center" of our being, where God dwells through the Holy Spirit, who has taken up residence there. We behold the beauty of the Lord and inquire in His temple (see Ps. 27:4).

In the first chapter of Colossians, Paul speaks of the saints *"to whom God willed to make known what is the riches of the glory of this mystery among the Gentiles, which is **Christ in you,** the hope of glory"* (Col. 1:27). The *"hope of glory"* is Christ *in us*. Some of the earlier Christian contemplatives and mystics, such as Madame Guyon and others, refer to this as "greater union with Christ." Let's look briefly at a quote about Jeanne Guyon as penned in my dear wife's book, *A Call to the Secret Place*.

> Most profoundly of all, Madame Guyon's life teaches us this wonderful truth about how we can experience intimacy with God. For she writes: "It is Jesus Christ Himself, the real and essential Word, who is in the center of the soul that is disposed for receiving Him. Never one moment ceases from His living fruitful, and divine operation."[1]

As we come into communion with God, who dwells inside of us, we come into fellowship with the *zoe*, the very life of God, which cleanses us and sets us apart for Him. That is what it means to be transformed.

Long ago I learned a statement that gives a simple explanation to all of this: *We must maintain the inner life to be effective in the outer life*. In order to be able to step out in confidence and authority to do God's will and minister in the power of the Spirit, we must nurture and maintain our inner communion and fellowship with God. We must regularly go to that abiding place in our hearts where His presence dwells.

Too often throughout Church history and even today, Christians tend to be divided into two camps over these truths. One camp is the "going and doing" camp, always going, always busy at the work, doing missions, serving the poor, and preaching the Gospel. The other camp is the "contemplative" camp, the meditative, quiet, and reflective ones who so love the "interior castle" that they just want to dwell there and stay there all the time.

Bernard of Clairvaux, the twelfth-century monk and mystic, identified three "vocations" in the Christian life: that of Lazarus, the penitent; that of Martha, the active and devoted servant of the household; and that of Mary, the contemplative. According to Jesus, Mary had chosen the best part. There was no reason for her to envy Martha or to leave her contemplation, unasked, to share in Martha's labors. Contemplation should always be desired and preferred. Activity should be accepted, though never sought for its own sake. In the end, the completion of the Christian life is found in the *union* of Martha, Mary and Lazarus in one person.

The *inner* life prepares us for the *outer* life; both are necessary. One of the lessons we must learn is to build a bridge between the two.

LISTEN, WATCH, WAIT

This type of communal prayer is not as much *doing* something as much as it is *being with* Someone, continuing in prayer with this Someone until we become the *expression* of Him in the world around us. One of the best things I have done in recent years happened in Spokane, Washington, when I participated in five days of the "vow of silence." For the first ten hours of each day, seven of us would meet together in the mornings just to share, and then we would take a vow of silence for the next ten or 12 hours. This meant no talking at all, not to ourselves or to any other person. What a spiritual discipline! What a hard day, but oh, how enriching!

That week really revved my engine! By the fourth and fifth days, I was being flooded with revelation that kept me fueled for months. This was nothing other than the spiritual discipline of quieting my soul before God, preparing myself to listen, and waiting to hear His voice. I can hardly describe the deep sense of inner peace and contentment that came upon me during that time.

The eighth chapter of Proverbs provides three important principles related to contemplative prayer:

> Now therefore, O sons, listen to me, for blessed are they who keep my ways. Heed instruction and be wise, and do not neglect it. Blessed is the man who listens to me, watching daily at my gates, waiting at my doorposts. For he who finds me finds life and obtains favor from the Lord. But he who sins against me injures himself; all those who hate me love death (Proverbs 8:32-36).

Verse 34 contains the three principles: *listens, watching,* and *waiting.* All three of these verbs are in the continuous passive tense in the Hebrew, meaning they are ongoing rather than momentary. Blessed are those who listen and keep on listening, who watch and keep on watching, and who wait and keep on waiting.

In order to listen, we have to shut our mouths. We cannot speak and hear at the same time. Watching at the gates means staying alert and wakeful. Joshua, Moses' servant and successor, faithfully stationed himself outside the tent of meeting every time Moses went in. Because he was watchful, Joshua was the first to see the glory that was on Moses' face when he came out after meeting with God. Waiting at the doorposts means standing by to hear what the Lord will speak, ready to do His bidding or to sit still in reverence and worship, whichever He desires of us.

What are the keys to contemplative experience? Listen, watch, and wait.

THE VOCABULARY OF THE CONTEMPLATIVE

Contemplative prayer is not a technique. It is not a relaxation therapy exercise or a form of self-hypnosis. It is not a paranormal or psychic phenomenon. Neither is it a New Age approach to self-improvement nor an attempt to empty one's mind. It is not a new thing or a remake of Eastern meditation dressed in "Christian clothing." Contemplation is an age-old biblical tool for coming into fellowship with God.

To *contemplate* means to gaze at intently, to think about intently, to study, to expect or to intend, to meditate, to muse. The word *muse* means to think about or to consider deeply, to meditate. To *meditate* means to plan, intend, to think deeply, to reflect upon. The word *reflect* means to throw back light, heat, or sound, to give back an image as in a mirror, to bring back or come back as a consequence or as reflected glory.

Any concept is confusing if we do not understand the terms or the vocabulary being used. For this reason, I want to define some of the terms commonly found in prophetic, contemplative Christian writings, both old and new.

- *False self.* This is the old sinful nature or "old self" that Paul talks about in Ephesians:

   In reference to your former manner of life, you lay aside the old self, which is being corrupted in accordance with the lusts of deceit, and that you be renewed in the spirit of your mind, and put on the new self, which in the likeness of God has been created in righteousness and holiness of the truth (Ephesians 4:22-24).

This "false self" is the ego-centered self that holds onto the things and values of the world and trusts in possessions, power, or other people in trying to find happiness, fulfillment, peace, purpose, meaning, and life.

- *True self.* This corresponds to the new spiritual nature we have as Christians, the "new self" of Ephesians 4:24 and Colossians 3:10:

  Do not lie to one another, since you laid aside the old self with its evil practices, and have put on the new self who is being renewed to a true knowledge according to the image of the One who created him (Colossians 3:9-10).

- *Centering.* Although used extensively by the Quakers, this term is not exclusive to Quaker theology and practice. It means simply to let go of all competing distractions until we are truly present with Him. I love that. *Centering* is the meditative art of quieting ourselves and focusing on the Lord, who is the center of all life.

- *Recollection* (re-collection). This is the process of bringing together disparate parts into a unified whole. It is allowing the Holy Spirit to cast light upon the fragmentations of our lives so as to bring cleansing and healing into our souls, our emotions, our remembrances, and our thoughts. A more familiar term that means the same thing is *integration.*

- *Union with God.* This means to be made one with our Master and our Creator God. It is a work that God does in our hearts, with two vital preparations on our part: love for God and purity of heart. First comes the revelation of God's vast love toward us; and second, this allows Him to produce in us a heart of purity as an expression of our love for Him.

- *Spiritual ecstasy.* This is essentially the same as what we saw in Chapter Nine on the ecstatic dimension: a supernatural trance state initiated by the Holy Spirit where one is caught up into the realm of the Spirit so as to receive those things—revelations, visions, or other experiences—that God desires.

All of these reflect an attempt by contemplative believers to describe the indescribable. In the end, we are reduced to the simple confession of Walter Hilton: "Contemplation is love on fire with devotion."

Contemplative prayer is an exercise in letting go of the control of our own lives and no longer leaning on the props of the false self. It is a kind of communion intended to increase our intimacy with God and our awareness of His presence. It is a step of submission, where we place our being at God's disposal, as we request His work of purification. In Christ Jesus, we open ourselves up to the Holy Spirit to get in touch with the new person, the true self, and to facilitate an abiding state of union with God.

RECOLLECTION

Richard Foster, a Quaker and author of the modern-day Christian classics *Celebration of Discipline: The Path to Spiritual Growth,* and *Prayer: Finding the Heart's True Home*, is a long-time student of various forms of prayer. Through his studies and experience, he has encapsulated contemplative prayer into three stages: *recollection,* the *prayer of quiet,* and *spiritual ecstasy*.[2]

Phase one is *recollection*, which, as we saw above, means letting go of all competing distractions. That is the idea behind Psalms 46:10: *"Cease striving and know that I am God...."* Some translations literally say it this way: *"Relax and let go, and know that I am God...."*

There is a correlation here between the inner knowing, in a revelatory way, of God's great love for us, and repentance on our part. Repentance means to turn away from sin and turn to God. In recollection, it means turning away from all competing distractions in order to focus on the Lord and His presence.

One example of a "competing distraction" is focusing on what has already happened, particularly when it causes us to dwell on our guilt and woundedness. As we continue in this journey, truth begins to become illuminated inside of us. One of the first things we will see is the depth of our own sinfulness—all of our failures, hurts, and wounds. Part of the recollection phase is learning to offer these things up as an act of faith and worship to the Lord and then dwelling in the simple reality of faith in the blood of Jesus and the healing process of the Cross in our lives. This process gets into the issue of casting all our anxieties, cares, worries, fears, and tensions upon Him, because He cares for us (see 1 Pet. 5:7).

While resting in quietness, we ask the Holy Spirit to make Jesus real to us and to close off everything else. Richard Foster teaches us that one way to help do this is to see Jesus sitting in a chair across from us. He truly is present, but sometimes we need help to visualize that reality. God created our imagination, and, like every other faculty we possess, we need to sanctify it, surrender it, and use it for God's purposes.

Our ability to flow in the gift of the working of miracles, including creative miracles, comes in part from our surrendering to the Lord this creative part of our lives, our imagination, because that is where we begin to believe the impossible. Utilizing our imagination in contemplation is perfectly appropriate and one of the best uses to which we can put it when we ask God to sanctify and fill our senses with His Spirit. This is not the same as New Age imaging, but simply what Brother Lawrence called "the practice of the presence of God."

If frustrations and distractions start to press in on us, we need a strategy for shutting them out. Madame Jeanne Guyon, the French Christian mystic of the late seventeenth and early eighteenth centuries, and a true pioneer of contemplative prayer whose writings we quoted from earlier, recommended meditation upon the Scriptures for this purpose. When competing distractions vie for our attention, she would tell us to muse, meditate, ponder, and mutter upon the Scriptures. (All of those words are contained in the meaning of the word *meditate*.) Meditating on the Scriptures helps us refocus our attention on the Lord, which is what it is supposed to do. As Madame Guyon writes in *Experiencing the Depths of Jesus Christ*:

> First, read a passage of Scripture. Once you sense the Lord's presence, the content of what you have read is no longer

important. The Scripture has served its purpose: it has qui-
eted your mind and brought you to Him.

The goal is to become quiet before the Lord, peaceful and still, and allow
the silence to still our noisy hearts. This is a skill that does not come easily or
quickly, but develops over a process of time. Being aware of the problem is
itself a step in the right direction. Recognizing our inability to conquer these
distractions on our own is a major stride forward. All of this is part of the
process of recollection.

THE PRAYER OF QUIET

As we grow accustomed to the unifying grace of recollection, we are ushered into the second phase of contemplative prayer, what St. Theresa of Avila
and many others called "the center of quiet" or the prayer of quiet.

Through recollection, we have put away all obstacles of the heart, all
distractions of the mind, and all vacillations of the will. Divine graces of love
and adoration wash over us like ocean waves, and at the center of our beings
we are hushed, and there is a stillness, to be sure, but it is a listening stillness.
Something deep inside of us has been awakened and brought to attention, and
our spirits now are on tiptoe, alert, and listening. Then out comes an inward
steady gaze of the heart, sometimes called "beholding the Lord."

Now we bask in the warmth of His dear embrace. As we wait before
God, He graciously gives us a teachable spirit. Our goal, of course, is to
bring this contentment into everyday expressions of life, but this does not
normally come quickly to us. However, as we experience more and more of
the inward attentiveness to His divine whisper, we will begin to carry His
presence throughout our days. Just as smoke is absorbed into our clothing
and we carry its smell with us, so the aroma of God's presence is seeping into
our beings, and we will likewise become carriers of His gracious fragrance
wherever we go. That is one of the benefits of communal prayer: basking in
the presence of this brilliant One. Then, when we have been in with Him,
we go out into the world, and we carry the brilliance of His great presence.

SPIRITUAL ECSTASY

The third phase of contemplative prayer is spiritual ecstasy. We looked at several aspects of this "state" in Chapter Nine. Anyone who has ever been around prophetic seer-type people knows that they tend to be quiet in nature. They calm themselves, many times even closing their eyes, and wait in an almost passive repose. In that place of quiet detachment from the reality around them, illumination—the spirit of revelation—is granted, and their beings become filled with God's pictures, God's thoughts, and God's heart.

This is the way it works with me. I apply the blood of Christ to my life, and I quiet my external being. Then I enter into worship of my dear Lord and bask in the beauty of His great presence. Then He takes me into rooms permeated with the light of His love and fills my being with visions that He desires me to see. At times, I am so captured by His love that He leads me up higher into a heavenly place where my spirit seems to soar. Oh, how marvelous are His dwelling places! Oh, how awesome is our Lord!

Spiritual ecstasy, this final step into contemplative prayer, is not an activity or undertaking that we do, but a work that God does in us. Ecstasy is contemplative prayer taken to the nth degree. Even the recognized authorities in the contemplative prayer life acknowledge that it is generally a fleeting experience rather than a staple diet.

Of this ecstatic state, Theodore Brakel, a Dutch pietist in the seventeenth-century, wrote:

> I was transported into such a state of joy that my thoughts were so drawn upward that seeing God with the eyes of my soul, I felt God's being at the same time. I was filled with joy, and peace, and sweetness that I cannot express it.

Another way to describe this ecstatic state is to be "inebriated" with God's presence. To an outside observer, someone caught up into the realm of the Spirit and taken to a rapturous place may appear drunk. The essence of this experience is to be overwhelmed with God's presence, whether or not we see any pictures or hear any words.

St. Augustine of Hippo, the fourth-century doctor of the Latin Church, turned his back on God during his early adult years. His mother, Monica, who herself became known as Santa Monica, prayed faithfully and earnestly for many years for her son, until he finally came into the Kingdom of God. Together they had an experience on the Tiber River in the city of Ostia. Augustine describes the experience in his *Confessions*:

> So we were alone and talking together and very sweet our talk was…discussing between ourselves and in the presence of Truth…what the eternal life of the saints could be like…. Yet with the mouth of our heart we panted for the heavenly streams of your fountain, the fountain of life. Then with our affections burning still more strongly toward the Selfsame, we raised ourselves higher and step by step passed over all material things, even the heaven itself, from which sun, and moon, and stars shined down upon the earth. And still we went upward, meditating, and speaking, and looking with wonder at your works. And we came to our own souls, and we went beyond our souls to reach that region of never failing plenty where thou feedest Israel forever with the food of truth. And, as we talked, yearning toward this Wisdom, we did, with the whole strength of our hearts' impulse, just lightly come into touch with her, and we sighed, and we left bound there the first fruits of the Spirit, and we returned to the sound of our voices, where a word was both beginning and end.

Part of the problem many people have with these hidden streams of the prophetic and other mystical experiences is that those who write about it—those contemplatives who have experienced it for themselves—cannot help but use the language of divine romance and poetic hyperbole, and that makes some folks nervous. Often, the language of the heart makes no sense to the mind except for those whose hearts are involved, because the heart lives in the language of love. The Old Testament Book Song of Songs is our biblical example of this type of message and inspired, poetic vocabulary.

THE GOAL OF OUR JOURNEY

Once we get to know these ways of Christ in us—the glory of God Himself living and dwelling in our beings—and come into union and fellowship with Him who now has taken up residence upon the throne of our lives, we will realize suddenly that we were created for that very thing. Walking in this inward life and light gives us the power to go forth into expressions of doing the works of Christ in the outward.

The glory of God was so brilliant upon Moses that he had to place a veil over his face. In the New Covenant in Christ, under which we live, we have an open invitation from the Lord, before whom the veil is rent—an invitation to look upon His face as long as we desire. The door is always open. Let us go in and gaze on His brilliant face! As we look at our Master, we will be changed from glory, to glory, to glory, to glory!

After all, isn't He the goal of our passionate pursuit? He is the stream of living water that makes my heart glad! Let us pursue the "hidden streams" of the prophetic and grow in greater intimacy with the lover of our souls. He is the goal of our journey.

Chapter Twelve

THE KEY OF INTIMACY
TO OPEN HEAVENS

Jacob was running for his life. His brother Esau was determined to kill him. Why the bad blood between brothers? First, Jacob had tricked Esau into selling his birthright to him for a bowl of stew. Second, Jacob had tricked their father, Isaac, into giving him the blessing that was rightfully Esau's as the firstborn son. Jacob, whose name means "supplanter," or "deceiver," was living up to his name. Cheated twice by his brother, Esau vowed to make Jacob pay for his trickery with his life.

This was the same Jacob who later wrestled with an angel, who many scholars believe was a pre-incarnate appearance of Christ Himself. The Lord lets Jacob think he has won, and in that winning, he obtains God's blessing. This blessing changes his life, and with that change comes a change of name. Jacob the "deceiver" becomes Israel, the "prince of God." He departs the wrestling match marked for life by his encounter with a permanent limp, because the angel dislocated his hip. So marked, Israel goes on to become the father of a nation that is to bless the whole earth. Twelve tribes arise from the loins of one man.

THE DREAM OF A LIFETIME

All of that was years in the future, however. At that time, Jacob was a young man running scared. Leaving Beersheba in the southern desert of what would one day be the nation of Israel, he traveled toward Haran, the homeland of his mother, Rebekah. Night was falling. Jacob was tired and looked for a place to sleep. He had no idea what was about to happen to him—let alone its eternal impact.

> *He came to a certain place and spent the night there, because the sun had set; and he took one of the stones of the place and put it under his head, and lay down in that place. He had a dream, and behold, a ladder was set on the earth with its top reaching to heaven; and behold, the angels of God were ascending and descending on it. And behold, the Lord stood above it and said, "I am the Lord, the God of your father Abraham and the God of Isaac; the land on which you lie, I will give it to you and to your descendants. Your descendants will also be like the dust of the earth, and you will spread out to the west and to the east and to the north and to the south; and in you and in your descendants shall all the families of the earth be blessed. Behold, I am with you and will keep you wherever you go, and will bring you back to this land; for I will not leave you until I have done what I have promised you"(Genesis 28:11-15).*

Jacob stopped for the night in a place so rugged that the only thing he could find for a pillow was a stone. Even this was a prophetic symbol: Jacob laid his head upon the rock, and Jesus—Yeshua—is the rock of our salvation. We who know Him are called to be living stones. Jacob laid his head upon the rock and was catapulted into another dimension.

Lying down to sleep, Jacob fell into a dream, but it was no ordinary dream. This dream was of massive proportion and changed his life. Like Jacob, just one night spent with the revelatory presence of God—just one impartation of revelation—can change our lives forever, more than years of learning and personal effort. When God changes *our* lives, then He can change *other* people's lives through us. Such was the case with Jacob.

In Jacob's dream, he saw a ladder reaching from earth to Heaven, with angels ascending and descending it. What really riveted Jacob's attention, however, was his vision of the Lord Himself standing at the top of the ladder. Jacob saw right into Heaven—which of us could do such a thing and *not* be changed? He experienced an open Heaven—such as we looked at in Chapter Eight—in which he saw a visible manifestation of God. One of the main characteristics of an open Heaven is that it opens to our view the activities that are going on in Heaven, and sometimes, even a visual image of the divine Personage.

As Jacob watched in awe (and probably petrified with fear!), the Lord spoke to him, reiterating the promises He had already given to Jacob's father, Isaac, and grandfather, Abraham. The land on which Jacob then lay was to be his and his descendants' forever. Here was Jacob, a fugitive and vagabond with perhaps little more than the clothes on his back, yet he was to become the father of a great nation. God assured Jacob that He would be with him wherever he went. When Jacob returned to this land, he would be a man of great wealth and prosperity—but also a man who knew God intimately.

THE GATE OF HEAVEN

Needless to say, Jacob was overwhelmed with fear and awe by what he witnessed that night:

> Then Jacob awoke from his sleep and said, "Surely the Lord is in this place, and I did not know it." He was afraid and said, "How awesome is this place! This is none other than the house of God, and this is the gate of heaven." So Jacob rose early in the morning, and took the stone that he had put under his head and set it up as a pillar and poured oil on its top. He called the name of that place Bethel; however, previously the name of the city had been Luz (Genesis 28:16-19).

When Jacob lay down to sleep that night, he did not have the foggiest notion where he really was. His dream changed his entire perspective. What had appeared as nothing more than a dry, rocky, barren waste suddenly became a holy place, the very house of God and gate of Heaven to earth. Jacob walked away from this experience with his senses heightened to the awareness of spiritual realities. Once he saw things from a heavenly point of view, his whole outlook changed.

There is a lesson in this for us. How many of us have looked at our surroundings, the city or town where we live, and seen nothing but a dry desert or a hard and rocky place, as unappealing as yesterday's leftovers? Too often we curse the place of our assignment because we cannot see it through God's eyes.

When we moved from the land of the Kansas City Prophets to Nashville, I had a hard time adjusting. I knew the Lord had sent us to a new land of promise, but for the first two years I could just not get it! I walked the floors; I cried out in the night times for answers. I would constantly ask myself and God, "Why is this place called Music City, U.S.A., when on every other street corner there are big brick edifices that are non-instrumental legalistic churches?" At that time, most nationally recognized prophetic voices either avoided Nashville or became encumbered by the "deaf and dumb spirit" that seemed to permeate the buckle of the Bible belt. So I determined to spend time with the Lord to get His understanding. I asked the Holy Spirit to allow me to experience being seated with Christ in the heavenly places to get His perspective.

Eventually I tapped into the "redemptive gift of God"— understanding of my new assignment. The surroundings had not changed (yet). God had not changed His mind. What changed? I changed! As this internal transformation took place, faith lit up on the inside of me to help change Music City into Worship City to the World! Yes, we can have the mind of Christ and believe and act accordingly.

In like manner, Jacob woke up from his dream with a different perspective. What changed? Not his physical environment; he was still surrounded by rocks and barren waste. Heaven had not changed; it was as eternal and changeless as ever. It was Jacob who changed. The open Heaven in his dream allowed him to make the link between Heaven and earth so that he could see his earthly reality from a heavenly perspective. That always changes the way we look at things. *"Surely the Lord is in this place, and I did not know it."* Perhaps you too need to take some time to sit with Christ Jesus and receive His heavenly view on your present assignment.

Through an open Heaven, Jacob received a moment of revelation that changed his life and his assessment of his situation. Prophetically, he laid his head upon the rock of Jesus, and revelation came down and changed his desert land into Bethel, the "house of God." For Jacob, an open Heaven was the key to intimacy of knowledge and fellowship with God.

All of us as believers, whether we are church leaders or not, need to get God's perspective on our present assignments. When we do, our whole outlook, attitude, and perspective will change. Insurmountable obstacles will suddenly become merely challenges to be faced. In faith, we will begin to call that which is not as though it already is. I now love my present assignment. It is one of my greatest privileges that I have been granted. Yes, Music City shall be Worship City to the world!

Jacob called the place where he was "the gate of Heaven." That is a good description of an open Heaven: a gateway, portal, or doorway into the spiritual realm opens up so that mortals can peer inside. This raises an interesting question: if there were gates of Heaven over specific geographical regions in Jacob's day, might not the same be true today?

"BEHOLD, THE HEAVENS WERE OPENED"

The baptism of Jesus was the occasion of another open Heaven event. Although all four Gospels record Jesus' baptism in one form or another, Matthew provides the most vivid account:

> Then Jesus arrived from Galilee at the Jordan coming to John, to be
> baptized by him. But John tried to prevent Him, saying, "I have need

to be baptized by You, and do You come to me?" But Jesus answering said to him, "Permit it at this time; for in this way it is fitting for us to fulfill all righteousness." Then he permitted Him. After being baptized, Jesus came up immediately from the water; and behold, the heavens were opened, and he saw the Spirit of God descending as a dove and lighting on Him, and behold, a voice out of the heavens said, "This is My beloved Son, in whom I am well-pleased" (Matthew 3:13-17).

The wording of this passage indicates that John, as well as Jesus, saw the Heavens open and the Spirit descend as a dove, and he heard the voice from Heaven. This open Heaven experience imparted to John information he would not have known any other way. By his own account, however, John was prepared before the fact, so that when he had this experience he would know what it meant:

The next day [John] *saw Jesus coming to him and said, "Behold, the Lamb of God who takes away the sin of the world! This is He on behalf of whom I said, 'After me comes a Man who has a higher rank than I, for He existed before me.' I did not recognize Him, but so that He might be manifested to Israel, I came baptizing in water." John testified saying, "I have seen the Spirit descending as a dove out of heaven, and He remained upon Him. I did not recognize Him, but He who sent me to baptize in water said to me, 'He upon whom you see the Spirit descending and remaining upon Him, this is the One who baptizes in the Holy Spirit.' I myself have seen, and have testified that this is the Son of God"* (John 1:29-34).

John the Baptist saw into a spirit realm and discerned that a sign would be given: the Holy Spirit would not simply come down, but would *light* upon Jesus or, in John's words, *remain* upon Him. The Heavens *did* open, the Spirit *did* come down, and the voice of God *spoke* from Heaven, *"This is My beloved Son, in whom I am well-pleased."*

The Spirit descending and remaining was the prophetic sign that enabled John to recognize the Son of God and to know that this man was different from any other man who had ever been born of woman.

SO HEAVENLY MINDED

Our desperate need today is to be so hungry for God that we cry out for open Heavens to come over our lives, our families, and our cities. How we need "Jacob's ladder" to descend again, not just for one night, but permanently! So many of us are famished for the bread of the Spirit; let us call out for Him to come down, not just to alight, but to remain—a manifested habitation of the Lord in our midst!

The depth of our hunger is the length of our reach for God. Just when we start to become satisfied is when God sends us a reminder of how much we still need Him. His desire is to create in us a greater desperation that will stir up a fiercer hunger that will release a longer reach. It isn't that He is far away, because He is always very near. The issue is our need for open Heavens again. Right here, right now!

I believe we are entering an apostolic era when this whole arena of open Heavens is going to break wide open. There will be teaching, revelation, expression, and experiencing of this on a scale unseen, at least since New Testament days, if ever. Homes, families, congregations, parks, hospitals, city halls—all will become "ground zero" for open Heaven manifestations. I am confident of this because I firmly believe that open Heavens are created over cities. I have experienced this in my own life. Michal Ann and I have experienced it for weeks on end in our home. Therefore, I have faith for this divine realm to be extended over entire regions for protracted periods of time.

From all my years of traveling in many nations, being a part of helping light fires in many places, and interviewing and walking with many "fire starters," I have learned one very important principle. *Before there is ever an open Heaven over a congregation or a city or a nation, there first is an open Heaven over a person.*

What kind of people might have Heaven open above them? It would have to be those who became radically undone in the Lord, those who are absolutely "wasted" on Jesus. These are the folks about whom the old saying in the Church speaks: "so heavenly-minded that they are no earthly good." That statement is not exactly true. In fact, I believe the time has come to modify it to say that visionary people who are radically wasted on Jesus are "so heavenly-minded that they are of *immense* earthly good." Whenever Heaven opens over individuals, they carry that open Heaven with them wherever they go and become climate-changers. They become history makers.

God is looking for candidates in this generation who will be seated with Christ in the heavenly places and call forth God's destiny and design into the earthly realm. It has happened before in all historic awakenings. I am talking about ordinary folks who surrendered to an extraordinary God. I am talking about people like Charles Finney and Evan Roberts.

PEOPLE OF AN OPEN HEAVEN

Charles Finney, the nineteenth-century evangelist and revivalist, walked under an open Heaven. I don't know if whole cities were gripped under an open Heaven at one time or not. But this I do know—he carried an open Heaven with him wherever he went. The anointing on his life was so strong that he would walk into a factory and before he could say a word, people would start weeping and coming under strong conviction of sin. Men, women, boys, and girls repented of their sins and turned to Jesus left and right. Finney had his critics, but he also had astonishing results. People who came into Finney's presence came under an open Heaven, and many, many of them were changed forever. Some people claim that this phenomenon is not biblical. On the contrary, it is very biblical. It is called "presence evangelism." It is being a carrier of His infectious presence.

Methods change, audiences change, culture and social mores change, but human nature does not. All humans are alike in that they share a common sinful nature. For this reason, the Gospel message must never change. No matter how we might alter our approach or tailor our methods in reaching people for Christ, one thing that must *never* change is our *message*. The Word of God is the "old, old story," and it is awesome and completely sufficient. There is no deeper truth than Jesus Christ crucified, risen from the dead, and returning one day to claim His Bride, the Church. Let's keep the main thing the main thing.

Evan Roberts was a young Welshman of 26 when Heaven opened above him, and he began to walk under a powerful anointing. The great revival that came to Wales in the early years of the twentieth-century did not begin with an open Heaven over a church or over a village or over a city. It began with one young man who was obedient to follow God's call on his life and who hungered for the moving of God's Spirit in power. Eventually, everywhere Evan Roberts went, the open Heaven followed.

His meetings were not typical for those times. They were more akin to what we would call worship and prayer meetings or, as it is often called today, "harp and bowl" gatherings. In a very real sense, the Welsh revival was a worship revival. Great singing abounded. The Welsh people have a rich and abundant hymn-singing tradition. Great hymns and other worship songs grew out of this world-impacting revival.

Intercessory prayer was a central focus to Roberts' meetings. In a typical gathering, he would have the first person stand and pray, "Send the Spirit now for Jesus Christ's sake." That person would sit down and the next person would stand and pray the same prayer: "Send the Spirit now for Jesus' sake." Roberts would go from one person to the next, and each would stand and pray the same way. Even people who had never prayed publicly stood and called to the Lord to send His Spirit now!

If the Spirit had not manifested His presence by the time the first row had finished praying, Roberts went on to the second row. After everyone had prayed, if the Spirit still had not come with conviction and power and manifested presence—if the "glory realm" of God had not showed up yet— Roberts simply started over. The second time around, however, he gave the people a second prayer. This time, when they stood up to pray they said, "Send the Spirit now, more powerfully for Jesus Christ's sake."

It was a simple, yet highly anointed approach, and God answered in a mighty way because Heaven was open over this young man. Those who came near caught the blessings. History was changed. The spiritual climate went from cold to hot.

Not long before the Welsh revival broke out, Evan Roberts spent several months at a Bible school in northern Wales, where he heard a young evangelist named Seth Joshua. At one point, Seth Joshua prayed, "Lord, bend the Church to save the world." When Evan Roberts heard that prayer, an arrow from God pierced his heart and gave him a burden for Wales and for the world.

Intimacy with God is the key to open Heavens. "Lord, bend the Church!" We possess the potential for earth-shaking revival, yet at the same time we are the biggest obstacles to it. "Lord, bend the Church! Bend the Church in a region. Bend the Church to save the world. Bend us, Lord!" We cannot allow ourselves to become resistant to God.

Once we see Him—once He really reveals Himself to us—we will be completely undone. When we see the One who is standing at the top of the ladder, we will be radically, totally wasted for Him! That is my goal—to see Him, to know Him, to become like Him; to become a *gate* for the sake of others.

OMNIPRESENCE VS. MANIFEST PRESENCE

In his inspiring book *The Secret of the Stairs*, author Wade Taylor identifies the differences between the omnipresence and manifest presence of the Lord:

> Many are not able to differentiate between these two aspects of His presence. First, there is His "*omni-presence*," which fills heaven and earth, and relates to our salvation and to its out-working within our lives. This speaks of the unconditional, "*abiding presence*," of the Holy Spirit within us.
>
> Second, there is the coming of the Lord to us as a Person, having intellect, will, and emotions. The Lord is eager to come

within our chamber, to personally *"share Himself with us"* in fellowship, and then lead us upward into His chambers, where *"we share with Him"* in the outworking of His purposes. This speaks of a *"conditional"* visitation from the Lord to us, and is referred to as His *"manifest presence."*

The first aspect of His presence is general, and relates to His redemptive grace. "Do not I fill heaven and earth? says the Lord." (Jer. 23:24b.) The second aspect of His presence is specific, and relates to His person. "He stands behind our wall, He looks forth at the windows, showing Himself through the lattice." (Song of Sol. 2:9b.)

Jesus expresses the conditions that allow Him to personally manifest Himself to us in the Gospel of John. *"He that has My commandments, and keeps them, he it is that loves Me: and he that loves Me shall be loved of My Father, and I will love him, and will manifest Myself to him. Judas says to Him, not Iscariot, Lord, how is it that You will manifest Yourself to us, and not to the world? Jesus answered and said to him, If a man love Me, he will keep My words: and My Father will love him, and We will come to him, and make Our abode with him."* (John 14:21-23).[1]

AT THE AGE OF SEVEN

When our oldest son, Justin, was but seven years old, he had a profound encounter with God. He was asleep in the top bunk, and his younger brother, Tyler, around three years old at the time, was asleep on the bottom bunk. Suddenly Justin was awakened. His eyes were opened in the Spirit, and he saw clouds fill his room. The throne of God was in the midst of the clouds with four unusual creatures surrounding it. A ladder unfurled from Heaven down into his room and one angel at a time would descend into his room carrying fire in its hand. The angel would release the fire and then ascend back up the ladder, only for several others to follow suit.

Finally one last angel descended into his room carrying a letter in its hand. The angel placed the letter on his dresser and then ascended up the ladder into the clouds of Heaven. Justin then watched as the clouds enveloped the throne and everything disappeared from his natural and spiritual sight. One thing remained in view though. The stationery on his dresser was left for a seven-year-old to read. He stared at the letter left for him from Heaven. It read, "Pray for your dad."

Angelic ambassadors sent a message to a seven-year-old boy, inviting him to participate in God's agenda. Heaven wanted Justin's prayers. The Lord knew his dear dad needed some reinvigorating, as I was involved in an assignment of major intercessory proportions in another city. Heaven is waiting for your prayers, too. Invitations are still being sent out. Will you be there to answer?

A Door in Heaven

John the Beloved received an open Heaven through which he saw the Lord. His experience came near the end of a long life of faithful and obedient service to Christ and His Church. Listen to his description:

> *After these things I looked, and behold, a door standing open in heaven, and the first voice which I had heard, like the sound of a trumpet speaking with me, said, "Come up here, and I will show you what must take place after these things." Immediately I was in the Spirit; and behold, a throne was standing in heaven, and One sitting on the throne. And He who was sitting was like a jasper stone and a sardius in appearance; and there was a rainbow around the throne, like an emerald in appearance* (Revelation 4:1-3).

Jacob saw One standing at the top of the ladder; John saw One sitting on the throne. This John—John the Beloved—is the same John who laid his head upon the chest of Yeshua the Messiah at the Last Supper; who heard the very pounding of the heartbeat of God; who heard the very breath of the Master, both in the natural and in the spirit realm as the *pneuma* or wind of the Holy

Spirit. This John is the one known as "the disciple whom Jesus loved." John the Beloved is the only disciple mentioned by name who stayed with Jesus even to the Cross, after all the others had fled.

Why did John stay at the Cross? I wonder if intimacy had something to do with his endurance and staying the course. Hearing the very heartbeat of God "ruined" John for life. He could never be the same again after catching the rhythm of that divine heart. Before long, John's heart began beating in union with the heart of God Himself, and now two hearts were beating in unison together. They were in agreement. This agreement, the coming together of the divine and human spirits in unison in an earthen vessel, is what is called in the old mystical Christian writings, *greater union with Christ.*

Many believers are just after intimacy, while many others are after souls. It is not an either/or proposition. There is a bridge between them both, a "leakage" between open Heavens. A powerful vision of the Almighty produces a passion for reaching souls. Intimacy eventually leads to evangelism.

OPEN THE DOOR

In Revelation 4:1 John says, *"After **these** things I looked, and behold, a door standing open in heaven."* After *what* things? Since the division of the Bible into chapters and verses was made long after it was written, it is only logical to look in the previous chapter to see what John was referring to.

Chapter one of Revelation relates John's initial vision of the Lord that he saw while "in the Spirit" on the Lord's day. Chapters two and three contain messages from the Lord to seven churches in Asia Minor: Ephesus, Smyrna, Pergamum, Thyatira, Sardis, Philadelphia, and Laodicea. The messages reveal the spiritual condition of each church, good or bad. Laodicea, the seventh church, is described as *"lukewarm, and neither hot nor cold"* (Rev. 3:16), and the Lord threatens to spit them from His mouth. Just four verses later, however, He gives a glorious promise to those who will listen and obey:

Behold, I stand at the door and knock; if anyone hears My voice and opens the door, I will come in to him and will dine with him, and he with Me (Revelation 3:20).

Whose door is Jesus standing before? This is a prophetic apostolic message, a heavenly message sent to a church in a city. It is not a word written just to an individual. Certainly, the invitation Jesus gives here applies to individuals, so it is quite appropriate to use this verse in evangelism as is so often done. Contextually, however, the word is for a group, a corporate body. Revelation 3:20 is an apostolic word about the voice of the Holy Spirit standing in front of a city. It is a city-transformation word where Jesus says in effect, "I am standing at the door of Laodicea." Many biblical scholars believe that our current age of the Church is the Laodicean age, characterized widely by lukewarm attitudes among churches and individual believers.

If we want open doors and open Heavens, then we have to do what precedes—what comes first. If we want the door to open in Heaven, we have to open the door to Jesus' knock on earth. Earthen vessels must answer the persistent, loving knock of God. As we respond, God responds. Intimacy with Him is the key that opens the door of Heaven. It begins with each of us as individuals—remember that an open Heaven comes first over a person—but the Lord's goal goes beyond individuals. He is after cities and nations.

Jesus says, "Behold I stand at the door of a whole city and knock. Is there anyone, a corporate Body of Christ in this region, that will open the door to Me, and let Me in? Are there gatekeepers in this region who are so desperate that they don't care what house gets built, as long as it is God's house?"

Sometimes the simple truths are the most easily overlooked. We use this verse for individual salvation, and rightfully so; but in context, it is an apostolic invitation for citywide transformation. Jesus stands at the doors of our cities and our churches, knocking. He is a persistent and loving Lord who will keep on knocking. Who will answer? If the people behind one door say no, He will go to another door, and another door, and another. He will keep knocking on doors until someone opens up and lets Him come in. He wants to come in and fellowship with His people. Too often we treat Him like He is a guest! But He is the owner of the House! He wants to come in for more than just a good meeting—He wants to dwell among His people!

Just don't be surprised when He ends up invading a place no one expects. Some hungry soul behind that door is crying, "Oh Lord, oh Lord, send Your Spirit now, for Jesus Christ's sake. Send your Spirit, Lord, powerfully, for Jesus Christ's sake."

His promise is for everyone—individuals, families, and communities. It is a city-transformation promise. "Open the door," Jesus says, "and I will come in to you and will dine with you and you with Me." He says, "Open the door, and I will sit down at your table and eat with you. This is not just a quick visit. I am here to stay."

WHAT DO YOU HEAR?

Does anybody hear the knock? Jesus is knocking, knocking, knocking. He comes to cities and knocks; many of them just say, "Go on somewhere else," and they miss the day of their visitation. He goes to the next city, and the next, looking for individuals hungry to be part of a prophetic revolution and an apostolic reformation. He is looking for gatekeepers of His presence—those prophets and seers and passionate Jesus-lovers who will say, "Oh Jesus, whatever you do, don't pass us by!"

Intimacy is the key that unlocks open Heavens over entire cities. It has happened before, and it can happen again. I firmly believe that it *will* happen again. Jesus did not stop knocking after Revelation 3:20 was written. He has been knocking for 2,000-plus years. Today, He stands at the doors of twenty-first-century cities, asking, "Who will answer?"

He stood at the door of a small nation called Wales, and somebody answered. He stood at the door of cosmopolitan Los Angeles, and somebody answered. He stood at the door of tiny Hebrides Islands, and somebody answered. He stood at the door of Shantung, China, and somebody answered. Jesus is knocking again, patiently knocking. I put the question to you: how will *you* respond to the Man who is knocking at *your* city's door?

"Behold I stand at the door and knock. Is there anyone...are there any gate-keepers who will let Me in?" Do you hear what I hear?

What will you do? Will you ignore the knock until He goes away? Or will you open the door and say, like Joshua, "As for me and my house, we will serve the Lord"? "For the sake of the city we represent, we will open the door to You. Come in, sit with us, eat with us, and fellowship with us. Let the Heavens open over this place, this home, this city, and let the blessings and power of our loving Father pour forth to bless the people!" *So be it, Lord!*

THE PURPOSE OF THE SEER

So what is the purpose of *the seer*? Like all true seers of old, we must reach high. We must look heavenward. We must think otherly. We must passionately pursue the God of visitation. John the Beloved said it this way, as recorded in Revelation 1:9-17:

> *I, John, your brother and fellow partaker in the tribulation and kingdom and perseverance which are in Jesus, was on the island called Patmos, because of the word of God and the testimony of Jesus. I was in the Spirit on the Lord's day, and I heard behind me a loud voice like the sound of a trumpet... Then I turned to see the voice that was speaking with me. And having turned I saw seven golden lampstands; and in the middle of the lampstands I saw one like a son of man, clothed in a robe reaching to the feet, and girded across His chest with a golden sash. His head and His hair were white like white wool, like snow; and His eyes were like a flame of fire. His feet were like burnished bronze, when it has been made to glow in a furnace, and His voice was like the sound of many waters. In His right hand He held seven stars, and out of His mouth came a sharp two-edged sword; and His face was like the sun shining in its strength. When I saw Him, I fell at His feet...* (Revelation 1:9-17a).

If there are true seers in the earth today, and there surely are, then we must have our aim and focus clear. We must see Jesus! In all our seeing, let's be like John the Beloved. Let's get in the Spirit and release the true prophetic spirit by revealing a testimony of Jesus (see Rev. 19:10). He is the One I long to see. He is the One for whom my heart yearns and pants. He is the goal and prize of my life.

May the key of intimacy be put in the door of our hearts, families, congregations, cities, and nations. May the prophetic power of visions, dreams, and open Heavens increase. May you receive an impartation of hunger for more of the Lord and may you increase in your spiritual capacity to "see in the Spirit realm." But always remember, the seer's goal is to reveal the Man Christ Jesus!

Oh, that we might see Jesus more clearly!

Section V

THE SEER DEVOTIONAL

The Seer Devotional is a added portion to this updated version of *The Seer*. Its aim is help the reader cultivate a devotional life with the Lord so that this book will not just lead to more head knowledge only. My desire is for you to experience more of the Holy Spirit activity in your very own life!

Therefore, this 40-day devotional has been compiled as a tool to complement the book, to give you practical tools to equip you to move further in your own personal pilgrimage. So whether in a group study or individual time of contemplation, drink deeply. This is composed just for you!

SEER AND PROPHET: TWO PROPHETIC STREAMS

Before I formed you in the womb I knew you, and before you were born I consecrated you; I have appointed you a prophet to the nations (Jeremiah 1:5).

TODAY'S DEVOTIONAL

In the spiritual realm, the flow of the prophetic from Heaven to earth resembles the Nile River. Just as the White Nile and the Blue Nile join to create the greater river called the Egyptian Nile, two streams of prophetic anointing come together to feed the greater concourse of the mighty prophetic river of God on earth. We can call these two streams the stream of the *prophet* and the stream of the *seer*.

Another way to look at this is to turn it around and think of a great prophetic river flowing from the throne of God that breaks into two streams—the *prophet* and the *seer*—which then give different degrees or dimensions or facets of prophetic impartation. Either way, it should be clear that both streams are important for the full expression of the Lord's prophetic word to His people in our day.

What is the difference between a *prophet* and a *seer*? *All true seers are prophets, but not all prophets are seers.* A prophet or prophetess, then, is a spokesperson for God, one who hears the voice of the Holy Spirit and speaks or pens God's mind or counsel through a divinely anointed manner.

1. From your understanding, how did God choose Old Testament prophets? Did they have to meet certain qualifications?

2. List five examples of Old Testament prophets. Look them up in the Bible and tell how God called each of them into service as a prophet or seer.

3. Why do you think God determined to have two streams of His great prophetic river? Have you seen these two streams in operation today?

4. What do you think this phrase means: "all true seers are prophets, but not all prophets are seers"?

5. How does a prophet or prophetess hear the voice of the Holy Spirit? Describe what you think is a "divinely anointed manner."

MEDITATION

Prophecy means the expressed thoughts of God spoken in a language that no people in their natural gift of speech could articulate on their own. The substance and nature of prophecy exceed the limits that the human mind is capable of thinking or imagining. Its purpose is to edify, exhort, and comfort either individuals or the corporate Body of Christ. Although prophecy comes *through* the mouths or pens of people, it comes *from* the mind of God.

Have you ever "heard" God speak in your inner person, speaking things that you could never have articulated on your own? How did you know it was God and not your own mind? Have you ever been able to use God's thoughts to edify, exhort, or comfort others?

THE SEER REALM

*Formerly in Israel, when a man went to inquire of God, he used to say, "Come, and let us go to the seer"; for **he who is called** a prophet now was formerly called a seer* (1 Samuel 9:9).

Today's Devotional

Within the overall realm of the prophet lies the particular and distinctive realm of *the seer*. The word *seer* describes a particular type of prophet who receives a particular type of prophetic revelation or impartation.

When it comes to prophetic revelation, a prophet is primarily an inspired hearer and then speaker, while a seer is primarily visual. In other words, the prophet is the *communicative* dimension, and the seer is the *receptive* dimension. Whereas *nabiy'* emphasizes the active work of the prophet in speaking forth a message from God, *ra'ah* and *chozeh* focus on the experience or means by which the prophet "sees or perceives" that message.

All true seers are prophets, but not all prophets are seers. A prophet may have the particular grace to hear and proclaim the word of the Lord, yet not necessarily function as profusely in the revelatory visionary capacity as a seer does. The seer, on the other hand, may move quite remarkably in this visionary dream capacity, yet not be as deep in the inspirational audible graces of hearing and speaking. Nevertheless, both move and operate in the prophetic realm, but in different capacities or dimensions.

1. One difference between a prophet and a seer is that a prophet hears revelation and speaks it while a seer sees revelation. Have you or anyone you know ever experienced these two types of revelation? What happened?

2. A seer is the receptive dimension of prophetic revelation, and the prophet is the communicative dimension. How does this help explain that all true seers are prophets, but not all prophets are seers?

3. What kind of faith does it take for a prophet to speak forth a message from God? What safeguards do you think a prophet should take to be sure the message is really what he or she has heard?

4. When a seer receives a prophetic revelation, how is it received? How does the seer's picture or vision bring God's revelation to others? Does the seer need to always speak what he or she sees?

5. From your experience, comment on seers and prophets and their usefulness in the Body of Christ. What are some of your immediate reactions to this teaching? Have you seen positive results from it?

MEDITATION

The seer realm of prophetic anointing has a lot to do with quietly waiting on God. Quite often, impartation in the seer realm comes only after a time of patient waiting and contemplative meditation upon the Lord. But thank the Lord, if we wait, He will come!

How much time do you spend waiting on God during an average day? During an average week? Is God asking you to increase your time waiting on Him so that He might impart more to you?

TWO PROPHETIC STREAMS: CONTRASTS AND COMPARISONS

[I pray] that the God of our Lord Jesus Christ, the Father of glory, may give to you a spirit of wisdom and of revelation in the knowledge of Him (Ephesians 1:17).

TODAY'S DEVOTIONAL

By contrasting and comparing the prophet and seer streams, we can gain a better understanding of how the two work together and complement each other in bringing out the fullest expression of God's prophetic revelation.

Prophets in this stream often work in a plurality of leadership. Seasoned and gifted individuals, both men and women, minister through the laying on of hands, relating prophecy to individuals or to the corporate body as it is revealed to them. This ministry often utilizes the spiritual gifts of tongues and the interpretation of tongues, prophecy and words of knowledge. *Nabiy'* prophets "hear" words in their spirits and begin by releasing this unction. This kind of prophecy tends to be more spontaneous and with a faster flow than "seer" prophecy, with inspiration as the general tone.

Ra'ah or *chozeh* seers, on the other hand, tend more toward single-person ministry versus the plurality of a team. The seer anointing emphasizes visions and the revelatory gifts mingled with the gift of discerning of spirits, rather than the audible, speaking gifts. Within the visionary dimension there are two basic levels of seeing: *visual* and *actual*.

Visual seeing involves insights, revelations, warnings, and prophecies from the Spirit of God that may come in supernatural visual dreams. In contrast, *actual* seeing involves supernatural dreams in which God's tangible presence is evident or manifested.

1. Have you ever been part of an experience where prophets laid hands on you or someone you know and ministered their revelation? Describe the experience. What was the atmosphere in the spiritual realm?

2. Why do you think the ministry of a prophet is usually spontaneous in its flow? Do you think this spontaneity helps keep prophets from adding their own thoughts, or do you think it could make the message more tainted with personal observations?

3. How are the spiritual gifts of tongues, interpretation of tongues, prophecy, and words of knowledge utilized by prophets? How have you seen them in operation?

4. Have you experienced the ministry of a seer who spoke of a vision or picture revealed by God? Why do seers operating in this ministry flow often receive the pictures of revelation *prior* to the time of ministry and delivery?

5. How would you explain these basic levels of vision: *visual* and *actual*? How do you think these ways of seeing work?

MEDITATION

Every born-again believer has two sets of eyes. We have our physical eyes, with which we view the physical, created world around us. Paul talks about a second set of eyes—the eyes of our hearts, or our inner selves—that can be enlightened to perceive spiritual truth. I am convinced that any believer can develop the seer capacity.

Pray that the Lord develops the eyes of your heart so that you will perceive spiritual truth.

DIMENSIONS OF THE PROPHETIC ANOINTING

For the testimony of Jesus is the spirit of prophecy
(Revelation 19:10b).

TODAY'S DEVOTIONAL

Essentially, the anointing is the supernatural enablement or grace—the manifested presence of the Holy Spirit—operating upon or through an individual or a corporate group to produce the works of Jesus. It means God with you and God in you; you are talking His talk and walking in His shadow.

As an anointed people, we as the Body of Christ have been called to carry a prophetic burden, which will cause us to live on the cutting edge of God's eternal purpose. The prophetic ministry is but one aspect of the fivefold calling of apostles, prophets, evangelists, pastors, and teachers. As such, it is resident to a degree in every ministry and is more evident and active in certain ones. God's ultimate weapon is a man or a woman who has encountered the prophetic anointing. God does not anoint *projects*; He anoints *people!*

People anointed with a prophetic ministry speak the word of the Lord in the name of the Lord. They carry weight in the Church by virtue of the ethical, moral, and spiritual urgency of their messages. Their credentials, credibility, and status as prophetic vessels stem not from birth or by official designation, but by the power of their inner call and by the response of those who hear them.

1. If the anointing is supernatural enablement or grace from the Holy Spirit, how does the Spirit determine who receives it? Is it available to all believers? Why or why not?

2. Consider what it means to have a supernatural anointing upon a corporate group. How does this work? Have you experienced corporate anointing? How did it affect the individual participants as well as the entire group?

3. Explain the statement, "God with you and God in you; you are talking His talk and walking in His shadow." How can people tell this is happening to you?

4. What is the "cutting edge of God's eternal purpose"? How can we live there? What part do we play in this type of life?

5. Though the prophetic ministry is resident to a degree in every ministry, in which of the fivefold ministries is it more evident and active? Why?

MEDITATION

The single most characteristic mark of true prophetic people is the evidence that they have stood in the counsel of God and have, therefore, faithfully declared what they heard from His mouth.

Have you stood in the counsel of God? Have you been faithful to declare what you have heard from the Lord? Whether these experiences are new to you, or your life has been marked by multiple incidents, you still need to grow further in His presence.

Plan time in your devotional time to wait and listen. Then follow through when you hear His direction.

UNDERSTANDING THE PROPHETIC ANOINTING

Blessed are the pure in heart, for they shall see God
(Matthew 5:8).

TODAY'S DEVOTIONAL

Today there is a new anointing for a new generation, a Joshua generation of people who will be born into the things of the Spirit in the midst of a great spiritual storm that is sweeping across our land. Let's take a closer look at this anointing.

Usually, prophets make no special claim to be heard, but are content to speak and act and leave the matter there—confident not in themselves, but in the fact that they have heard from God, and that every word from Him will find fulfillment. Their primary concern is not with the distant future, but to tell forth the will of God in the crisis of their own day. Prophets, then, are essentially interpreters of God.

The prophecies of the Old Testament prophets foreshadowed Christ. The major task of New Testament prophets and beyond has always been to declare that in Christ all the prophecies of the Bible have been fulfilled.

Remember that prophecy itself is the expressed thoughts of God spoken in a language that no people in their natural gift of speech could articulate on their own. The substance and nature of prophecy exceed the limits of what the natural mind could conceive. Prophecy comes *through* the mouths of people, but *from* the mind of God—spiritual thoughts in spiritual words.

Look at the variations of prophetic grace listed below and make comments in each box:

Variation	How God Uses My Experience in This Area
Dreamers and Visionaries: Prophets Who Proclaim God's Corporate Purpose	
Prophets Who Proclaim God's Heart Standards for His People	
Prophets Who Proclaim the Church's Social Responsibilities and Actions	
Prophets Who Speak Forth the Administrative Strategy of God With a Political Slant	
Leaders Who Usher in the Manifested Presence of God Through Prophetic Worship	
Prophetic Intercessors, Spirit-Bearers, Counselors, Equippers, Writers, and Evangelists	

MEDITATION

The prophetic anointing of the Spirit makes itself known in a wide variety of ways. People are different, with different personalities, cultures, ethnic backgrounds, and gifts. It should not be surprising then, that there is a great divergent expression of the ministry and office of the prophet. These various models represent what the Spirit is doing and desires to do in the Church. Together they present a more complete picture of the fullness of the Lord's prophetic anointing.

How does your personality, culture, and background bring uniqueness to the expression of your spiritual gifts? How do they present a part of the picture of the fullness of the Lord's prophetic anointing?

DAY 6

POISON AND ANTIDOTE

*Now, there are varieties of gifts, but the same Spirit. And there are varieties of ministries, and the same Lord. And there are varieties of effects, but the same God who works all things in all **persons***
(1 Corinthians 12:4-6).

Today's Devotional

Clearly, the prophetic anointing manifests in many diverse ways. All arise from the same Holy Spirit, who gives as He wills. With this in mind, a warning is in order. There is a deadly poison that can kill our ministry and our ability to walk in our anointing, whatever it may be: the poison of covetousness. Comparing ourselves to someone else and wanting what they have produces death. We should never judge or evaluate our anointing by someone else's anointing. It is vitally important to avoid jealousy and insecurity. God has plenty of anointing to go around. Let's be satisfied to seek our own calling and walk in our own anointing.

The antidote to this poison is to learn to walk in accountability with others, cultivating faithfulness while giving ourselves to the unique expression of grace that God has imparted to each of us. Sometimes we are prone to allow ourselves to be hindered by rejection, criticism, legalistic traditions, and the restrictive yokes and molds of others' unrealistic and erroneous expectations.

The Holy Spirit will help us and liberate us to be unique and varied expressions of His wonderful prophetic presence, and yet to walk circumspectly with integrity within the Church.

1. When God assembles His people, the anointing manifests itself in diverse ways. Why do people tend to think that there is a formula or one-size-fits-all anointing?

2. Why does covetousness become a major deterrent to the anointing? How does this happen? Have you ever coveted another per- son's anointing or experience?

3. Have you ever judged or evaluated your gifts or anointing by someone else's anointing? What dangers lie in such an evaluation? How can we be freed from such comparisons?

4. When we are satisfied with our own calling, we acknowledge certain aspects of God's character. What are some of these? How does faith come into play in order to walk in our own anointing?

5. Do you have accountability to people with whom you can cultivate faithfulness to your gifts? If so, how do they call you to accountability? If not, who could become your team of exhorters to keep you on track?

MEDITATION

God has never been in a box. We are the ones in boxes! It is time to let the Holy Spirit take the lid off, so that, in gratitude *to* Him, we can become all that we can be *in* Him. Let's let His anointing break the yoke. Instead of wishing we were somebody else or had what somebody else has, let's be faithful and accountable to walk in the unique expression of grace that God has given to each of us.

What box are you in? What will you do to let the Holy Spirit take the lid off your box?

VISION: THE POWER THAT SUSTAINS

Where there is no vision, the people are unrestrained, but happy is he who keeps the law (Proverbs 29:18).

TODAY'S DEVOTIONAL

This verse in the New International Version reads: *"Where there is no **revelation,** the people cast off restraint; but blessed is he who keeps the law."* Some other translations, such as the New Revised Standard Version, use the word *prophecy* instead of *vision* or *revelation*. The point is clear: Without prophecy, without divine revelation or vision, people will cast off all restraint. They will run wild because they have no guidance—no *vision*. The Word of God—His *law*—provides vision and guidance for living, and those who follow it are blessed.

All people need vision to sustain them in life. The apostle Paul set his sights on knowing Christ, which he acknowledged was a lifelong process.

> *Brethren, I do not regard myself as having laid hold of it yet; but one thing I do: forgetting what lies behind and reaching forward to what lies ahead, I press on toward the goal for the prize of the upward call of God in Christ Jesus. Let us therefore, as many as are perfect, have this attitude* (Philippians 3:13-15a).

Like Paul, we need to be a people of vision. Let us set our sights on the Lord and aim at His goals.

1. Looking at the different translations of Proverbs 29:18 above, make your own "amplified version" that explains the words of this verse in the terms of your life.

2. How does the Word of God provide vision for our lives? Besides the Ten Commandments, where can you find guidance for living? In what ways have you received blessings when you followed the Word?

3. "All people need vision to sustain them in life." What does this mean for someone who is in the 20-40 age bracket? What about those in their 50s and 60s? What about senior citizens?

4. What do you believe is "lying ahead" (see Phil. 3:13-15a) for you in the near future? What has God spoken about your long-term future?

5. How do you set your sights on the Lord when you make major life decisions? How do you ensure that you are aimed at His goals and not merely your own?

MEDITATION

As Christians, we are called to be a people of vision. We must learn to set a goal or target in front of our eyes to gaze upon. It is only when we aim at something that we have any chance of hitting it!

How do your priorities reflect your goal or target? Is your target easy to aim at? Are you easily distracted from achieving your goal?

THE VISION THAT SUSTAINED ZECHARIAH

On the twenty-fourth day of the eleventh month, which is the month of Shebat, in the second year of Darius, the word of the Lord came to Zechariah the prophet, the son of Berechiah, the son of Iddo...
(Zechariah 1:7).

TODAY'S DEVOTIONAL

Zechariah was a visionary prophet whose visions related specifically to the time after the Babylonian exile and the beginning of the Messianic period in Israel's history.

In one of his visions, Zechariah saw an elaborate golden lampstand with two olive trees on either side of it. His first response was very intelligent. He asked the angel, *"What are these, my lord?"* Asking a question is a wise course of action whenever visionary revelation occurs. That is a lesson I learned from Zechariah. No matter what I see or how many times I think I may have seen it before, I always ask, "What is this, Lord?" I am confident that the same God who gives me the revelation can also interpret it for me.

Even when the angel asks him specifically, *"Do you not know what these are?"* Zechariah answers with humility, *"No, my lord."* (See Zechariah 4:4-5.) Had Zechariah not responded with humility and openness, he probably would not have gained much from the whole experience. People who think they know it all already cut themselves off from learning anything new.

This vision sustained Zechariah, Zerubbabel, and all of the returning exiles. It encouraged and motivated them to rebuild the temple in Jerusalem, as well as the walls of the city and the city itself, which had been destroyed by the Babylonians. Vision sustains a people, and humility is a key that releases understanding!

1. Have you ever had a vision or revelation that had to do with governmental or social concerns? Why would God give such visions or revelations to nongovernmental or social leaders?

2. When God has spoken or revealed something to you that you did not understand, have you asked questions to receive further clarification? Do you ask your Christian leaders for clarification when you need it?

3. Humility and openness characterized Zechariah's response to the angel. Why are these two traits important to anyone involved in revelation or visionary gifts?

4. Understanding the message of a revelation or vision is important, but why is it also important to "gain from the experience"? What can be learned through the experience?

5. It must have been exhilarating to Zechariah to see the faith that accompanied the exiles and the leaders as they rebuilt what had once been destroyed. What has been destroyed in your life, community, or church that needs to be rebuilt? What can stir the faith of those who need to be motivated to make a difference?

MEDITATION

Zechariah's vision had to do with a message for Zerubbabel, the civic official of the returning exiles under whose leadership the temple in Jerusalem would be rebuilt. The word of the Lord to Zerubbabel was, *"Not by might nor by power, but by My Spirit"* (Zech. 4:6). This was meant as an encouragement to Zerubbabel and the rest of the returning exiles that a new era was beginning, an era characterized by the working of God's Spirit in power, and the coming day of the Messiah.

God spoke to a civic official through an established prophet. Does God still desire to speak to civic officials today? Whom might He choose to speak through?

SEEKING THE VISION
THAT SUSTAINS US

[I pray] *that the eyes of your heart may be enlightened, so that you will know what is the hope of His calling, what are the riches of the glory of His inheritance in the saints, and what is the surpassing greatness of His power toward us who believe...* (Ephesians 1:18-19a).

TODAY'S DEVOTIONAL

Keeping our vision of the Lord clear before us will sustain us through the many labors of our lives and ministries.

Over the years, I have become convinced that in the Christian life, at least two things are certain: God *never* changes, and we are *always* changing. Our lives as Christians are a continual transition from one place to another, one level to another, one understanding to another. The purpose of spiritual light is to bring us into change and growth. The more light we have, the more change we experience, and the more we change (for the better), the more we are brought into higher levels of glory. Unless we are in constant transition, we will stop somewhere along the way and settle down. The Christian life is a frontier. God did not call us to be settlers, but to be pilgrims and pioneers. This is the point of Paul's prayer in the first chapter of Ephesians.

The more enlightenment we have, the more wisdom and revelation we are open to receive, and the greater understanding we can develop of the hope of His calling, the glory of His inheritance, and the surpassing greatness of His power as they apply to our lives.

1. How has keeping your vision of the Lord clear before you sustained you through your labors in ministry and in your life?

2. How do you personally know that God never changes? What Scripture confirms this to you? What experiences have you had to testify that this is true?

3. How do you know that humanity is always changing? Where do you find this in the Scriptures? Have you seen this to be true in your experience?

4. How well do you weather transitions in your life? Do you see your transitions as bringing you from one level to the next? Do they help you grow in your understanding?

5. What factors help us develop the understanding of the hope of God's calling and His surpassing greatness? How can you develop these factors?

MEDITATION

We need a vision to sustain us as a people—a vision that shows us clearly how the promises of God are more than all the power of evil. Let us then be a people of vision who will not perish, but walk together in hot pursuit of the Lord, that we too will be able to hold before our eyes an all-consuming vision of the conquering Son of Man and the Ancient of Days sitting upon His throne.

Do others have the same vision as you? Are you walking in hot pursuit with others of like vision?

THE DIVERSITY
OF VISIONARY STATES—PART 1

*But one and the same Spirit works all these things, distributing to
each one individually just as He wills* (1 Corinthians 12:11).

TODAY'S DEVOTIONAL

There is only one Holy Spirit, but He works in a multiplicity of ways.
There are many spiritual gifts, but only one gift-giver: the Holy Spirit of
God. The prophetic anointing manifests itself in many diverse ways, but they
all derive from the same Spirit.

This same diversity by the one Spirit applies also to visionary states and
experiences. In fact, the New Testament uses a variety of Greek words to
express different visionary states. None of these states are "higher" or "better"
than any of the others. They are simply different, and the Holy Spirit uses
them with different people for different purposes.

Let's take a closer look at some of these visionary states.

Onar

In Greek, *onar* is the common word for "dream." It refers simply to the kind
of dreaming we all do when we sleep. Everyday dreams are themselves visionary in
nature, because our minds generate images that we "see" while we are asleep. As the

Bible makes clear, God can and does use these common dreams to communicate with ordinary people.

Enupnion

Like *onar*, the word *enupnion* refers to a vision or dream received while asleep. The difference with *enupnion* is that it stresses a surprise quality that is contained in that dream.

1. Why is it important to know that even though there are diverse spiritual gifts, there is only one Giver of those gifts? How does this bring us to respect the gifts that others have?

2. Look up the word *anointing* in a common dictionary. Then find three Scriptures that use this word. What have you learned about what *anointing* is? Are there specific ingredients that are necessary, even if it is manifested in various ways?

3. Do you have the ability to "sense" or know when the prophetic anointing is ready to manifest itself in you or others? In your experience, what takes place before prophecy is given in a corporate setting?

4. Have you or someone you know had an *onar*? What makes this visionary state different from "ordinary" dreams?

5. Have you or anyone you know experienced an *enupnion*? Why would God want to give a surprise in a dream?

MEDITATION

Sometimes a "surprise element" is released through seer encounters. Watch out: ready or not, here He comes!

How regular are seer encounters in your life? Do you take the time to wait and pray to receive visions and revelation from the Lord? Do you prepare for sleep by asking the Lord to speak to you while you sleep? Begin a regimen of preparation for bed that includes inviting God to bring revelation in the night hours.

THE DIVERSITY
OF VISIONARY STATES—PART 2

*Boasting is necessary, though it is not profitable; but I will go on to
visions and revelations of the Lord* (2 Corinthians 12:1).

TODAY'S DEVOTIONAL

Here are three more New Testament Greek words that express different
visionary states.

Horama

Horama is another general term for vision, meaning "that which is seen." It
carries the particular sense of a "spectacle, sight, or appearance." New Testament examples commonly associate this word with *waking visions*.

You can be a candidate for *horama* visions. Just tell the Lord of your desire
to be a person who receives the spirit of revelation and sees visions. It is in
His Word. It is for today. It is there for the asking!

Horasis

A *horasis* occurs when the Spirit who lives within us looks out through
the "windows" of our eyes and allows us to see what He sees. Are we seeing
in the natural or in the spiritual? Sometimes it is hard to tell, and sometimes
it is *both*. When our spiritual eyes are open, sometimes our natural eyes can

see into the spiritual realm. We may see dual images as visionary spiritual pictures that are superimposed over the images we are seeing with our physical eyes.

Optasia

Another visionary state found in the New Testament is denoted by the word *optasia*—literally meaning "visuality," or in concrete form, "apparition." *Optasia* has the very specific connotation of self-disclosure, or of letting oneself be seen. The word always occurs in the context of someone seeing a divine or spiritual personage.

1. Have you ever had a *horama* vision, or do you personally know someone who has had one? What did the vision entail? Why do you think God revealed it? What resulted from its revelation?

2. Have you asked God for the spirit of revelation and the gift to see visions? Why does this type of revelation "scare" some people? Why should we seek *horama* visions?

3. Have you experienced a *horasis*, or do you know of someone who has experienced one? How do both the natural and spiritual work in this visionary state?

4. What is your understanding of the *optasia* visionary state? Have you or someone you know experienced this? What impact can this visionary state have on one's life?

5. Looking at the three visionary states above, which would you say the Lord needs to develop more in His Body? Why?

MEDITATION

We all have two sets of eyes: our physical or natural eyes, and the eyes of our hearts, with which we see into the spiritual realm; the latter are the eyes through which we see and understand spiritual truth. The Bible says that our bodies are temples for the Holy Spirit. Every temple has windows and doors. When the Lord comes to dwell in our temples, He likes to be able to look out His windows. Our eyes—physical and spiritual—are the windows to our souls.

How well do your eyes work in seeing what the Lord wants you to see?

THE DIVERSITY
OF VISIONARY STATES—PART 3

*Therefore, prepare your minds for action, keep sober **in spirit,***
fix your hope completely on the grace to be brought to you at the
revelation of Jesus Christ (1 Peter 1:13).

TODAY'S DEVOTIONAL

Here are the remaining New Testament Greek words that express differ-ent visionary states.

Ekstasis

Ekstasis, from which our English word *ecstasy* is derived, means "amaze-ment, astonishment, or a trance." Literally, *ekstasis* means "a displacement of the mind," or "bewilderment." When translated as "trance," *ekstasis* refers to one being caught up in the Spirit so as to receive those revelations that God intends.

Apokalupsis

With *apokalupsis*, we come to the most frequently used word in the New Testament to describe a visionary state. *Apokalupsis* literally means "disclo-sure," an "appearing" or "coming," a "manifestation." It carries specifically the sense of something hidden that has now been uncovered or revealed.

Egenomehn ehn pneumati

The phrase *egenomehn ehn pneumati* literally means "to *become* in the Spirit," a state in which one could see visions and be informed or spoken directly to by the Spirit of God. Therein lies the secret to how we get revelation. We do it by first getting in the Spirit. The more we are filled with the Spirit and walk in the Spirit, the more we become one with the Spirit, and the more our eyes will be opened to see in the Spirit. He will give us the perception to look into the spiritual realm.

1. Have you ever had an *ekstasis* vision, or do you personally know someone who has had this type of vision? What did the vision entail? Why do you think God revealed it? What resulted from its revelation?

2. Have you or someone you know experienced an *apokalupsis?* How do hidden things become revealed in this vision?

3. What is your understanding of the *egenomehn ehn pneumati* visionary state? Have you or someone you know experienced this? What impact can this visionary state have on one's life?

4. Looking at the three visionary states above, which would you say the Lord needs to develop more in His Body? Why?

5. In order to get revelation, we must first get in the Spirit. What does this mean to you? How does a person become one with the Spirit?

MEDITATION

Have you ever had an experience where you suddenly felt like a little light went on inside? You may not necessarily have had an actual vision, but just a sense that something that you did not understand, something that was hidden from you, was now revealed. That is an *apokalupsis*-type experience.

If you have experienced this type of vision, how did God use it? If you have not experienced this, how can you prepare yourself to receive such revelation?

WISELY JUDGING
REVELATORY ENCOUNTERS

*But examine everything **carefully**; hold fast to that which is good*
(1 Thessalonians 5:21).

TODAY'S DEVOTIONAL

There is only one dependable, unshakable guide through the minefield of supernatural encounters. In a world filled with spiritual voices of the New Age and voices of every other type and description, Christians need to know how to make their way through a spiritual field littered with hidden (and deadly) weapons of the enemy designed to wound or destroy the unwary and the undiscerning.

Entire segments of the Body of Christ have "written off" the supernatural aspects of God's Kingdom and His workings in the Church today because of fears about being deceived and led astray. Others have written these off due to excess, abuse, and the bad testimony left behind by lone rangers who are not accountable to anyone in the Body of Christ. The prophetic has been given a bad rap at times, but some of the wounds have been self-inflicted. Nonetheless, God *does speak* to His people today, and He is very capable of preserving us from harm and deception.

Since the Bible is our absolute standard against which we must test *all* spiritual experiences, it should be obvious that we need to know and study God's Word.

God has also ordained that we find safety in our relationship to a Bible-believing fellowship.

The following building blocks must be firmly in place before we begin to investigate the principles of testing spiritual experiences. Soberly estimate your personal status for each question.

1. Am I regularly studying the Scriptures?
2. Am I maintaining a life of prayer?
3. Am I seeking purity, cleansing, and holiness in my life?
4. Am I a worshipful member of a local Christian congregation?
5. Am I committed to a few peer relationships with people who can speak into my life?

MEDITATION

What would you think if you had a spiritual experience that made your hair stand on end? Would you write it off as absolutely satanic or "off the wall" because it didn't fit your theological code? Many people would and do. Supernatural encounters are real. The seer dimension into the spirit world is not something relegated to yesterday—it exists today and is on the rise! The question we must answer is: do all such revelatory encounters come from the one true God, or can there be other sources? How can we tell the source or nature of the spirit beings we encounter? What are the marks of a truly God-initiated encounter or revelatory experience?

Answer these questions with the Holy Spirit's help, and allow God to speak direction as to where you need to go from here.

SOURCES OF REVELATION

Son of man, prophesy against the prophets...who are following their own spirit and have seen nothing (Ezekiel 13:2-3).

TODAY'S DEVOTIONAL

The Scriptures indicate that spiritual revelation or communication comes from any one of three sources: the Holy Spirit, the human soul, or the realm of evil spirits. The need for discernment in this area is obvious.

The Holy Spirit is the only true source of revelation (see 2 Pet. 1:21). It was the Holy Spirit who "moved" the prophets of the Old Testament and the witnesses of the New Testament. The Greek word for "moved," *phero*, means "to be borne along" or even "to be driven along as a wind"

The human soul is capable of voicing thoughts, ideas, and inspirations out of the unsanctified portion of our emotions (see Ezek. 13:1-6; Jer. 23:16). These human inspirations are not necessarily born of God. As Ezekiel the prophet said, they are prophecies *"out of their own hearts...Woe unto the foolish prophets, that follow their own spirit, and have seen nothing"* (Ezek. 13:2-3 KJV).

Evil spirits operate with two characteristics common to their master. They can appear as "angels of light" (or as "good voices"), and they always speak lies, because they serve the chief liar and the father of lies, satan. We need to "test" every source and aspect of the revelation—whether it be a dream, apparition, spoken word, or other type.

Check yourself with the following questions:

The Self Test:

1. Is there any evidence of influences other than the Spirit of God in my life?

2. What is the essence of the "vision" or revelation? (How does it compare to God's written Word?)

3. Was I under the control of the Holy Spirit when I received the vision?

    • Have I presented my life to Jesus Christ as a living sacrifice?

    • Have I been obedient to His Word?

    • Am I being enlightened with His inspiration?

    • Am I committed to doing His will, no matter what it is?

    • Am I yielding my life to the praises of God or to critical speech?

    • Am I waiting quietly and expectantly before Him?

Understand **The Source Test:**

1. Have I cut off all pictures put before my mind's eye by satan using the blood of Jesus?

2. Have I presented the eyes of my heart to the Lord for Him to fill?

3. Has the Holy Spirit projected on the inner screen of my heart the flow of vision that He desires?

NINE SCRIPTURAL TESTS

1. Does the revelation edify, exhort, or console?

2. Is it in agreement with God's Word?

3. Does it exalt Jesus Christ?

4. Does it have good fruit?

5. If it predicts a future event, does it come to pass?

6. Does the prophetic prediction turn people toward God or away from Him?

7. Does it produce liberty or bondage?

8. Does it produce life or death?

9. Does the Holy Spirit bear witness that it is true?

Look at a recent revelation you have either received or witnessed. Go through each test and evaluate the revelation based on these nine questions. What have you learned doing this exercise?

FIFTEEN WISDOM ISSUES

Beloved, do not believe every spirit, but test the spirits to see whether they are from God, because many false prophets have gone out into the world (1 John 4:1).

TODAY'S DEVOTIONAL

The 15 wisdom issues listed below will help us learn how to wisely judge the various forms of revelation we will encounter in our adventure with Christ.

1. Search for proper exegesis and Scriptural context.

2. Focus on Jesus.

3. Major on the "main and plain" things.

4. Follow biblical principles—not the rigid letter of the law.

5. Build bridges. We must keep ourselves clean from spiritual pride.

6. Honor and pray for leaders.

7. Be aware of times and seasons. We can predetermine by His guidance, but also welcome spontaneous occurrences.

8. Let love rule.

9. Maintain balance. There is a godly tightrope of dynamic tension between the reality of subjective experience and biblical doctrine.

10. Understand the relationship of divine initiation and human response. Although some external, visible, and audible signs

are divinely initiated, some of them are human responses and reactions to the Holy Spirit.

11. Be known by your fruits.

12. Perceive the works of God and the motives of people.

13. Control your flesh and cooperate with God.

14. Be alert and aware. Let us search the Scriptures, review Church history, seek the Lord, and receive input from those who are wiser and more experienced than us.

15. Avoid spiritual ditches. There are two deep ditches we should avoid. We should watch out for analytical skepticism and fear (of people, rejection, fanaticism, and so forth).

Looking over the 15 items above, evaluate where you currently stand in each one:

1. How does your personality affect the rating of the wisdom items above?

2. Pick three of the wisdom issues that you have rated most operational in your life. How will you help transfer these to someone else? How can you formally or informally mentor him or her?

3. Look at the three wisdom issues that you rated the lowest. What will you do to bring them forward?

4. Do you see any of these wisdom issues as more important than the others? Why or why not?

MEDITATION

If you can't jump in the middle of it, bless it. If you can't bless it, then patiently observe it. If you can't patiently observe it, then just don't criticize it! Do not stretch out the rod of your tongue against those things you do not understand!

What does this mean to you?

DAY 16

DISCERNING OF SPIRITS

But solid food is for the mature, who because of practice have their senses trained to discern good and evil (Hebrews 5:14).

TODAY'S DEVOTIONAL

Let me clarify that we are talking about two overlapping but different issues here: general discernment, which is a product of experience, discipline, and study; and discerning of spirits, which is a spiritual gift imparted by the Holy Spirit. Discernment or distinguishing of spirits is different because it goes beyond our natural learning abilities. It is a supernatural gift from the Lord; we cannot earn it. No amount of human insight or learning will enable us to discern between spirits. Only God can impart that ability, and He does so by His sovereign choice. General discernment and the discerning of spirits are different, but related. The principles for growing in both arenas are the same, however: regular meditation on the Word of God and the crucible of life experience.

Discerning of spirits is the supernatural ability to distinguish not only between good and bad spirits, but also between various classes of spirits:

- The Holy Spirit
- Good angels
- Fallen angels
- Demons or evil spirits
- The human spirit

Sometimes when dealing with the spiritual realm, we can find ourselves facing "gray" areas where things are unclear. That is one time when we need the gift of discerning of spirits to clear away the gray and separate matters into black and white.

1. How would you rate your level of general discernment? What experiences, discipline, and/or study have helped shape your general discernment?

2. How is discerning of spirits different from general discernment? Why is the Holy Spirit needed to impart this gift?

3. If general discernment and discerning of spirits are different, why are the principles for growing in both arenas the same? What are these principles? In what ways have these principles been effective in your life?

4. From your understanding, explain the various classes of spirits listed above. Have you been able to distinguish these classes? How can you grow in your awareness of these?

5. What "gray" areas have you had to contend with when discerning spirits? What can help you distinguish between spirits?

MEDITATION

Basically, discernment is perception, which can come in a variety of ways. Sometimes it is as simple as an inner knowledge, a "gut feeling," that we cannot explain, yet somehow know is real. This kind of spiritual perception is often so subtle that we can easily miss it or attribute it to something else, such as a "hunch."

Have you had "hunches" that turned out to really be spiritual discernment? Have you thought you had spiritual discernment in something, when in actuality it was your own "hunch"? Think about how you will be able to tell the difference in the future.

DISCERNING THE HOLY SPIRIT, ANGELS, HUMAN SPIRITS, AND EVIL SPIRITS

And they were all filled with the Holy Spirit and began to speak with other tongues, as the Spirit was giving them utterance (Acts 2:4).

TODAY'S DEVOTIONAL

When the Spirit came on that Day of Pentecost, He appeared in two forms: wind and fire. There is no indication that these believers knew beforehand *how* the Spirit would appear, but when He came, they knew He was there. Once again, only the gift of discernment could impart this knowledge.

Another area of discernment is the ability to discern the human spirit—the true character or motive behind a person's words or actions—even if hidden from casual view. Jesus possessed this ability to an exceptional degree. No one can "see" faith. We can observe faith in action as it is demonstrated, but only the Spirit of God can impart the ability to discern faith in another.

One area of discernment where we must exercise care, caution, and maturity is in the discerning of evil spirits. Have you ever been in a place or situation where you simply felt the presence of evil? What about a time when a rotten or unpleasant odor was present with no identifiable natural source?

Some of the common "symptoms" of the possible presence of evil spirits in a place are an oppressive atmosphere, a sense of confusion, a pervading sense of loneliness or sadness, a feeling of pressure, and depression. These are just a few examples; there are many more.

1. Why do you think the Spirit appeared in two forms on the Day of Pentecost? What were these, and what symbolism do you see in them?

2. What causes you to believe that the disciples used discernment to know the Holy Spirit had come and did not think it was merely an unusual work of nature? How is this type of discernment useful to the Church?

3. How is the ability to discern the human spirit useful to you as a believer? How can you develop this gift?

4. Why do you need to exercise care, caution, and maturity when discerning evil spirits? Do you need to be afraid of these spirits? Explain your answer.

5. Look at the list of "symptoms" of the possible presence of evil spirits above. Have you ever experienced these symptoms and received the revelation that they were due to an evil spirit? How can you be sensitized to this possibility in a greater dimension?

MEDITATION

Not every illness is caused by an evil spirit, but we find some people today who are not healed immediately through prayer or the laying on of hands. In some of these cases, a spirit of infirmity may be at work, which must be taken care of before healing will occur. In a visionary sense, such a spirit may be revealed as appearing like a leech on a person, sucking the strength out of whatever part of the body is afflicted.

As graphic as this is, have you ever seen such a vision of someone? Why would God use such a graphic picture?

THE PURPOSE OF THE GIFT
OF DISCERNMENT

*The wind blows where it wishes and you hear the sound of it, but do
not know where it comes from and where it is going; so is everyone
who is born of the Spirit* (John 3:8).

TODAY'S DEVOTIONAL

God never gives gifts or imparts spiritual abilities for no reason. Why is the gift of discernment, and the discerning of spirits in particular, so important? There is a sixfold purpose for this gift in the life of the Church:

1. ***Deliverance from demons.*** Demons must be discerned and exposed before they can be dealt with. The New Testament contains numerous accounts of demon-possessed people who were delivered by Jesus or His followers. This ministry is still essential today.

2. ***Reveal the servants of satan.*** Once, when Paul was sharing the Word of God with a Roman proconsul, he was opposed by a magician named Elymas (see Acts 13:8-12).

3. ***Expose and defeat the work and utterance of demons.*** This is clearly illustrated in Acts 16:16-18 when Paul casts the spirit of divination out of the slave girl.

4. ***Expose error.*** Discerning of spirits reveals not only the workers of satan, but the errors of their teachings as well.

5. ***Acknowledge and confess Christ.*** As the spirit of prophecy is poured out, people will fall on their faces and declare that Jesus is Lord (see 1 Cor. 14:24-25).

6. ***Know the moving of the Holy Spirit so as to cooperate with Him.*** Unless we recognize (discern) where and how the Holy Spirit is moving, we may find ourselves unintentionally working at cross-purposes to Him.

When we understand these six purposes, we can begin to see the incredible importance of discernment in the Church today.

1. God never gives gifts or imparts spiritual abilities for no reason. What does this mean to you? Has your life experience borne this out?

2. Explain why the gift of discernment and the discerning of spirits are so important. Has this been true in your life? How do these gifts help us in life decisions?

3. Look at the six purposes for the gift of discernment and the gift of discerning of spirits in the life of the Church. Think through the experiences you have had with each one. Which purpose has been most demonstrated in your life thus far?

4. Of these six purposes, which seems to be the most important to you at this time? Why?

5. How do these purposes help express the desires of God for the Church to be wise? How do these purposes demonstrate the effectual work of the Holy Spirit to train us?

MEDITATION

The operation of the Holy Spirit is especially needed in "religious" cities. God have mercy on us and deliver us from the slumbering effects of religious spirits. Where the Spirit of the Lord is, there is freedom!

Is the city or town you live in "religious"? How do you need to pray for your city so that it would receive the Spirit of the Lord and the freedom that accompanies Him?

GUIDELINES FOR OPERATING IN THE GIFT OF DISCERNMENT

By this you know the Spirit of God: every spirit that confesses that Jesus Christ has come in the flesh is from God (1 John 4:2).

TODAY'S DEVOTIONAL

I want to share six guidelines for walking uprightly and effectively in the gift of discernment.

1. *Cultivate the gift.* We can cultivate the gift of discernment by regularly exercising our spiritual senses—learning to give a spiritual interpretation of what our normal senses perceive during a visionary experience.

2. *Test the spirits.* Don't automatically assume that every vision or spiritual presence is from God. He commands us to test the spirits in order to distinguish the true from the false.

3. *Examine the fruit.* One of the best ways to test the spirits is to look at the results, keeping in mind that fruit takes time to develop.

4. *Discerning of spirits is not the gift of suspicion.* It is easy to fall into the trap of improperly using this gift to "see" things about other people and to "report" what we see in a way that could hurt or damage them.

5. ***Wisdom, wisdom, wisdom!*** Wisdom is an *absolute* necessity in exercising the gift of discernment. Such wisdom comes only from God.

6. ***Intercede!*** Along with the gift of discernment may come faith to act or pray with authority. The key, however, is to *always* pray first for discernment so that we will know what to do in any specific situation.

These guidelines will help you to use the gift of discernment with maturity, yielding great fruit for the Kingdom.

1. How do you cultivate your gift of discernment? How do you exercise your spiritual senses?

2. In what ways do you test the spirits? Are you easily able to distinguish between what is true and what is false?

3. How thoroughly do you examine the fruit of those who are prophets in today's world? Why are younger prophets under more scrutiny than those who have been in ministry a long time?

4. Explain the difference between *suspicion* and *discernment*. Have you been able to avoid suspicion? Are you able to discern without judgment?

5. Why is wisdom so important when using the gift of discernment? How do we get wisdom? Do you spend time with the Lord so that you receive all the wisdom you need? Explain.

MEDITATION

The gift of distinguishing of spirits is needed today. Deliverance is needed today. Supernatural strength and aid are needed today! The term *seer*, though used in the Old Testament, technically is not used in the New. It is my view that the gift of discerning of spirits encompasses these seer perceptive capacities. Let's call them forth and welcome them for *the edifying of the Body of Christ*.

Take time to pray, calling these gifts forth first in yourself and in your church.

DREAM LANGUAGE

If there is a prophet among you, I, the Lord, shall make Myself known to him in a vision. I shall speak with him in a dream
(Numbers 12:6b).

TODAY'S DEVOTIONAL

The Lord spoke these words to Miriam and Aaron when they challenged Moses' position as God's sole spokesman to the Israelites. He went on to say that His relationship with Moses was different, because He spoke to Moses face-to-face or, literally, *"mouth-to-mouth"* (Num. 12:8). For our purpose, the pertinent point is that God clearly states here that dreams and visions are avenues He will use to speak to His prophets—in the past, the present, and the future.

While dreams are a specific portion of the prophetic ministry, they are not limited only to the prophetically gifted. Joel 2:28 says, *"It will come about after this that I will pour out My Spirit on all mankind; and your sons and daughters will prophesy, your old men will dream dreams, your young men will see visions."* This Scripture was fulfilled on the Day of Pentecost and continues to be fulfilled in our own day. It is time for the Church to return to a biblical understanding of dreams as an avenue of discerning God's voice.

Dreams are closely associated with visions. The primary difference is that dreams occur during the hours of sleep, while visions usually take place while one is fully awake or conscious. Both means of visual revelation have solid biblical precedent.

Look at the following examples of times when God spoke to heathens through dreams. Complete the following chart:

Person	Scripture	Important Result	Aspects of Dream Result
Abimelech	Gen. 20		
Laban	Gen. 31		
Midianite soldier	Judg. 7		
Pharaoh's butler and baker	Gen. 40		
Pharaoh	Gen. 41		
Nebuchadnezzar	Dan. 2		
The wise men	Matt. 2		
Pilate's wife	Matt. 27		

MEDITATION

May the Lord raise up men and women of revelation and excellence once again to give the timely counsel of God to those in authority.

Take time to pray that God would do this in your life, the life of your local church, and the Church at large.

THE SYMBOLIC LANGUAGE
OF DREAMS

*And it will come about after this that I will pour out My Spirit on
all mankind; and your sons and daughters will prophesy, your old
men will dream dreams, your young men will see visions*
(Joel 2:28).

TODAY'S DEVOTIONAL

Dreams are the language of emotions and often contain much symbolism. Generally speaking, biblical symbols can be classified into seven different categories:

1. ***Symbolic actions.*** In Ephesians 2:6 two symbolic actions—raising and seating—describe what God has done for us spiritually through Christ.

2. ***Symbolic colors.*** In prophetic dreams, specific colors often symbolize specific things.

3. ***Symbolic creatures.*** In Revelation 12:9, two symbolic creatures—the dragon and the serpent—are used to represent satan.

4. ***Symbolic directions.*** For example, "up" often means toward God or toward righteousness, while "down" means the opposite.

5. ***Symbolic names.*** One common characteristic of names in the Bible is that they often reflect the character of the individual. Names carry weight in the spiritual realm. Often their meaning is more than just symbolic.

6. ***Symbolic numbers.*** Numbers have great symbolic meaning throughout the Bible. Humanity was created on the sixth day, and God finished His work and rested on the seventh. The introduction and the interpretation of these numbers are consistent throughout the Scriptures.

7. ***Symbolic objects.*** A rock as a symbol for the Lord is quite common in the Bible (see Ps. 18:2; 1 Cor. 10:4). Many other common objects are used in a similar way, such as shields, bowls, harps, candlesticks, and so forth.

Looking at the experiences you have had thus far in dreams and visions, fill out the chart below:

	What You Know	**What You Would Like to Learn**
Symbol		
Actions		
Colors		

Creatures		
Directions		
Names		
Numbers		
Objects		

MEDITATION

One important point to remember in trying to understand dream language is that God is consistent with His symbolic language. How He speaks in Genesis is similar to how He speaks in Revelation. Throughout the Bible, the types and symbols remain very much the same. This same consistency of symbolism holds true in our own lives as well.

Can you see the use of symbolism in your dream language? Ask the Lord to give you the knowledge to interpret symbols that He can use to guide you.

WISDOM POINTS TO REMEMBER

If a prophet or a dreamer of dreams arises among you and gives you a sign or a wonder, and the sign or the wonder comes true, concerning which he spoke to you, saying, "Let us go after other gods (whom you have not known) and let us serve them," you shall not listen to the words of that prophet or that dreamer of dreams; for the Lord your God is testing you to find out if you love the Lord your God with all your heart and with all your soul (Deuteronomy 13:1-3).

TODAY'S DEVOTIONAL

Dreams and visions can be exciting and wonderful as a means of receiving insight and revelation, as long as they come from the right source. Remember that dreams and visions can arise from three places: the demonic realm, the soulish realm (our own human minds and spirits) and the Holy Spirit. In order to be effective in either giving or receiving visionary revelation, we must be able to distinguish the source. This is where the gift and discipline of discernment is so important.

Another important factor is giving careful attention to our environment. There may be occasions, for example, when we will have to remove from our homes some things that should not be there, such as certain cultic, occultic, or even soul-tie objects, before our sleep will be sweet and clean and our environment ready to receive pure revelation. We must be careful to identify and close off all potential demonic entrances to our home in Jesus' name.

Dreams and visions are wonderful, but our lives are more than just dreams and visions. Our lives are in our Master, Jesus Christ. Someone may reveal true and accurate information and still be a deceptive tool of the enemy to seduce us, draw us in by fascination, and lead us away from Christ.

1. What have you learned about understanding the source of revelation as it comes to your life? Of the three sources of revelation, what tools do you have to distinguish between them?

2. How does the discipline of discernment work in your life at present? How would you like to grow in this discipline? What will be your first steps to do so?

3. Have you looked throughout your house to be sure there are no objects that represent cults or the occult? If not, plan to do so. What can "cleaning" these things out of your home do for you and your family?

4. What are soul-tie objects? How do you identify them? Have you taken time to rid your home of these? If not, plan a time when you will.

5. How can someone "reveal true and accurate information and still be a deceptive tool of the enemy to seduce us…"? Have you experienced such a deception? How can you identify such a person?

MEDITATION

Don't get caught up simply in the glitter and glamour of revelatory seers. Examine their message. Look at their lifestyle. What is their conduct? What actions are they calling for? If they call for something that is contrary to the principles found in the written Word of God, then they are deceived, immature at best, or even false prophets, no matter how genuine their visions seem to be or how powerful the message.

Think about these cautions, and pray these into your life so that you will have wisdom in terms of revelatory gifts.

DAY 23

LEVELS OF SUPERNATURAL VISIONS

I speak the things which I have seen with My Father (John 8:38a).

TODAY'S DEVOTIONAL

How do visions "happen"?

A mental "snapshot" is a good way to describe how visions can happen. Think of how an instant camera works. The shutter opens, allowing light to enter through the lens, imprinting on the film the image that is in front of the lens. The film develops "instantly" so the image can be viewed and analyzed. In a vision, "light" from the Lord enters the "lens" of our spiritual eyes and imprints an image on the "film" of our hearts and minds. As the image "develops," we gain a better understanding of what it means. Most visions are internal in nature. An image is ingrained in our memory, and we can take it out, look at it, and study it any time we need to.

Another way to understand how visions happen is to think of each believer in Christ as a house or temple. First Corinthians 6:19 says that our bodies are temples of the Holy Spirit. Houses generally have windows that let in light. Our eyes are the windows of our souls. Sometimes Jesus, who lives in our houses, likes to look out of His windows and share with us what He sees. That is when a vision occurs—we see what Jesus sees when He looks out the windows of His houses.

1. Have you had a vision? Does the camera analogy fit for the visions you have had or ones you have heard about? Explain.

2. "An image is ingrained in our memory, and we can take it out, look at it, and study it any time we need." How does this boost the usefulness of a vision?

3. As a house or temple of the Holy Spirit, how do your eyes provide "windows" to your soul? What have they seen that has helped you in your life?

4. Is the concept new to you that Jesus looks out the windows of your soul and shares with you what He sees? What does this say about the importance of keeping your windows clean and clear?

5. How would you evaluate the average Christian's experience with visions? What needs to be done to help encourage visions in mature believers?

MEDITATION

Jesus walked by faith and always pleased His Father (see John 8:29). He discerned (saw) His Father's acts and acted accordingly. It seems that in the life of Jesus, His spiritual eyes perceived things that His mind did not always visualize. Such spiritual perceptions could be the operation of the gift of a word of wisdom, word of knowledge, discerning of spirits, the gift of faith or even the gift of prophecy. Often, the higher the level of spiritual vision, the higher the dimension of spiritual sight occurs. I, like you, want to follow Jesus' example and do what we see the Father doing.

How much do you walk by faith like Jesus did? Do you reflect His ability to perceive what His Father was doing both by His spiritual eyes and His mind? How can you become more like Him in these areas?

VISIONS, DREAMS, AND MESSAGES

*If there is a prophet among you, I, the Lord, shall make Myself
known to him in a vision. I shall speak with him in a dream*
(Numbers 12:6b).

TODAY'S DEVOTIONAL

The following are brief descriptions of different ways we receive messages.

A *pictorial vision* is an image revealed in a picture, which can also be identified and described in terms of pictures. They are Holy Spirit visual aids! Symbols may or may not be involved.

A *panoramic vision* is one in which a person sees a pictorial vision, not in snapshot form, but in motion in his or her mind.

A *dream* is a visionary revelation from the Holy Spirit that one receives while asleep. Supernatural dreams can occur in any level of sleep: light rest, regular sleep, deep sleep, or even in a trance state.

Audible messages in the spiritual realm can involve people speaking words or objects making sounds. We can perceive such messages inside of us by our inner ears, or outside of us by our physical ears.

An *appearance or apparition* is different from a pictorial vision in that it is an actual—perhaps tangible and audible— visitation occurring outside of the person.

More than just a spiritual vision, a *divine sight* is an actual disclosing of a supernatural event. It is like an appearance or apparition in that it is an actual occurrence outside of the person or persons experiencing it. However, it is not of a being, but an object or activity.

Use the following chart to check your understanding of the different ways we receive messages

Method	Your Definition	Your Experience
Pictorial vision		
Panoramic vision		
Dream		
Audible message		
Appearance or Apparition		
Divine sight		

MEDITATION

God is not the author of doubt, confusion, or fear. When God releases His message to us, even through one of His angels, we should sense purity and holiness, a reverence to the Lord, and openness, because His messengers have nothing to hide. The Spirit of God is not afraid to be tested. We should never fear offending God by testing the spirits. On the contrary, God is honored when we do, because He told us in His Word to do so (see 1 John 4:1-3).

Do you have doubts, confusion, or fears about messages you have received? How do you test the spirits?

OPEN HEAVEN

Now it came about in the thirtieth year, on the fifth day of the fourth month, while I was by the river Chebar among the exiles, the heavens were opened and I saw visions of God (Ezekiel 1:1).

TODAY'S DEVOTIONAL

An open Heaven is a vision where a hole seems to appear in the immediate sky, the celestial realm is disclosed, and heavenly sights of God become seeable. The term *open Heaven* originated in historic revivals to describe those times when the manifested presence of God seemed to come down in a tangible manner as conviction of sin, conversions, and healings took place. We are now moving from an era of prophetic renewal into a new epoch of the Holy Spirit. We are crossing a threshold into a period of apostolic open Heavens for whole cities and regions to be visited by the presence of the Almighty.

Examples of an open Heaven are found throughout the Scriptures. Here are four instances:

- Ezekiel states that *"the heavens were opened."* He then describes a great cloud sent by God to protect Ezekiel from His brightness. Then he sees flashing lightning, brilliant light, living creatures, and other details (see Ezek. 1:1-4).

- At Jesus' baptism, the *"heavens were opened"* and the Holy Spirit descended upon Him in the form of a dove. Then the Father spoke audibly (see Matt. 3:16-17).

- As Stephen was being stoned for preaching the Gospel, he looked up into Heaven and saw *"the sky loosened and the clouds rolled back"* and Jesus standing to receive him (see Acts 7:55-56).

- The apostle John, while meditating on the Lord's day, heard a voice and saw *"a door opened in heaven."* He was then shown the One who sits upon the throne, and he received many detailed messages from the Lord (see Rev. 4).

These open Heaven experiences in the Scriptures show us that such encounters are part of God's plan.

1. Does an open Heaven seem to be a common occurrence or one that is rare? Explain your answer.

2. The results of an open Heaven are tangible. What are some of these? Why are tangible results like these important for the legitimacy of the vision?

3. At Jesus' baptism, what were the tangible results of the open Heaven?

4. When Stephen was being stoned, what tangible results might have occurred?

5. With the one-of-a-kind revelation that John received when the door opened in Heaven, what tangible results have come about?

MEDITATION

There are examples of humble, authentic vessels in our day who are receiving open Heavens and other levels of revelatory activity in their lives. These experiences are on the increase. As the last days unfold, such encounters will only multiply!

Has this been part of your experience? Why or why not?

DAY 26

HEAVENLY VISITATION

I know a man in Christ who fourteen years ago—whether in the body
I do not know, or out of the body I do not know, God knows—such a
man was caught up to the third heaven (2 Corinthians 12:2).

TODAY'S DEVOTIONAL

The Bible refers to three heavens:

1. The lowest heaven, the atmospheric sky that encircles the earth (see Matt. 16:1-3).

2. The second heaven, the stellar heaven that is called outer space, where the sun, moon, stars, and planets reside (see Gen. 1:16-17).

3. The third Heaven, which is the highest one, and the center around which all realms revolve, is Paradise, the abode of God and His angels and saints (see Ps. 11:4; Neh. 9:6).

A heavenly visitation is like an out-of-body experience, except that the person's spirit leaves the earth realm, passes through the second heaven, and goes to the third Heaven. This can occur while the person is praying, while in a trance or a deep sleep from the Lord, or at death.

In the same way that people can visit the third Heaven by having an out-of-body experience, they can also visit the various regions of hell. If they are sinners, they approach hell by descending—in death or a near-death experience or in a supernatural vision—and are shown where they are destined to spend eternity unless they repent and accept Jesus Christ as their personal Lord and Savior. Then they are brought back to earth into their bodies by the mercy of God.

1. A Scripture is listed as a reference for each of the three heavens. Research these in your Bible and note the distinctions. Use a concordance and find other references as well.

2. Have you ever had a heavenly visitation? Do you know someone who has? Read Second Corinthians 12 about Paul's experience. What was the message to Paul? How did he use the experience to teach the Corinthian church?

3. Have you heard or read of people, both Christian and non-Christian, who have had near-death experiences that allowed them to see Heaven or hell? How does God want to use these experiences for them personally? Is there a message that goes beyond the person who has experienced it? If so, what?

4. Does God mean to frighten non-Christians by allowing them to visit hell? Why does He use this type of experience?

5. Why would God allow Christians to visit hell? How might He use such an experience in the life of a believer?

MEDITATION

I believe heavenly visitations have occurred not only in the Bible, but also throughout history. Such experiences will increase as true apostolic ministry emerges in these last days. Join me and express your desire to step into all that our Father God has prepared for you.

Take some time to tell God about your desire to move into everything He has planned for your life.

THE ECSTATIC REALMS
OF THE SPIRIT

On the next day, as they were on their way and approaching the city, Peter went up on the house-top about the sixth hour to pray. But he became hungry and was desiring to eat; but while they were making preparations, he fell into a trance (Acts 10:9-10).

TODAY'S DEVOTIONAL

I decided to study the subject of supernatural encounters in depth and spend time around godly people who had a lot more experience with trances and out-of-body experiences than I did. What I learned is that these kinds of phenomena originated with God; satan merely usurped and corrupted them as he did everything else. *When properly understood and when initiated by the Spirit of God, a trance is an exciting, fabulous, wonderful thing—another powerful visionary experience that brings a person into the heavenly realm.* The *key* is that such an experience *must* be initiated by the Holy Spirit *only*.

It must *never* be self-induced.

A trance brings us into the "ecstatic" realm of the Spirit. Literally, an *ecstatic trance* is a displacement of the mind, a bewilderment that is commonly accompanied by amazement or astonishment. It is a distraction, especially one resulting from great religious fervor, and which often includes feelings of great joy, rapture, and delight that arrest the whole mind.

According to Vine's Expository Dictionary, *ekstasis* refers to "any displacement, and especially, with reference to the mind, of that alteration of the normal condition by which the person is thrown into a state of surprise or fear or both; or again, in which a person is so transported out of his natural state that he falls into a trance."

1. Have you experienced trances or out-of-body experiences? Do you personally know someone who has? If you know of someone, take time to talk with him or her about the experiences and the effect they have had.

2. How has satan corrupted trances and out-of-body experiences from what you have seen and heard of them? What important criteria assure us as to whether the ecstatic experience is from God or not?

3. The ecstatic realm of a trance can be described as "a displacement of the mind." What do you think this means? Why would God want us to experience this?

4. If a trance often results from great religious fervor, why would God want to distract us and bring us into "feelings of great joy, rapture, and delight"? Why would He want to "arrest the whole mind"?

5. What is your opinion of the ecstatic realm of the Spirit as you understand it thus far? Does fear or excitement characterize your answer? What might you do to understand this dimension to a greater level?

MEDITATION

In a trance, one can be shocked, amazed, and joyfully "caught up" in one's emotions due to the wondrous activity of the Holy Spirit. In a higher level of trance, one's natural bodily functions are temporarily "put on pause," and the person is caught up in the Spirit (whether in the body or out of the body is not the primary issue), and sees, hears, feels, tastes, touches, or even smells the presence of the Lord in an otherworldly or heavenly sort of way.

Does this sound like something you would like to experience to a greater degree than you have thus far? If so, plan time with the Lord regularly where you do not have to hurry, but can linger to receive more of His ecstatic experiences.

CAUGHT UP IN THE SPIRIT

After these things I looked, and behold, a door standing open in heaven, and the first voice which I had heard, like the sound of a trumpet speaking with me, said, "Come up here, and I will show you what must take place after these things." Immediately I was in the Spirit; and behold, a throne was standing in heaven, and One sitting on the throne (Revelation 4:1-2).

TODAY'S DEVOTIONAL

The Bible contains numerous instances of people undergoing possible trance-like experiences, even though the word *trance*, or *ekstasis*, is not used.

The prophet Ezekiel described many of his visionary experiences as him being "lifted up" by the Spirit, which can also describe a trance-like condition:

The Spirit lifted me up and took me away... (Ezekiel 3:14).

The Spirit lifted me up between earth and heaven and brought me in the visions of God to Jerusalem... (Ezekiel 8:3).

And the Spirit lifted me up and brought me in a vision by the Spirit of God to the exiles in Chaldea (Ezekiel 11:24).

*And the Spirit lifted me up and brought me into the inner court; and
behold, the glory of the Lord filled the house* (Ezekiel 43:5).

It is important to note here that one does not have to be in a trance to "be
in the Spirit." However, one who has experienced a trance may be properly
said to have been "in the Spirit."

God does nothing without a purpose. His purpose in imparting visionary
revelation, whether through a trance or any other means, is not just to give
us an "experience," but that we might see and know *Him*.

Using the four examples from Ezekiel, read the texts surrounding the verses
and fill in the chart below.

Scripture Reference	Setting or Situation	Main Points of the Vision Ezekiel Received
Ezekiel 3:14		
Ezekiel 8:3		
Ezekiel 11:24		
Ezekiel 43:5		

1. From the information in your chart, draw conclusions as to why God spoke to Ezekiel using this method. Are there situations in your life when you could use a vision to give you direction or information to move forward?

2. What does it mean to "be in the Spirit"? Does this describe a state of being, an attitude, or a mentality? Is it figurative or literal? Explain your answers.

3. Why can you be "in the Spirit," but not be in a trance; and yet, if you are properly in a trance, you are "in the Spirit"? Explain the difference.

4. What is the purpose of trances and visions? Why does God use these things in our lives? Have you been in a trance or vision? Do you know someone who has? What have been the results of such experiences?

MEDITATION

We should not desire or seek visionary experiences for their own sake, but for how they can help us draw closer in deeper intimacy with our Lord. Lest we think that supernatural trances were limited to biblical days, I want to share that trances from the Holy Spirit can be and are being experienced by "ordinary" Christians today.

As an "ordinary" Christian, do you crave deeper intimacy with the Lord?

EXAMPLES OF VISIONARY REVELATION

*And the spirit lifted me up and brought me in a vision by the spirit
of God to the exiles in Chaldea. So the vision that I had seen left me*
(Ezekiel 11:24).

TODAY'S DEVOTIONAL

Lest we think that supernatural trances were limited to biblical days, there are testimonies of such experiences that date more closely to our own day.

Dr. Mahesh Chavda tells how he took the final step to receive Christ as his Savior and Lord, becoming the first in his family to embrace Christ. Mahesh's account is an incredibly beautiful and accurate description of how the Holy Spirit brings a person into contact with the love and grace of God. Through the years since that night, Mahesh has been used mightily by God in a world-wide ministry of evangelism, healing, and other miracles.

The life and ministry of Kenneth E. Hagin were profoundly influenced by his visions of Jesus. Dr. Hagin describes how the gifts of the Spirit and, par-ticularly, the gift of discerning of spirits, were in operation in him *only* when he was in the realm of the Spirit. In other words, it was not at his choice or volition, but only when he was, in his words, "in the anointing."

Maria Woodworth-Etter was a powerful evangelist and revival leader of the late nineteenth and early twentieth centuries. Wherever she went, the power of God fell: people were slain in the Spirit, saw visions, received rev-elation, and were converted by the thousands.

These three people had profound experiences in visionary revelation. Use the chart below to trace their experiences. (Refer back to Chapter Nine of *The Seer* for more information on each person.)

	Dr. Mahesh Chavda	Kenneth E. Hagin	Maria Woodworth-Etter
Condition Prior			
Character of God			
Results of the Trance Revealed Through the Person's Life and the World He/ She Touched			

Studying your chart, can you see why God used trances to speak to these people and change their lives? Do you think He desires to do the same for you?

MEDITATION

Biblically and historically, the trance has been a legitimate method God has sometimes used to impart visionary revelation, and it continues to be so today. Ultimately, God's desire is to bring us close to Himself and impart His will and His ways to us, so that we can minister to others in wisdom because we have spent time standing in the council of God.

God can impart His will and His ways to us in many different ways. Why, then, do you think He uses trances to communicate to us?

STANDING IN THE COUNCIL OF GOD

But who has stood in the council of the Lord, that he should see
and hear His word? Who has given heed to His word and listened?
(Jeremiah 23:18)

TODAY'S DEVOTIONAL

The Lord gives vision to those who, in the words of Jeremiah, have *"stood in the council of the Lord"*:

> But if they had stood in My council, then they would have announced
> My words to My people, and would have turned them back from their
> evil way and from the evil of their deeds (Jeremiah 23:22).

What does it mean to "stand in the council of the Lord"? Jeremiah speaks of seeing, hearing, giving heed to, and listening to the Word of God. Habakkuk refers to seeing an oracle and describes himself as a guard on the rampart keeping watch to see what the Lord will speak to him.

In the prophetic realm, to stand in the council of God means both to see and to hear the Word of God. But for what purpose? Jeremiah 23:22 gives the answer: to announce God's Word to God's people in order to "[turn] *them back from their evil way and from the evil of their deeds."* In other words, the purpose of standing in the council of God is to produce fruit in the lives of

God's people: the fruit of holiness, repentance, the fear of the Lord, and a godly lifestyle.

1. What does the "council of the Lord" mean to you? Have you ever stood there?

2. Take the four components of the Jeremiah passage and explain how these work in your life. Do they all need to be present each time? Explain.

    *   Seeing—

    *   Hearing—

    *   Giving heed to—

    *   Listening to the Word—

3. How do seeing and hearing combine to bring obedience to the Word of God? Have they done so in your experience?

4. Do you think that every time someone stands in the council of God, fruit automatically appears in the lives of God's people? Why or why not? What principle do you see here?

5. Look at the four fruits mentioned above. Think about your experience in seeing and hearing the Word of God. Do these fruits easily come forth from your life? Do you share these with others?

    *   Holiness—

    *   Repentance—

    *   The fear of the Lord—

    *   Godly lifestyle—

MEDITATION

How can anyone "see" what the Lord "speaks"? The simplest answer is that God has more than one way of speaking. His speech is not limited to audible words or, indeed, to words of any kind.

Think about your answers to these questions: what has your experience been—is it easier to hear or see? Do you understand more clearly by sight or sound?

IN CLOSE DELIBERATION

Also we have obtained an inheritance, having been predestined according to His purpose who works all things after the counsel of His will (Ephesians 1:11).

TODAY'S DEVOTIONAL

The Hebrew word for "council" in Jeremiah 23:18 is *cowd*, which means "a session," or "a company of persons in close deliberation." It implies intimacy, as in secret consultation. By comparison, our English word *council* refers to a group of people called together for discussion or advice.

Just as there are earthly councils of men and women that come together to discuss and advise, there is also a council that takes place in Heaven, presided over by Almighty God, where we can hear and receive the *counsel* of the Lord—the wisdom and vision and direction that derive from the council of God. By His sovereign and personal invitation, we can enter God's "hearing room" to listen to the deliberation of His council so as to be able to announce His Word on an issue.

The Lord has revelation—secrets, if you will—that He wants to open up to us. One of the highest characteristics of a prophetic person is that he or she is supposed to be a trusted friend of God. God has secrets, and He is looking for some friends to share His counsel with. It is an open invitation; we *all* can be friends of God.

1. Compare the Hebrew meaning of *cowd* with our English word *council*. How does it differ or become more distinct?

2. The intimacy—as in a "secret consultation"—aspect of the Hebrew word infers what about the council of God? What would be the purpose of His counsel being in secret?

3. What does Ephesians 1:11 mean by the *"counsel of His will"*? Who is at the council? Who gives the wisdom and direction from this council? How does the process of listening to the deliberation of His council help us?

4. What is the purpose of the council of God? What are we supposed to do after we have heard the counsel of His will?

5. Have you ever thought of God telling you His secrets? Have you ever felt you have heard something that was not to be revealed until a later time or, perhaps, not at all? To receive a "secret" from God, what disciplines do you need to exercise regularly?

MEDITATION

God's prophetic people are to be His friends. They are to be the ones in whom He can entrust His word, His message, and His revelation, often speaking to them beforehand about what He is going to do.

Why do you need to know what God says ahead of the rest of the world? What purpose would this serve? Ask the Lord to share more with you so you can know what is and what will be.

GOD SPEAKS BEFORE HE ACTS

Surely the Lord God does nothing unless He reveals His secret counsel to His servants the prophets (Amos 3:7).

TODAY'S DEVOTION

Why does God speak to His servants the prophets before He acts? Is God not sovereign? Can He not do whatever He wants to do without informing any of us? Absolutely, but God has chosen to work this way because at Creation He gave the stewardship of this earth to humanity. He established a chain of command, so to speak. God has never rescinded His original decree giving humankind dominion over the earth. That is why He says, in effect, "Before I do anything, I will let someone—My friends—know what I am about to do."

God always acts with purpose. He reveals His secret counsel to us because we are His friends, but He also reveals it in order to get a job done—to accomplish His will.

As believers, we *are* God's friends—just as we are co-heirs with Christ—but our friendship with God is characterized by love as well as by faithful obedience and service. We find our identity not in who we are or what our title is, but in Christ and in servanthood. Who we are is not determined by what we do, but to whom we belong. If we are "in Christ," our lives are in Him. He *is* our life.

1. How does our job description as stewards of the earth tie into the way in which God speaks to us before He acts? How are we capable of making changes, setting course corrections, and adjusting the way we operate due to pre-knowledge?

2. Have you ever heard God speak something to you before it happened, or do you know of someone who has experienced this? When God speaks this way, how are we to act upon what is spoken? Are we to alert people? Are we to do something different than we have been doing?

3. Because God always acts with purpose, why do we disavow His sovereignty when we credit circumstances to "coincidence" and "luck"? Why do we blame circumstances for so much of our misfortune? Why don't we readily ask God for understanding regarding how He is using the circumstances to accomplish His will?

4. Looking at your answers to No. 3, how would you tell an unbeliever these things? How should you address the sovereignty of God so that it might gain a hearing and not close the person off?

5. How is your friendship with God characterized—by love, faithful obedience, and service? If you are receiving the counsel of God, do you need to remain humble and ready to do what it takes to serve as needed? How do you intend to do this?

MEDITATION

There are two sides to the coin of standing in the council of God. On one side is the sovereignty of God, and on the other, the initiative of people. One of the amazing truths of the Bible is that the announced intention and counsel of God can be altered by our intercession!

Where are you in terms of the two sides of the council of God? Are you able to merge the sovereignty of God and the initiative you have in your mind? In your heart? In your daily walk? Explain.

BEING THERE

Thus says the Lord of hosts, "If you will walk in My ways and if you will perform My service, then you will also govern My house and also have charge of My courts, and I will grant you free access among these who are standing here" (Zechariah 3:7).

TODAY'S DEVOTIONAL

An experience of "being there" in the council of God is significant for several reasons. First of all, it is an honor when God grants this kind of audience. Second, the more subjective the experience, the greater the possibility of pure revelation. Finally, our own thoughts are out of the process, and reception in the spirit realm is in clearer focus.

These are important factors to consider because they help us establish the proper mind-set for walking in that realm. After all, if God grants us the privilege of such a supernatural encounter as standing in His council, we had better know how to act when we are there. God gives us instruction for this in His Word.

Zechariah 3:7 contains God's conditions for standing in His council: *"walk in My ways and…perform My service."* This involves progressive steps of faithfulness. If we do those things, God promises that we will govern His house, have charge of His courts, and have free access to those who are standing there.

There are three important guidelines to help protect us from error during supernatural encounters:

1. Avoid unhealthy familiarity and fascination with their personage.

2. Watch out for the issue of "commanding angels" in spiritual warfare encounters.

3. Be careful to use proper discernment in the distinction between true angelic encounters and demonic counterfeits.

Following God's conditions for entering His council—walking in His ways and performing His service—as well as following these three guidelines for how to avoid error will position us to be among those who "stand there."

The significance of being in the council of God is threefold (see Zech. 3:7b). Look at these and give input on each using the following chart:

Attribute	Significance
The mind-set this helps me establish.	
The honor to be granted an audience.	
The more subjective the experience, the greater the possibility of pure revelation.	
The reception in the spirit realm is in clearer focus.	

1. How would you act if God granted you to stand before His throne at this very moment? Would you know what to say? What to do? How to follow heavenly protocol?

2. Look at the promises we can look forward to if we perform His service in progressive steps of faithfulness. Of these—governing His house, having charge of His courts, and having free access to those who are standing there—which is most exciting and why? Which are you most unsure of? Why?

3. The three guidelines to help protect us from error during supernatural encounters show what traps we need to avoid. Of these three, which would be the trap that might ensnare you the most easily? Why?

4. How do you intend to seek the counsel of God? What will put you in a position to be in the council of God and receive its benefits or promises?

MEDITATION

How then should we walk among those who are standing by in the council of the Lord? What should be our demeanor in His presence? The key—the only acceptable posture—is a spirit of humility in the holy fear of the Lord.

How do you enter the presence of God? Does humility accompany your communion?

DAY 34

GIVING OURSELVES TO THE PROCESS

*"For I know the plans that I have for you," declares the Lord, "plans
for welfare and not for calamity to give you a future and a hope"*
(Jeremiah 29:11).

TODAY'S DEVOTIONAL

God is looking for people to share His counsel with. He is looking for people who have a passionate desire for Him. If our passion is for the Lord Himself—not visions or prophecies or manifestations or anything else like that for their own sake—then He will reveal Himself to us in any number of ways. God rewards all who seek Him with their whole hearts.

Along with our passionate seeking, we must learn how to balance between the *objective* and the *subjective* experience. An objective experience is not determined by impressions, feelings, inner vision, or voices, but is based upon convictions concerning God's character—His faithfulness to keep His promises. A subjective experience, on the other hand, is the cry of the soul for a clearer awareness of God, the passionate desire for a distinct hearing of His voice.

Whatever else we do, we must maintain our balance between the subjective and the objective. We must not become so fixated on prophetic or visionary revelation that we throw away the Bible. Let us keep our objectivity. The revelatory word is not a competitor with the written Word, but a complement to it and *always* subordinate to it. The written Word of God is the unwavering standard by which *all* revelatory word *must* be measured.

1. Jeremiah 29:11 tells us that God has only good plans for us. Is this easy for you to believe when you look at challenges you face in your life? Read verses 12 and 13 of the same chapter and meditate on the conditions for this kind of blessing.

2. When we are passionate to be with God, He will reveal Himself to us in any number of ways. What are some of the ways that God reveals Himself? What ones have you experienced?

3. God rewards all who seek Him with their whole hearts. What kind of rewards does God give us? What rewards have you received from the Lord?

4. Explain the balance between the objective and subjective experience. What are the limitations of each? What are the benefits?

5. How do the revelatory word and the written Word of God work together? Which is greater? Why?

MEDITATION

Depending on their background and the teaching they have received in their churches, Christians respond to the phenomena of mystical experiences in different ways. Some are suspicious, while others condemn and reject them outright. There are still others, however, who embrace these experiences, sometimes cautiously at first, and then with increasing enthusiasm.

What has been your experience as to how Christians respond to mystical experiences? How have you embraced these experiences? Have you been cautious or enthusiastic?

Think about how the Lord wants you to respond.

HIDDEN STREAMS
OF THE PROPHETIC

But we all, **with unveiled face, beholding as in a mirror the glory of the Lord,** *are being transformed into the same image from glory to glory, just as from the Lord, the Spirit* (2 Corinthians 3:18).

TODAY'S DEVOTIONAL

I have found that the most direct road to greater intimacy with God has come through the practice or discipline of an almost lost art—something called contemplative prayer.

In contemplative prayer, we as Christians do not primarily relate to God as the One who sits upon His throne in Heaven, but through the reality of our new birth in Christ, connecting with Him as the One who has taken up residence inside us. We each have a throne in our hearts where He dwells in a very personal way. In contrast, in intercessory prayer, we approach God who is seated on His throne in Heaven. We then, as priestly believers, make our appeal, stand in the gap, and remind God of His Word.

The phrase *communion with God* is commonly understood to mean coming into fellowship with God through the power of the Holy Spirit in Jesus Christ, who dwells in the born-again believer. Communion with God is a way of fellowshipping with the Holy Spirit by learning to quiet the distractions of our souls and of the world, calming the inner chaos and noise from outside that tends to vie so strongly for our attention. We come into the heart or "center" of our being, where God dwells through the Holy Spirit, who has taken up residence there.

1. Have you engaged in contemplative prayer? On a regular basis? What does the term *contemplative prayer* mean to you?

2. Think through the difference between intercessory prayer and contemplative prayer. How would you explain the difference to someone who is new in the prayer arena?

3. How does Second Corinthians 3:18 describe our journey of maturity? How does contemplative prayer help make the transformation?

4. Evaluate your communion with God. Do you fellowship regularly through the power of the Holy Spirit in Jesus Christ? What is your fellowship with the Holy Spirit like—intimate and full or staid and shallow? What can you do to grow in this area?

5. Describe the "center" of your being. How does God dwell there? Why does God choose to take up residence within you?

MEDITATION

Christians tend to be divided into two camps. One camp is the "going and doing" camp, always going, always busy at the work, doing missions, serving the poor, and preaching the Gospel. The other camp is the "contemplative" camp, the meditative, quiet, and reflective ones who so love the "interior castle" that they just want to dwell there and stay there all the time. The *inner* life prepares us for the *outer* life; both are necessary. One of the lessons we must learn is to build a bridge between the two.

Think about where you are in terms of these two camps. How do you need to bridge between the two?

DAY 36

LISTEN, WATCH, WAIT

Now therefore, O sons, listen to me, for blessed are they who keep my ways. Heed instruction and be wise, and do not neglect it. Blessed is the man who listens to me, watching daily at my gates, waiting at my doorposts. For he who finds me finds life and obtains favor from the Lord. But he who sins against me injures himself; all those who hate me love death (Proverbs 8:32-36).

TODAY'S DEVOTIONAL

Communal prayer is not *doing* something as much as it is *being with* Someone, continuing in prayer with this Someone until we become the *expression* of Him in the world *around us.*

The eighth chapter of Proverbs provides three important principles related to contemplative prayer. Verse 34 contains the three principles: *listens, watching,* and *waiting.* All three of these verbs are in the continuous passive tense in the Hebrew, meaning they are ongoing rather than momentary. Blessed are those who listen and keep on listening, who watch and keep on watching, and who wait and keep on waiting.

Contemplative prayer is an exercise in letting go of the control of our own lives and no longer leaning on the props of the false self. It is a kind of communion intended to increase our intimacy with God and our awareness of His presence. It is a step of submission where we place our being at God's disposal as we request His work of purification. In Christ Jesus, we open ourselves up to the Holy Spirit to get in touch with the true self and to facilitate an abiding state of union with God.

1. Explain communal prayer as you would to a person new to prayer. How does it bring one closer to God? How does it help the person become more of the expression of God to the world?

2. What is your experience in communal prayer? Have you found it to be something that you seek to do often? Are your experiences rewarding and full? Have you found that it has changed you more and more into the image of God?

3. Look at the three principles in Proverbs 8:32-36. Of listening, watching, and waiting, which is easiest for you to do and why? Which is most difficult and why? What might you do to increase your capacity to listen, watch, and wait?

4. How does someone "let go" of his or her own life? What is the process one goes through to quit leaning on the props of false self? Have you experienced it to some degree? Explain.

5. How does submission enter into our communion? What impact does it have? Why is it a prerequisite to purification? Do you find that you embrace or endure submission? Why?

MEDITATION

To *contemplate* means "to gaze at intently, to think about intently, to study, to expect or to intend, to meditate, to muse." The word *muse* means "to think about, or to consider deeply, to meditate." To *meditate* means "to plan, intend, to think deeply, to reflect upon." The word *reflect* means "to throw back light, heat, or sound, to give back an image as in a mirror, to bring back or come back as a consequence or as reflected glory."

Take time to muse, meditate, and reflect. Give yourself a spiritual retreat, even if only for a part of a day, and bring yourself into balance.

THE GOAL OF OUR JOURNEY

Fixing our eyes on Jesus, the author and perfecter of faith, who for the joy set before Him endured the cross, despising the shame, and has sat down at the right hand of the throne of God (Hebrews 12:2).

TODAY'S DEVOTIONAL

As we grow accustomed to the unifying grace of recollection, we are ushered into the second phase of contemplative prayer called "the center of quiet" or the prayer of quiet. Through recollection we have put away all obstacles of the heart, all distractions of the mind, and all vacillations of the will. Divine graces of love and adoration wash over us like ocean waves, and at the center of our beings, we are hushed. There is a stillness, to be sure, but it is a listening stillness. Something deep inside of us has been awakened and brought to attention, and our spirits now are on tiptoe—alert and listening. Then out comes an inward steady gaze of the heart, sometimes called "beholding the Lord."

Another phase of contemplative prayer is spiritual ecstasy. In that place of quiet detachment from the reality around us, illumination—the spirit of revelation—is granted and we are filled with God's pictures, God's thoughts, and God's heart. Spiritual ecstasy is not an activity or undertaking that we do, but a work that God does in us. Ecstasy is contemplative prayer taken to the nth degree.

Once we get to know these ways of Christ in us—the glory of God Himself living and dwelling in our beings—and we come into union and fellowship with Him who now has taken up residence upon the throne of our lives, we will realize suddenly that we were created for that very thing.

1. What is a "prayer of quiet" in your experience? Do you use this type of prayer in your devotional disciplines? How does it strengthen the unifying grace of recollection?

2. What does recollection do for the heart? What does it remove? What does it leave room for?

3. What does it mean to "behold the Lord"? Have you beheld Him? Does it seem ironic to you that you gaze inward and not outward to behold God?

4. How are contemplative prayer and spiritual ecstasy linked? Do you see why the church fathers wanted to get away in order to use these in their relationship with God? How can you come into contemplative prayer and spiritual ecstasy in today's hustle-and-bustle world?

5. What is the goal of your journey? How do you know you are moving in the right direction? What signs are there in your life?

6. How does it feel to know you were created for God to reside within you? How can you be sure He has taken up residence on your throne?

MEDITATION

Isn't God the goal of our passionate pursuit? He is the stream of living water that makes my heart glad! Let us pursue the "hidden streams" of the prophetic and grow in greater intimacy with the lover of our souls. He is the goal of our journey.

Is your journey steadily pulling you to God? What course corrections do you want to make on your journey?

THE KEY OF INTIMACY
TO OPEN HEAVENS

After being baptized, Jesus came up immediately from the water; and behold, the heavens were opened, and He saw the Spirit of God descending as a dove and lighting on Him (Matthew 3:16).

TODAY'S DEVOTIONAL

The baptism of Jesus was the occasion of another open Heaven event. Matthew 3:13-17 indicates that John as well as Jesus saw the Heavens open and the Spirit descend as a dove, and he heard the voice from Heaven. This open Heaven experience imparted to John information he would not have known any other way. The Spirit descending and remaining was the prophetic sign that enabled John to recognize the Son of God and to know that this man was different from any other man who had ever been born of woman.

How we need for the Heavens to open again, not just for one moment, but permanently! So many of us are famished for the bread of the Spirit; let us call out for Him to come down—not just to alight, but to remain, a manifested habitation of the Lord in our midst!

What kind of person might have Heaven open above them? It would have to be someone who became radically undone in the Lord, someone who was absolutely "wasted" on Jesus. Whenever Heaven opens over individuals, they carry that open Heaven with them wherever they go, and they become climate-changers. They become history makers.

1. Meditate on the baptism of Jesus. Read Matthew 3:13-17. How was John's life changed by the experience?

2. Read Genesis 28:11-19. Think about the dream Jacob had when he was in such desperate circumstances. In what ways did this dream change Jacob's life?

3. Have you had Heaven open before you? If not, do you know someone who has experienced this? Is there a certain qualification a person needs before experiencing such a vision? Why or why not?

4. What have been the results for those who have had Heaven open over them? Are there only good results? What kind of life change does God expect?

5. Why does God let us have these open Heaven experiences? Of what use are they? What power can they bring to your life?

MEDITATION

God is looking for candidates in this generation who will be seated with Christ in the heavenly places and call forth God's destiny and design into the earth realm. It has happened before in all historic awakenings. I am talking about ordinary folks who surrendered to an extraordinary God. I am talking about people like Charles Finney and Evan Roberts.

Are you one of these candidates? If not, do you want to become one? Surrender to your extraordinary God!

DAY 39

A DOOR IN HEAVEN

After these things I looked, and behold, a door standing open in heaven, and the first voice which I had heard, like the sound of a trumpet speaking with me, said, "Come up here, and I will show you what must take place after these things"(Revelation 4:1).

TODAY'S DEVOTIONAL

John the Beloved received an open Heaven through which he saw the Lord. His experience came near the end of a long life of faithful and obedient service to Christ and His Church. Once we see Him—once He really reveals Himself to us—we will be completely undone. When we see the One who is standing at the top of the ladder, we will be radically, totally wasted for Him! That is my goal—to see Him, to know Him, to become like Him—to become a *gate* for the sake of others.

Jacob saw One standing at the top of the ladder; John saw One sitting on the throne. This John—John the Beloved—is the same John who laid his head upon the chest of Yeshua the Messiah at the Last Supper; who heard the very pounding of the heartbeat of God; who heard the very breath of the Master, both in the natural and in the spirit realm as the *pneuma* or wind of the Holy Spirit. This John is the one known as "the disciple whom Jesus loved." John the Beloved is the only disciple mentioned by name who stayed with Jesus, even to the Cross, after all the others had fled.

1. What was John doing when he received the revelation we have as our last book in the Bible? His revelation was very detailed and very long. What do you think sustained him to receive all of the vision?

2. Are you in such a place of intimacy in your life that God could give you as intense a revelation as John? Why or why not? What is needed to become this open? What in John's history made him this available for God's ultimate revelation? What is your history?

3. How does one hear the "pounding of the heartbeat of God"? How is it possible to hear "the very breath of the Master"?

4. Of John the Baptist, Jacob, and John the Revelator, who do you most identify with and why? Whose experience of an open door to Heaven do you most relate to?

5. If you had been John, what would have been your reaction to seeing such an array of pictures, creatures, and experiences? How would the experience change your life?

MEDITATION

Many believers are just after intimacy, while many others are after souls. It is not an either/or proposition. There is a bridge between them both, a "leakage" between open Heavens. A powerful vision of the Almighty produces a passion for reaching souls. Intimacy eventually leads to evangelism.

What kind of "leakage" are you experiencing currently? Do you have enough "water" to leak? Do you affect those around you?

DAY 40

OPEN THE DOOR

*Behold, I stand at the door and knock; if anyone hears My voice and
opens the door, I will come in to him and will dine with him,
and he with Me* (Revelation 3:20).

TODAY'S DEVOTIONAL

In Revelation 4:1, John says, *"After these things I looked, and behold, a door standing open in heaven…."* After what things? Since the division of the Bible into chapters and verses was made long after it was written, it is only logical to look in the previous chapter to see what John was referring to. Take the time now to read Revelation chapters 2 and 3 to understand the context.

In Revelation 3:20, whose door is Jesus standing before? This is a prophetic apostolic message, a heavenly message sent to a church in a city. It is not a word written just to an individual. Certainly, the invitation Jesus gives here applies to individuals, so it is quite appropriate to use this verse in evangelism, as is so often done. Contextually, however, the word is for a group, a corporate body. Revelation 3:20 is an apostolic word about the voice of the Holy Spirit standing in front of a city.

Intimacy is the key that unlocks open Heavens over entire cities. It has happened before, and it can happen again. I firmly believe that it *will* happen again. Jesus did not stop knocking after Revelation 3:20 was written. He has been knocking for 2,000-plus years. Today, He stands at the doors of twenty-first-century cities, asking, "Who will answer?"

1. How have you traditionally viewed Revelation 3:20's picture of Christ at the door? Does the context of this verse change the way you see it?

2. When Revelation 4:1 describes an open door, does it mean that He has opened the door or that we have opened it? What does it take to open a door of Heaven?

3. Do you see yourself as a person who stands in the gate of a city to hear the invitation of Jesus? Why or why not? Do you think God wants you to become a door opener? In what ways?

4. How can your local church be a city-changer? How should you pray for the corporate Body of Christ in your city?

5. What will you do? Will you ignore the knock until He goes away? Or will you open the door and say, like Joshua, *"As for me and my house, we will serve the Lord"*? (Josh. 24:15).

MEDITATION

So what is the purpose of *the seer*? Like all true seers of old, we must reach high. We must look heavenward. We must think otherly. We must passionately pursue the God of visitation. May the key of intimacy be put in the door of our hearts, families, congregations, cities, and nations. May the prophetic power of visions, dreams, and open Heavens increase. Because the seer's goal is to reveal the Man Christ Jesus!

Are you a seer? If so, how will you increase your availability to reach higher? If not, what will you do to become available for this prophetic power?

ENDNOTES

CHAPTER 1

1. Kenneth Hagin, *The Holy Spirit and His Gifts*. (Tulsa, OK: Faith Library Publications, 1974).

2. Dick Iverson, *The Holy Spirit Today* (Portland, OR: Bible Temple Publications, 1976).

3. Derek Prince, *The Nine Gifts of the Holy Spirit* (tape series) (Fort Lauderdale, FL: Derek Prince Publications, 1971).

4. David Pytches, *Spiritual Gifts in the Local Church* (Minneapolis, MN: Bethany House Publishers, 1971).

5. Quoted in Ern Baxter, *Prophetic Seminar* (teaching notes) (Mobile, AL: Integrity Communications, 1984).

6. Michael G. Maudlin, "Seers in the Heartland: Hot on the Trail of the Kansas City Prophets," *Christianity Today* 35.1 (January 14, 1991).

7. All information in this section on Paul Cain and the Kansas City Fellowship is drawn from Michael Maudlin, "Seers in the Heartland," *Christianity Today* 35.1 (January 14, 1991).

CHAPTER 2

1. William Robertson Smith, The prophets of Israel and their place in history to the close of the eighth-century B.C., New York: Appleton and Company, 1895. 182.

CHAPTER 3

1. Clifton Fadiman and André Bernard, eds., *Bartlett's Book of Anecdotes*, Revised Edition. (New York: Little, Brown and Company, 2000), 67.

2. *Ibid.,* 138.

CHAPTER 5

1. James Strong, *Strong's Exhaustive Concordance of the Bible* (Peabody, MA: Hendrickson Publishers, 1988), s.v. "moved" (Greek #5342).

2. Mark and Patti Virkler, *Communion With God* (Shippensburg, PA: Destiny Image Publishers, 2001), 77.

3. *Ibid.*, adapted from a diagram (78) and from a table entitled "Testing Whether an Image Is From Self, Satan, or God" (79). Used by permission.

4. David Neff, "Testing the New Prophets," *Christianity Today*, 35.1 (January 14, 1991), 4.

CHAPTER 6

1. Derek Prince, *The Nine Gifts of the Holy Spirit,* tape series (Fort Lauderdale, FL: Derek Prince Publications, 1971).

2. John Wimber, *Spiritual Gifts Seminar*, vol. 2, tape series (Anaheim, CA: Vineyard Ministries International, 1985).

3. Dick Iverson, *The Holy Spirit Today* (Portland, OR: Bible Temple Publications, 1976).

4. Kenneth Hagin, *The Holy Spirit and His Gifts* (Tulsa, OK: Faith Library Publications, 1974).

5. Francis Frangipane, *Discerning of Spirits* (Cedar Rapids, IA: Arrow Publications, 1991), 6.

CHAPTER 7

1. For the information in this section on the symbolism of colors, numbers, and other items in dreams, I am indebted to Kevin J. Conner and his book, *Interpreting the Symbols and Types* (Portland, OR: Bible Temple Publications, 1980).

CHAPTER 8

1. Anna Rountree, *The Heavens Opened*. (Lake Mary, FL: Creation House, 1999), paraphrased from page 114 and the back cover of the book.

2. W.E. Vine, Merrill F. Unger, William White, Jr., *Vine's Complete Expository Dictionary of Old and New Testament Words* (Nashville, TN: Thomas Nelson Publishers, 1996), New Testament section, 639.

CHAPTER 9

1. W.E. Vine, Merrill F. Unger, William White, Jr., *Vine's Complete Expository Dictionary of Old and New Testament Words* (Nashville, TN: Thomas Nelson Publishers, 1996), New Testament section, 24.

2. David Blomgren, *Prophetic Gatherings in the Church: The Laying on of Hands and Prophecy* (Portland, OR: Bible Temple Publications, 1979).

3. David A. Castro, *Understanding Supernatural Visions According to the Bible* (Brooklyn: Anointed Publications, 1994).

4. *Ibid.*, 47-49.

5. Mahesh Chavda, *Only Love Can Make a Miracle* (Ann Arbor, MI: Servant Publications, 1990), 45-51.

6. Kenneth E. Hagin, *I Believe in Visions* (Tulsa, OK: Faith Library Publications, 1989), 65-66.

7. Maria Woodworth-Etter, *Signs and Wonders* (Tulsa, OK: Harrison House, 1916), 63-65.

8. R. Edward Miller, ed., *I Looked and I Saw the Lord* (East Point, GA: Peniel Publications, 1971), 22-23.

CHAPTER 10

1. For much of the basic material in this chapter I am deeply indebted to the teaching and ministry of Carlton Kenney, an outstanding Bible teacher and missionary statesman who has lived and worked in Japan for many years.

2. Shawn Bolz, *The Throne Room Company* (North Sutton, NH: Streams Publishing House, 2004), 20-21.

3. Carlton Kenney, *Standing in the Council of the Lord* (Hampton: Masterbuilder Ministries, 1992).

4. *Ibid.*

CHAPTER 11

1. Michal Ann Goll, *A Call to the Secret Place* (Shippensburg, PA: Destiny Image Publishers, 2003), 66.

2. For more on this three-stage process of contemplative prayer, read the classic book by Richard Foster, *Prayer: Finding the Heart's True Home* (San Francisco: HarperSanFrancisco, 1992).

CHAPTER 12

1. Wade Taylor, *The Secret of the Stairs* (Hagerstown, MD: McDougal Publishing Company, 1996).

ABOUT
JAMES W. GOLL

James W. Goll is the president of Encounters Network, based in Franklin, Tennessee, which is dedicated to changing lives and impacting nations by releasing God's presence through prophetic ministry, intercessory prayer, teaching, and compassion ministry. James is also the international director of Prayer Storm—an Internet-based, 24/7/365 prayer ministry. Further, he is the director of the EN Alliance, a coalition of leaders, and founder of the God Encounters Training—eSchool of the Heart—where faith and life meet. James has his Doctorate of Practical Ministry through the Wagner Leadership Institute, in Pasadena, California.

After pastoring in the Midwest, James was thrust into the role of itinerant minister, equipping and training around the globe. He has traveled extensively to every continent, carrying a passion for Jesus wherever he goes. James desires to see the Body of Christ become the house of prayer for all nations and carries a heart for God's purposes in Israel.

James is the author of numerous books and training manuals, and is a contributing writer for several periodicals. James' books are translated into numerous languages. He has also produced numerous study guides on subjects such as "Equipping in the Prophetic," "Blueprints for Prayer," and "Empowered for Ministry," all of which are available online through the Encounters Resource Center.

James is an instructor at the Wagner Leadership Institute, a member of the Harvest International Ministry Apostolic Team, and a consultant to several national and international ministries. James and Michal Ann Goll were married for 32 years before her graduation to Heaven in the fall of 2008. Together they have four wonderful adult children. James continues to make his home in the beautiful hills of Franklin, Tennessee.

ADDITIONAL BOOKS BY JAMES W. AND MICHAL ANN GOLL

The Lost Art of Intercession

The Lost Art of Practicing His Presence

The Coming Prophetic Revolution

Compassion—The Call to Take Action

A Radical Faith

God's Power in You

The Beginner's Guide to Hearing God

Exploring the Gift and Nature of Dreams

Empowered Women

Prayer Storm

Prayer Storm Study Guide

A Radical Faith Study Guide

The Seer 40 Day Devotional Journal

Deliverance from Darkness Study Guide

The Lost Art of Pure Worship

The Call of the Elijah Revolution

Women on the Frontlines— A Call to Courage

A Call to the Secret Place

Intercession

The Reformer's Pledge

The Beginner's Guide to Signs, Wonders and the Supernatural Life

Discovering the Seer in You

Empowered Prayer

God Encounters

Praying for Israel's Destiny

The Coming Israel Awakening

Shifting Shadows of Spiritual Experiences

The Coming Prophetic Revolution

Adventures in the Prophetic   *Deliverance from Darkness*

The Prophetic Intercessor   *Angelic Encounters*

Dream Language   *The Seer*

For more information contact:

Encounters Network
P. O. Box 1653
Franklin, TN 37075
Office Phone: 615-599-5552
Office Fax: 615-599-5554
For orders call: 1-877-200-1604

For more information, to sign up for weekly e-mail communiques, or to view over 200 free video and audio messages, visit the following websites:

www.encountersnetwork.com

www.prayerstorm.com

www.compassionacts.com

www.jamesgoll.com

www.GETSchool.com

www.ENMedia.com

E-mail:

info@encountersnetwork.com

info@prayerstorm.com

prayer@encountersnetwork.com

FREE E-BOOKS?
YES, PLEASE!

Get **FREE** and deeply-discounted **Christian books** for your **e-reader** delivered to your inbox **every week!**

IT'S SIMPLE!

VISIT lovetoreadclub.com

SUBSCRIBE by entering your email address

RECEIVE free and discounted e-book offers and inspiring articles delivered to your inbox every week!

Unsubscribe at any time.

SUBSCRIBE NOW!

LOVE TO READ CLUB

visit **LOVETOREADCLUB.COM** ▶